Financial Analysis and Business Decisions on the Pocket Calculator
  Jon M. Smith
Managing Innovation
  Edwin A. Gee and Chaplin Tyler
The Management System: Systems Are for People
  Leslie H. Matthies
Forecasting Methods for Management, Third Edition
  Steven C. Wheelwright and Spyros Makridakis
Decision Making and Planning for the Corporate Treasurer
  Harold Bierman, Jr.
Corporate Financial Planning Models
  Henry I. Meyer
Strategies in Business
  Shea Smith, III, and John E. Walsh, Jr.
Program-Management Control Systems
  Joseph A. Maciariello
Contemporary Cash Management: Principles, Practices, Perspective
  Paul J. Beehler
Dynamic Cost Reduction
  Irving Dlugatch
Inventory Control for the Financial Executive
  Thomas S. Dudick and Ross Cornell
Handbook for Budgeting
  H. W. Allen Sweeny and Robert Rachlin, Editors
Accounting Estimates by Computer Sampling, Second Edition
  Maurice S. Newman

Accounting Estimates
by Computer Sampling

ACCOUNTING ESTIMATES BY COMPUTER SAMPLING

Second Edition

MAURICE S. NEWMAN
University of Alabama

A Ronald Press Publication

JOHN WILEY & SONS
New York   Chichester   Brisbane   Toronto   Singapore

Library of Congress Cataloging in Publication Data:

Newman, Maurice S.
   Accounting estimates by computer sampling.

   (Systems and controls for financial management series)
   "A Ronald Press publication."
   Previous ed. published as: Financial accounting
estimates through statistical sampling by computer.
   Includes index.
   1. Accounting—Statistical methods.   2. Accounting—
Data processing.   3. Sampling (Statistics)   I. Title.
II. Series.
HF5657.N5   1982   657'.028'54   81-12955
ISBN 0-471-09147-2   AACR2

FOREWORD

The day is past when accountants could ignore the power and efficiency of statistical methods. They have for too long tried to teach statistical methods to one another, writing papers and giving speeches on statistical methods that, when examined by a competent statistician, turn out to be mostly propagation of error, the effect being to delay use of statistical methods by accountants. A good book for accountants is rare. Comes now my friend Dr. Maurice Newman, with long experience in accounting and auditing, and with his doctorate earned with a dissertation on statistical methods in auditing, presenting to accountants a book that will help accountants to learn and appreciate statistical methods. It is with much satisfaction that I review the contents of this book, with the hope that it will inspire accountants to continue their studies of statistical theory. The usual excuses:

Our problems are different.
We have to turn out our work on short-time fuses: there is no time for statistical design.
Statistical methods leave no room for judgment.
Statistical methods can only lead us to uncertain inference.

Such excuses are merely various synonyms for inertia.

It is true that few men can achieve competence in both accounting and statistics. It is not necessary. Both pursuits are scholarly and difficult, yet it is possible for accountants to be statistically minded, to work under the general direction of a competent statistician, and to carry out procedures and to draw by the appropriate statistical theory inferences from the results, with appropriate margins of uncertainty from all sources.

Investigation of errors found in a statistical sample will lead the auditor to a cross-section of causes of error.

Nothing in statistical practice forbids an auditor to use judgment-samples, to supplement what he learns from statistical sampling. In fact, he has not only a right but a duty to examine in full or with high intensity any group of accounts that in his judgment are liable to special types of error.

W. Edwards Deming

SERIES PREFACE

No one needs to tell the reader that the world is changing. He sees it all too clearly. The immutable, the constant, the unchanging of a decade or two ago no longer represent the latest thinking—on *any* subject, whether morals, medicine, politics, economics, or religion. Change has always been with us, but the pace has been accelerating, especially in the postwar years.

Business, particularly with the advent of the electronic computer some 30 years ago, has also undergone change. New disciplines have sprung up. New professions are born. New skills are in demand. And the need is ever greater to blend the new skills with those of the older professions to meet the demands of modern business.

The accounting and financial functions certainly are no exception. The constancy of change is as pervasive in these fields as it is in any other. Industry is moving toward an integration of many of the information gathering, processing, and analyzing functions under the impetus of the so-called systems approach. Such corporate territory has been, traditionally, the responsibility of the accountants and the financial people. It still is, to a large extent—but times are changing.

Does this, then, spell the early demise of the accountants as we know them today? Does it augur a lessening of influence for the financial specialists in today's corporate hierarchy? We think not. We maintain, however, that it is incumbent upon today's accountants and today's financial people to learn *today's* thinking and to *use today's* skills. It is for this reason the Systems and Controls for Financial Management Series is being developed.

Recognizing the broad spectrum of interests and activities that the series title encompasses, we plan a number of volumes, each representing the latest thinking, written by a recognized authority, on a particular facet of the financial person's responsibilities. The subjects contemplated for discussion within the series range from production accounting systems to planning, to corporate records, to control of cash. Each book is an in-depth study on one subject within this group. Each is intended to be a practical, working tool for the business people in general and the financial people and accountants in particular.

ROBERT L. SHULTIS
FRANK M. MASTROMANO

PREFACE

A new edition of a book gives the author an opportunity to revise the ideas presented in the light of subsequent experience and criticism. A new edition also allows any errors to be corrected and new material to be added. All of this has been done.

Of particular interest to those with a theoretical interest in the use of applied statistics will be the newly added appendix on formulas, constants, and relationships. This appendix not only sets forth the most commonly suggested formulas for accounting uses but compares them so that their relationships and particular advantages or disadvantages are brought out point by point.

Another appendix has been added in response to questions about how certain statistical techniques may be accomplished. This includes the FORTRAN coding for all of the important statistical requirements to design, select, and evaluate stratified regression estimates. With these program modules available, one should be able to develop and assemble a working program quickly and easily as these modules have been tested thoroughly.

This book fulfills three purposes of interest to professionals in the areas of management, finance, accounting, data processing, and statistics. The primary purpose is to show how statistical sampling can be used to produce satisfactory estimates for financial and accounting objectives. A secondary purpose is to explain, in simple terms, the nature and limits of statistical estimation sampling when applied to business records and data. The final purpose is to demonstrate how the computer can be used effectively to provide stratified regression estimates of financial data as well as less sophisticated types of estimates.

A stimulating reason for the employment of statistical sampling in the development of financial estimates, such as the annual physical inventory, is the use of electronic data processing in accounting practices. The statistical knowledge and procedures described in this book represent 15 years or more of work experience with some of the largest companies in the world, developing general-purpose computer programs that would provide satisfactory financial estimates together with substantial cost savings.

The application of estimation sampling to situations arising from large scale accounting records is an interdisciplinary problem that requires knowledge of accounting, data processing, and statistics in order to obtain a satisfactory estimate that is sufficiently precise for financial statement purposes. Only recently have the schools of accountancy been graduating students with a reasonable knowledge in each of these fields.

The unique characteristic of the computer programs that have been developed is the way in which a number of statistical concepts have been put together in an accounting-oriented approach to obtain reasonably accurate estimates of asset or liability values. The material contained herein will enable any professional to apply estimation sampling through use of packaged programs. The book also contains adequate information so that a professional team could develop internal programs for estimation sampling and evaluation, thereby avoiding many pitfalls and obstacles that might otherwise be encountered.

The case study contained herein shows specifically how a stratified regression estimate may be made of the value of a physical inventory at considerable savings of cost and time over the alternative of a full complete count. The feature of sampling interest is the relationship between the physical inventory and the book record. The strata limits are determined by the computer program so that the resulting estimate is adequately precise for accounting needs.

In the development of these programs I am indebted particularly to my partner, Kenneth W. Stringer, for his suggestions and support; to Dr. W. Edwards Deming for his instruction, advice, and encouragement; to the late Professor Frederick F. Stephan for his clarifying explanations of troublesome statistical points; and to my wife, Ann, who bore much of the burden of these studies without complaint.

In addition to those mentioned above, special thanks are due to Valerie Walters, Wanda Fisher, and other members of our secretarial staff for the production of the final copy.

MAURICE S. NEWMAN

Tuscaloosa, Alabama
October 1981

CONTENTS

Accounting Estimates
by Computer Sampling

CHAPTER 1

ROLE AND IMPORTANCE
OF ESTIMATES IN BUSINESS

NATURE OF MODERN MANAGEMENT

The business environment in which a company operates today is a set of complex interacting forces. The outputs of one industrial process are the inputs to many other industrial processes, so that a change in supply or demand for one product will affect the production and marketing of many other products.

In addition, labor turnover, absenteeism, work stoppages, and energy restrictions create situations within a company that affect operations in subtle ways not easy to detect. A great amount of information is generated daily within a company, but the processing priorities frequently are such that answers are not readily available in situations where time is of the essence.

Early Development

At an earlier stage in our economic development it was possible for a manager to get the information required to plan and control the business directly. A manager could review the sales orders, walk out in the shop to oversee the production, and check the bank statement to determine liquidity. Business, in general, was less complicated, and more time was available to make decisions.

As companies grew larger, the manager hired subordinates for first-line supervision and had, perforce, to rely on summary reports and financial statements to maintain control of the business. Companies began hiring controllers and financial executives in the 1930s and 1940s to assist in analyzing the increased flow of business information. Many of them came from the accounting profession where they had learned how to accumulate and analyze data. The emphasis in the earlier years was primarily on financial analysis but gradually extended to sales analysis and all types of business analysis. Graduates of business schools began to fill the ranks of middle management from 1950 on, and professional management came of age.

Need for Information

Professional managers today need information with which to plan and control their businesses, and most of them are forced to rely on summary data and reports prepared by electronic computers. In many cases the managers do not get the necessary information when they want it. Generally there are far more computerized data available than are necessary to make a decision, but the problem for managers is to obtain the essential information and use it to improve management control.

Information Gap

There is, unfortunately, a gap between those professional managers who know the business problems and need the information with which to plan and control their operations, and those who understand and thus effectively control the computer technology to supply these needs. Despite the fantastic operating speeds of electronic equipment, most installations are geared up for the routine daily processing of orders, invoices, payroll checks, and accounts receivable, leaving little time or talent free to meet the more crucial business problems that arise occasionally and require quick answers.

The daily routine processing provides input to summary reports which present the manager with a tremendous amount of information. Some of this data may be related to budgets or projections so that a divisional head may manage by exception. Quite often these reports are not sufficiently timely for action to be taken and nonroutine information is very difficult to come by.

Consider, for instance, a situation where an employee in a foreign-based operation dies unexpectedly. Management may require a list of all people with the language fluency, functional experience, education, training, age, and marital requirements needed for this position in less than 24 hours so that a decision on replacement can be made immediately. This type of problem can be handled quickly by a computer with a general purpose extractive program.

Then there is the type of problem that might arise during a merger discussion as to how sales coverage of the two companies might overlap and thus result in opportunities for cost savings. The company reports and records may not be set up in a way which provides a timely answer for a competent decision.

High echelon executives are often told that it will take several days or even several weeks of programming to obtain an important report. As a consequence, they are forced to make a critical decision based on little or no information, when they could have made a reasonable decision based upon a sample estimate extracted quickly from available data.

Professional managers face practical problems of considerable importance where facts are pertinent to the decision. The purpose of this book is to show how a sophisticated tool such as "estimation sampling" can be applied to obtain helpful solutions to many of the problems faced today by managers and accountants.

PRACTICAL PROBLEMS AND THEIR IMPORTANCE

There are a number of practical problems that business people face for which a ready solution can often be provided by estimation sampling. Although it is not possible to list all of them, some problems that have been solved through this process may serve as examples to managers of how estimation sampling may be effective.

Determination of Physical Inventories

Most businesses of any size can use estimation sampling to advantage in the determination of physical inventories. Most manufacturing companies have inventories of raw materials, work-in-process, finished goods, and parts and supplies. Sampling may be used in any of these areas to provide reasonable estimates of inventory values. It is more usually applied to finished goods or to parts and supplies as sampling is particularly adaptable to those inventories where the sample items can be well defined and easily counted. Chemicals and gasoline are examples of the types of inventory items that are not well defined or easily measured, whereas boxes of machine parts are well labeled and easily counted.

Each year it is necessary, for income determination, to take a physical inventory of parts and supplies in stockrooms or warehouses. In many types of businesses this is a major operation, as the number of different parts may run into the hundreds of thousands. Establishing control over the inventory for accounting purposes may require a work stoppage. It is not unusual for such a physical inventory to require several days during which time shipments to customers must be delayed. Incoming goods pile up on the loading docks and cannot be processed until the counting is completed. Anything that will reduce this downtime has to benefit a company, as no one has ever made money by taking physical inventory. Suffice it to say, as will be shown later, that a satisfactory statistical estimate for financial statement purposes can be made with minimum effort and a minimum amount of downtime.

Valuing Loans and Receivables

There are many situations in which an executive may need to make a review of a large number of installment loans or accounts receivable. This may occur during the normal course of business, in a special examination, during a purchase investigation, or in the course of an audit by certified public accountants. Whatever the reason, the problem is usually one of many thousands of loan accounts on which an opinion needs to be formed as to the overall collectibility of these accounts. A full investigation would be prohibitive, but a satisfactory estimate can be obtained by examining a small sample and forming opinions as to the collectibility of the accounts in the sample.

The ability to make such estimates reasonably and quickly would mean that a credit manager could experiment with various credit and collection techniques to see if there was any significant difference between one technique and another. There is a variety of credit and collection techniques to choose from, and some may work well with people in one location but be unsatisfactory if used in a different city or state. Sample estimates would provide answers quickly as to which technique to use.

Establishing Reserves

The financial reporting responsibilities of a company require that various reserves be provided to present fairly the financial results of the company. The amount of these reserves is often not easy to determine but financial management must make a reasonable effort to estimate these reserves to the best of its ability and to the satisfaction of the company's outside auditors.

There are many situations that require the establishment of reserves: life insurance companies must establish a benefit reserve on each policy; most companies establish reserves for collectibility of their accounts receivable; others establish reserves for obsolescence of parts and supplies. Where such reserves need to be established, an appropriate sample can be extracted from the accounts, the required reserves determined for each item in the sample, and, based on the sample results, the total reserve may be estimated.

Computation of Discount Earned

Banks and finance companies need to determine what part of the original unearned discount on loans receivable to include in income of the current period. Some systems have been devised that provide a reasonable accurate solution to this problem, but many involve a tremendous amount of calculation. These calculations may be reduced considerably by taking an appropriate sample from the accounts, determining the amount of discount earned on each individual account, and thereby estimating the total amount of discount earned for the period.

Determining Cost of Sales

Public companies that have made offerings of their stock are required to determine income in accordance with generally accepted accounting principles. Private companies that do not have stock in the hands of the public may neither have outside auditors nor be as careful in the determination of income. At some point, a private company may decide to make a public offering, and may engage auditors who are required to audit the financial statements for the past three years. At this time the determination of income in past years becomes important, and the auditor has to determine that these income figures are fairly presented.

In those situations where the auditor has not observed the taking of the physical inventories at the beginning of the first year nor at the end of each of the three years involved, reliance must be placed on other auditing procedures to be able to express an opinion. One possibility is to estimate the cost of sales for each year based on samples of the sales invoices for each of these years. These selected invoices may be costed to provide a basis for an estimate of the cost of sales for each annual period. This estimate will enable the auditor to check the reasonable accuracy of the opening and closing inventories for those periods that were not observed.

LIFO Method of Inventory

In those situations where alternative accounting practices are permissible it may be desirable to disclose the effect of using a particular practice rather than an alternative practice as, for instance, when a company prices inventory on a LIFO (last-in, first-out) basis rather than on a FIFO (first-in, first-out) basis. The LIFO method of determining inventory has been an acceptable accounting method for many years past but the increased rate of inflation has made it a preferable way of measuring net income in many cases. While there are a number of problems attendant upon the use of the LIFO method, its use during periods of inflation may improve the cash flow from operations, thus making it more attractive when there is a shortage of available credit or when interest rates are exceptionally high.

In recent years, many companies have switched to LIFO and have then discovered that the necessary calculations are not easy to make. In most cases, the underlying records will be on a FIFO or average cost basis. In order to proceed to a LIFO basis, a sample could be selected and priced out on a last-in, first-out basis to obtain an estimate of the value of the entire inventory on a LIFO basis and thus determine the effect on the income statement of using the alternative procedure.

Changing Prices

During the past decade there has been constant discussion among accounting bodies worldwide about how the effects of changing prices and general inflation can be dealt with in financial reporting. Experimentation in this area has centered around either constant dollar accounting or current cost accounting or both.

Starting in 1976, the Securities and Exchange Commission required certain large companies to provide information on the replacement costs of inventory and property. In other countries such as England, Canada, and Australia, income statements have been issued on a current cost basis or as supplementary information.

Starting with 1980, larger companies in the United States are required to provide information both on a constant dollar basis and on a current cost basis. The LIFO method of inventory discussed above would be similar to current cost. Measurement of the assets owned by a company will also have to be presented on a current cost basis, whereas the property records are undoubtedly on an historical cost basis. A sample of property and equipment items could be selected from the fixed asset record and a reasonable estimate made of the current cost of the machinery and equipment items selected. This would permit a statistical estimate to be made of the fixed assets at current cost.

Oil and Gas Reserves

The passage of the Energy Policy and Conservation Act in 1975 set in motion provisions for disclosure of oil and gas reserves as later defined by the Securities and Exchange Commission in Accounting Series Release No. 257 adopted December 19, 1978. In general, oil and gas producing companies will have to determine, by internal or external means, the proved reserves as defined. Sample estimates could provide the necessary reserve data.

In addition, external auditors will need to satisfy themselves as to the reasonableness of the reserve information supplied by the company and this could be achieved with a sample estimate.

Testing Equipment

Public utilities are usually required by law to test a certain number of their meters periodically. There may be other situations where companies may want to test equipment on a periodic basis. This may be done quite readily by selecting a sample and using the results of that sample to provide an estimate of the effectiveness of the equipment. The sample may be quite small if it is selected on a proper basis, so that a considerable amount of time and money can be saved in the testing process.

Complying with Government Regulations

From time to time it may be necessary for a company to be able to prove compliance with government regulations—for instance, that it has not increased prices above a permissible level. From the government point of view, a similar procedure might be required to ascertain compliance with the regulations or to prove noncompliance. A satisfactory test may be made by selecting an appropriate sample and estimating the overall price increase or any substantial deviations from a specified price level.

Regulatory Hearings

Proceedings before the Interstate Commerce Commission or other regulatory bodies may require that estimates of traffic or usage be presented to the hearing examiner. In merger situations between railroads, for example, it may be necessary to estimate traffic that might be diverted from one railroad to another in a proposed merger. In these situations a sample may be selected to determine the amount of traffic that would be diverted if the merger were permitted to take place. In utility rate hearings the current value of assets may be a factor in setting rates. A sample could provide the basis for an estimate of current replacement cost of the property, plant, and equipment where such estimates are germane to the rate hearings.

NEED FOR ESTIMATION SAMPLING

The purpose of this book is to show how estimation sampling may be used effectively in many business situations. Business life is full of estimates. In the sense that a financial manager would use the term, an estimate means a valuation based on either first hand observation or roughly calculated from incomplete data. Estimates are useful for many business purposes, such as planning market strategy and developing new products, but a large number of estimates arise from the need for periodic financial statements and the necessity of allocating operating results to discrete periods. For some purposes, estimates do not need to be precise, but for financial statement purposes many accountants often require a complete verification. This is particularly so in the case of inventory although it is not often necessary.

On the other hand, it must be realized that there are considerable costs, even on an incremental basis, in shutting down operations for a complete count. Part of these costs certainly could be avoided with a sample count. Although it may be difficult to pinpoint or segregate these costs, they will often amount to a considerable sum. There are costs associated with the complete count and costs associated with the shutdown.

The costs of making a complete count include those of preparation and data processing as well as the time required to make the actual counts and to verify, price, and summarize the inventory. A complete count may take several days to a week before the stock may be released and operations can begin again. Quite often stockroom personnel need assistance from other departments with the counting that has to be done. The individuals from other departments may not be familiar with the stock and their efforts may be marginal in this type of activity.

The time required for a sample count may be two hours to half a day, and a sample count can usually be performed by trained stockroom personnel and internal auditors with aid from accounting personnel who will be responsible for the final results. Thus the reduction in personnel and time requirements, the greater competency of those assigned, and the elimination of overtime can amount to a significant saving that could easily be realized by using a sample rather than a complete count.

Possibly even more important might be the recapture of sales that would otherwise be lost during an inventory shutdown, or the elimination of an interruption to procurement, production, or distribution that might otherwise add to manufacturing overhead costs. These costs may be hard to isolate but they are often quite expensive.

Nature of a Statistical Estimate

One form of sampling that has been around for years is the counting scale. By means of this device, which utilizes leverage, a small number of parts can be used to offset hundreds or thousands of small pieces. Only a small number of parts needs to be counted and extended by the leverage factor. Similarly, a company needing a product analysis might make a distribution of sales invoices for one month and multiply the results by twelve to approximate an annual sales distribution. Estimates of this nature may be useful for certain purposes, but there are situations in which they would not be considered sufficiently reliable.

There is some risk involved in any estimate made from a sample, but the degree of risk may be measured objectively by obtaining a statistically unbiased estimate. When a sample is taken subjectively or intuitively there is, unfortunately, no way to determine the degree of risk involved in using such estimates. The estimate may be quite wrong, or hopelessly biased, with the eventual user being unaware that this is the case.

Probability Sample. Objectivity and lack of bias are obtained by random selection from a given population in such a way that an equal or determinable probability of selection may be assigned to the selection of each sampling unit. Tables of random numbers are available, or pseudo-random numbers may be constructed through computer programs, that will provide an acceptable degree of randomness for selection purposes.

By using a random process to select only a small sample, it may be inferred, with a specified degree of reliability, that the estimate obtained from the sample is correct within a certain mathematically determined range of precision. For example, the evaluation of a sample taken of a physical inventory might result in an estimated value of $1,000,000 with precision limits of plus or minus $25,000 at a 95 percent reliability level. It is usually inferred, although this is not strictly rigorous, that if the entire inventory were counted using identical procedures, the most likely value of the inventory would be $1,000,000. While this may not be the exact value that would be obtained from a full count, there is a small chance (less than 5 percent) that the full value of the inventory would be less than $975,000 or more than $1,025,000.

This raises the question as to what might be gained from a result that is more precise but not necessarily that much closer to the actual value which would be obtained from a full count. The costs associated with a full count could be appreciably greater than the possible error, but there is also a 5 percent chance that the inventory is $25,000 over or short. Such an error would not make or lose money for the company as it would be offset in the next year.

In most companies that have sizable annual inventories, this degree of possible error would be considered as immaterial. At worst it would increase or decrease profits after taxes by about $12,500 (assuming a 50 percent tax rate) and the most likely case is that the net effect upon profits would not be material. For most purposes, this would be a risk that could be assumed without altering any decisions that might be based on these data.

A further consideration is the purpose for which the estimate is to be taken. In a purchase investigation or merger study, the emphasis may be on supporting the balance sheet value for inventory. In these cases, it is satisfactory to know that the inventory is no less than $975,000 without being overly concerned that it might be somewhat greater than $1,000,000. In such situations the estimate can be considered as even more satisfactory and the time-saving may be critical to the decision.

The mathematical concepts of probability sampling may be found in any one of a number of recognized statistical textbooks[1] and will only be covered in this book to the extent that they may be important to the development of a discussion.

The elementary principles, however, are easy to understand and few in number. A random sample from a given population is a selected number of units which is considered as representative of the whole population. We expect that it is representative by using the laws of probability to eliminate any bias or subjectivity.

We develop from this random sample certain statistics which may be used as estimators of similar values, or parameters, of the parent population. The principle estimators are the mean, or average value, and the standard deviation which is a measure of variability or dispersion. If the random sample is large enough, we assume that these estimators are valid for estimates of the population.

We use the mean estimator to estimate the mean value of the population, and thus by multiplying by the total items in the population, the estimate of the population. We use the standard deviation of the sample as an estimator of the range in which we might expect the estimated population mean to differ from the true population mean at a given reliability.

When two values may be compared for each item in the sample, as would be true where a record exists to which the sample value may be compared, other stastistics such as the regression slope and constant of the sample may be developed. More sophisticated estimates such as stratified regression estimates can then be produced with the help of a computer.

Some measure of doubt will surround every sample, no matter how well taken, just as complete counts may suffer from counting errors made by insufficiently trained people. The point that should be stressed is that by application of these statistical measures it is possible to ensure that the degree of risk is suitable to the circumstances.

Business Application

There are many business situations where estimation sampling can be usefully employed, a number of which are discussed later in this book. The

[1]Cf. W. Edwards Deming, *Sample Design in Business Research*, Wiley, New York, 1960.

statistical principles used are similar in most of these circumstances so that any one case can serve as a suitable example of the application of the principles. Because most companies must take a physical inventory, and because this is currently one of the principal uses of estimation sampling by accountants, aside from having a good potential for saving money, the taking of a physical inventory will be used as the principal example of the use of estimation sampling throughout the remainder of this book. In this way, the reader will be able to follow the sampling process from beginning to end.

Economic Viewpoint. An annual physical inventory is required for income determination. The evaluation of a statistical sample provides an estimate of the value of the physical inventory that may be relied upon as accurate within the achieved precision limits and prescribed confidence. An estimate of this nature can be obtained much more quickly than a completely priced full count and at a reasonable cost.

The annual ritual of a full-scale and lengthy counting procedure followed by many days of recounting, pricing, and extending the physical quantities may not be the best approach to income determination. Attempts to make a complete count of hundreds of thousands of different parts at one time have to be viewed as a waste of manpower and an unnecessary disruption of normal productive activity. Sales can be lost during this nonproductive period, and it may be several days or weeks before normal productive efficiency is regained.

Any company that maintains a perpetual inventory record on computer may design and select a stratified random sample quickly and efficiently by use of the procedures and programs that will be described hereafter. Even a small company can benefit from the use of statistical sampling in connection with an annual physical inventory, and the larger the company, the more obvious are the savings.

In addition to income determination, there is a continuing need to reconcile the physical quantities on hand with the perpetual records from time to time for production purposes. These two needs are often confused and do not have to be done at the same time. Logically, it would be better to do them separately. For production control there is no need to (1) count low value expendable items, (2) count everything at the same time, (3) price and extend these physical counts, or (4) use supervisory or clerical personnel in making the counts. Such reconciliations for inventory control purposes can be made more economically by the stockroom clerks on a routine cyclical count basis. This is an operating requirement that has no particular financial significance and very little connection with income determination.

Management Viewpoint. The most obvious advantage to management in using a statistical sample to estimate the physical inventory is that the taking of the inventory requires a few hours rather than days. Profits can be determined but not made by an operating shutdown. The sooner normal operations can begin again, the better it will be for the company.

The cost savings that may accrue from reduction of the peak load of counting, pricing, and extending have amounted to hundreds of thousands of dollars in some situations. Even where these costs are not incremental in nature, in that the persons would still be on the payroll doing other work, there is still a significant diversion of time and effort in a complete coverage from what might otherwise be classed as productive time.

There are other advantages that are more subtle and must be seen to be believed. These have to do with improving the effectiveness of the warehousing operations and management and will be discussed in more detail later. In sampling from accounting records, a principal objective of the sampling plan, or statistical feature of interest, is to determine the overall relationship between the perpetual records and the physical inventory. This can serve as a measure of the effectiveness of the perpetual records in keeping control of the physical quantities. The more closely these records agree, the tighter the precision that would be achieved for a given sample size. An analysis of the results, in terms of sample size and precision, from one period to the next can give an indication as to whether the overall performance is improving.

A further advantage of statistical sampling comes from a better analysis of the types of differences that seem to occur. Some of the time that is saved by sampling may be spent in an in-depth study of why there is not substantial agreement between the perpetual records and the physical quantities. This should lead to improvements in the recordkeeping procedures and in the warehouse locator records. Warehousemen will be quick to see the correlation between the records and the physical movement of goods. Improvements in housekeeping and storage are the likely result.

The closer the reconciliation of physical quantities to perpetual records, the tighter the control that management maintains over the warehousing operations. Immediate knowledge will be available from the record of goods on hand as to what may be shipped at customer demand. This control can be reinforced by a routine program of cyclical counts that will help keep the records in line with actual counts. There will be a greater awareness of losses or pilferage which may lead to better storage or security procedures which, in turn, may increase company profits.

Accounting Viewpoint.   One of the traditional reasons for complete physical count each year is an auditing procedure that required certified public accountants to observe the taking of a physical inventory. This procedure was introduced in 1939, primarily as a result of the McKesson & Robbins case[2] in which there had been a failure to observe the taking of certain inventories, some of which, in actual fact, did not exist.

The requirement for an annual physical count of each item was to remain until 1966 when the Auditing Committee of the American Institute of Certified Public Accountants issued its Statement on Auditing Procedure No. 36, which recognizes inventory sampling as a permissible substitute for complete physical counts. The statement says:

In recent years some companies have developed inventory control or methods of determining inventories, including statistical sampling, of sufficient reliability to make an annual physical count of each item of inventory unnecessary in certain instances. The purpose of this statement is to recognize this development.[3]

In the past many companies have been cognizant of their total inventory value only when the complete physical count was made, priced, and extended. If these annual valuations were in reasonable agreement with the book values no particular problem would arise. It would then be assumed that the book values were in substantial agreement at the end of each month or quarterly period when management reports or interim financial statements may have been distributed or published. When there has been a substantial gain or loss in the inventory value, however, questions arise as to when this gain or loss may have occurred and whether the financial statements were correctly stated at the interim periods.

The basic reason, and really the only compelling reason, for taking a physical inventory at or near the end of a year is to determine the cost of unsold goods. This is a necessary and preliminary step in the determination of income for the current year. A similar inventory having been taken at the end of the previous year, the difference between these inventories is combined with purchases, labor costs, and other expenses into the cost of goods sold.

To achieve this purpose, the inventory must be counted with accuracy clearly in mind, and these physical quantities must be fairly priced. Large errors in counting or pricing cannot be tolerated, as they will result in substantial inventory adjustments and a distortion of net income both for the current year and for the following year. Minor errors in counting or pricing may go unnoticed because they do not materially affect net income for the current year.

[2]Report on Investigation in the Matter of *McKesson & Robbins, Inc.*, Securities and Exchange Commission, 1940, p. 11.
[3]Statements on Auditing Procedure No. 36., American Institute of Certified Public Accountants, New York, August 1966.

It is desirable to take the physical inventory with reasonable speed and at a minimum cost. Speed is essential so that the goods may be released and the operating personnel may resume service to their customers quickly enough to avoid losing any sales. A trade-off will often exist between speed and cost, for the work may be completed more quickly by employing additional people or by incurring the costs for overtime.

Where perpetual inventory records are used and entries are made as sales are recorded, the cost of goods sold may be determined from these entries subject to any inventory adjustment for loss or obsolescence. This adjustment may be determined when the physical inventory is taken. When the perpetual inventory records are considered to be adequately maintained, and the periodic adjustments are not material, the physical inventory need not be taken at the year-end, since the perpetual record will provide a reasonable basis for the necessary year-end computations.

For a perpetual record to be adequately maintained, some form of reconciliation of the detail records is necessary on some regular basis. This is often accomplished by cyclical counting, a procedure by which a certain number of different items are counted and reconciled to the perpetual records on a daily, weekly, or monthly basis. This is necessary to ensure the integrity of the perpetual inventory records for operational or control purposes. Quite often a value distinction is made so that the more valuable or more critical items may be counted and reconciled daily or weekly. Less valuable or less critical items might be reconciled monthly and low value, non-critical items such as nuts and bolts may never be counted.

There is an unfortunate tendency to combine the control requirement mentioned above, which is essential to production, with the annual physical inventory necessary for financial purposes. An adjustment once a year may be sufficient for financial purposes, but the daily usage of the perpetual records is clearly not adequate for operational or control purposes if these records are only likely to be correctly adjusted once a year. The need for complete coverage for operational purposes is best served by partial coverage at regular times during the year. This requires counting only, and the counts do not have to be priced or extended.

It is questionable whether complete coverage has ever been the right approach to serving the financial purpose of income determination. At best, it only provides another sample of unknown reliability. No complete count of an inventory with a large number of parts will ever be "accurate" as there will always be a few errors in count or measurement as well as in pricing, extending, and summarizing the values. In most cases, these will be kept to a minimum and large differences will be found and corrected through checking and review procedures. There will always be some possible degree of error in a complete count and some possible degree of error in a sample. It is usually a surprise to most people to find out that the possible error associated with a relatively small sample is quite reasonable and that a much larger sample or a complete count will not improve the results proportionately. The fact that the range is slightly narrower would not justify the additional effort. Untold hours have been consumed in counting, pricing, and extending the physical quantities in annual physical inventories. Large amounts of overtime have been spent in an activity that can never make money for the company. Differences between book and physical inventories are gradually narrowed to an acceptable level after many hours of recounting and repricing the physical quantities. The best that can be said of the complete count is that it is reasonably accurate within a narrow range that may be dismissed as immaterial to income determination. The same may be said of an estimate based on a sample count.

INTERDISCIPLINARY SCOPE

The statistical estimation of a computer-based inventory, or any major accounting record is an interdisciplinary problem that requires knowledge of accounting statistics, and data-processing in order to reach a satisfactory solution. Professionals in each of these areas have certain expertise that is necessary to an understanding of the problem and to the development of a solution. At some point in time, an individual must obtain a working knowledge of the other disciplines to approach estimation sampling in a realistic manner, or there has to be a substitute either in the form of a pooling of professional resources or by use of packaged programs, as described later.

Accounting Knowledge

The professional accountant has received adequate training in accounting, cost accounting, auditing, financial statement preparation, and data analysis to make it possible to visualize the inherent problems in the estimation of major financial statement values. Financial statements contain many estimates, and the professional accountant is knowledgeable as to the precision and reliability that must be associated with these estimates in order to make a fair presentation of the financial results of a company for a given period.

Certain words or terms may have a particular meaning within a particular discipline, and those words or terms would not necessarily be understood to have the same meaning by persons with other disciplinary backgrounds. To minimize any confusion, some of the common accounting terms used in this book are defined and discussed in Appendix 3.

Statistical Knowledge

The professional statistician is well versed in all the statistical methodology required for estimation sampling. The statistician is familiar with probability distributions, the types of estimates that may be made, the use of stratification, and sampling procedures in general. A financial manager, accountant, or auditor may acquire a considerable degree of statistical knowledge through informal education and actual use. Formal courses are available and consultants can provide valuable help in specific situations.

Statisticians have applied their skills in engineering, marketing, the physical sciences, and the social sciences but have had much less influence in the field of accounting. Many statisticians have had experience with large-scale data handling, but again not in the accounting environment. Statisticians can be useful in this area, but they should be conscious of their relative inexperience when working in an unknown accounting environment.

Many terms used in statistics employ common words that are assigned a special meaning in statistical usage. Some of the more important statistical terms used in the discussion that follows are defined and discussed in Appendix 3.

Data Processing Knowledge

Data processing has developed in several stages from the manually performed operations of the past to the magnetic records and electronically performed operations of the present. It has expanded with the growth of business and involves the basic functions of classifying, sorting, calculating, summarizing, and recording data into accounting records and management reports.

The electronic computer has brought about communication between these various data processing functions together with a substantially increased amount of programmable capability and readily accessible memory. The advent of the computer also raised data processing to a professional status. The data processing manager has the necessary knowledge of programming skills, operating procedures, and computer scheduling to get the job done. The computer specialist is familiar with record formats and is a necessary member of the estimation sampling team whenever the basic records have been computerized.

Some of the more important data processing terms that will be used in the following discussions are also defined and discussed in Appendix 3.

CHAPTER 2

ESTIMATES AND THEIR APPLICATION

The purpose of this chapter is to explain the simple statistical notation that will be used and to introduce some of the statistical concepts that are a part of the computer programs. This will provide a satisfactory base for the following chapters that discuss accounting populations, sample design, selection, and evaluation, as well as statistical sampling applied to financial accounting estimates through use of the computer programs.

STATISTICAL NOTATION

The use of mathematical notation is customary in literature about statistical sampling, and specialized notation is often necessary to indicate the particular way in which a statistical estimate is made. Unfortunately, notation has not been standardized, so that a reader must often convert formulas to his own notation in order to understand them. In recent years, however, an attempt has been made to standardize statistical notation in certain respects, such as by using capital letters for population items and lowercase letters for sample items. Greek letters denote population parameters, with ordinary letters representing sample estimates of the corresponding population parameters. Parameters are constant values for a specific population that help to define its statistical properties. Certain changes have also been suggested to simplify typewriting and typesetting.

The simple notation defined below will be used in this discussion:

N The number of separate accounts or identifiable parts in an accounting population that is to be sampled. For example, $N = 2500$ if there are 2500 different part numbers whose extended value makes up the book inventory value.

n The sample size as a number of accounts or part numbers that are statistically selected from an accounting population to make up a random sample. The determination of sample size is part of the sample design.

X The known dollar value of the book population such as the sum of the extended book values in the accounting population. For example, $X = \$10,000,000$ if the sum of the extended book values of 2500 different part numbers amounts to $\$10,000,000$.

Y The unknown dollar value of the accounting population, such as the actual physical inventory value, that we wish to estimate.

$\hat{Y}$ An estimate of the unknown accounting population. The carat sign ($\hat{}$) indicates an estimator of any population parameter.

X_i An individual item in the known accounting population that may be identified by a value given to the subscript i from 1 to N. Thus X_{25} would be the twenty-fifth account as determined by an assigned number or by sequence. All book values are defined whether selected for the sample or not. These items are selected at random for the sample and then may be designated as x_i where $i = 1$ to n.

x The total of the extended book values selected at random for the sample.

y The total of the extended physical values of the items selected at random for the sample. These sample items are the only items in the actual population about which anything is known.

y_i The actual physical value associated with one of the x_i drawn in the sample, where i is a number from 1 to n.

$\mu(X)$ The average of the population values is an important location parameter commonly called the *mean*. By tradition, the Greek lowercase letter mu is used followed by a parenthetic modifier or subscript that identifies the variable to avoid confusion.

$\bar{y}$ The mean, or average, of the sample values is indicated by a bar over the appropriate lowercase letter. The sample mean may be used as an estimator of the parent or population mean.

σ The standard deviation of a population is a scale parameter and may be known in the case of the book values or unknown for the actual physical values. Again, by tradition, the Greek lowercase letter sigma is used for the known population parameter followed by a parenthetic modifier or subscript if necessary.

σ^2 The known variance of a population which is the square of the standard deviation.

s   The standard deviation of a sample is indicated traditionally by the lowercase letter *s*. Its principal use is as an estimator of the parent or population standard deviation.

b   The slope or coefficient of a regression line obtained from a regression analysis of the *x* and *y* sample values. The regression line is defined in the form

$$\bar{y} = a + b\bar{x} \tag{2.1}$$

where *a* designates a constant value measured at the point where the regression line intersects the *y* axis. The principal purpose of the sample coefficient obtained from the regression of *y* sample values on *x* sample values is as an estimator of the similar unknown coefficient in the parent population.

β   The slope of a regression line that would be obtained from a regression analysis of all the *X* and *Y* values if the latter all were known. This population parameter is indicated by the Greek lowercase letter beta. This value is not likely to change much from year to year unless there is a basic change in the method of operation.

Σ   The sum of a number of specified items from 1 to *n* may be indicated by the Greek capital letter sigma.

r   An estimator of the population correlation coefficient of two random variables, such as *X* and *Y* populations, as developed from the sample data. Subscripts or parenthetic modifiers may be added where confusion might arise.

STATISTICAL ESTIMATES

There are many different types of statistical estimates which serve different purposes depending on the results required. These vary from the simple mean estimate, often used in sampling public opinion, to the stratified regression estimate, required for more precise estimation of financial values, which is the subject of this book.

All these types of statistical estimates are related to some degree and their use may depend on the information that is available or obtainable. Unless the cost of sampling is an important factor, one would tend to use the type of estimate that makes the best use of the available information.

MEAN ESTIMATE

Of these various types of estimates the most easily understood is the mean estimate which is based simply on knowledge of the average sample value, or sample mean, of the feature of sampling interest. For example, if we take a random sample of 100 from 2500 accounts we might sum the 100 sample items and find the total to be $3600. The mean sample value would be $36 ($3600 ÷ 100) and the mean estimate of the population would be $90,000 ($36 × 2500).

Simple Form

If we disregard any knowledge concerning the book inventory or if we have no book inventory, we may estimate the physical inventory by using the following formula for a mean estimate:

$$\hat{Y} = \frac{N}{n} y \tag{2.2}$$

To illustrate, we use a sampling interval of 80, take a sample of 250 items from a total number of 20,000 items, and determine the extended value of each of the 250 part numbers. We sum these extended values to determine the total sample value ($125,000) and multiply by 80 to obtain a mean estimate of the physical inventory of $10,000,000.

If we were to take 100 or more samples from the same population and determine their means, the means of each of these 100 different samples would not be the same. We do know, however, that if we made a graph of these sample means with *number of samples* on the vertical axis and *mean value* on the horizontal axis, the graph would approximate a *normal distribution*[1] as shown in Figure 2.1.

If we were to go further and take all possible samples of all sizes from the same population, we would find that the mean of all the possible sample means would coincide exactly with the true population mean. This can be tried out manually on a small population or can be run on a computer for a large population and is a good exercise for a better understanding of the statistical principle involved.

The usefulness of this knowledge to a financial manager or accountant lies in the fact that, regardless of whether or not the population distribution is normal, a large enough sample permits the use of the normal distribution to draw inferences as to an estimate of the population value and a range of

[1] Cf. John E. Freund, *Mathematical Statistics*, Prentice-Hall, Englewood Cliffs, NJ, 1962, p. 187.

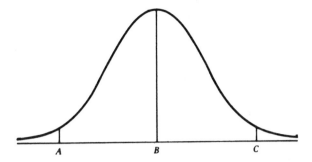

Figure 2.1 A normal distribution.

precision surrounding that estimate. Accounting populations are likely to have an exponential distribution, or at least something other than the normal distribution, but a distribution of the means of samples drawn from any accounting population will approximate the normal distribution if the number and size of samples is sufficiently large. The distinction between large and small is not easy to make but there is little justification for assuming that small samples in the accounting area will be normally distributed.

From our knowledge of the *normal distribution* we would expect the largest number of these 100 sample means to be clustered around *B*, the central point of the distribution in Figure 2.1. For this reason we would consider *B* as our best estimate of the unknown *mean* of the population. We also expect that a certain number of the sample means will fall between points *A* and *C*, both of which may be determined mathematically.[2]

If we establish points *A* and *C* so that each is approximately two standard errors from *B*, we can expect that about 95 out of 100 sample means would fall between those points. Given a sample mean of $500 and a standard error of $10, our points *A* and *C* would be $480 and $520 respectively. From this we may infer that a population of 20,000 items would have an estimated value of $10,000,000, and the normal distribution allows us to be 95 percent sure that the true value would not exceed $10,400,000 (20,000 × $520) nor be less than $9,600,000 (20,000 × $480). These precision limits, as they are usually referred to, might be too wide for many accounting purposes but the limits can be narrowed by increasing the sample size.

We are not likely to take 100 or more samples of any given population. Nor would we want to as it would dissipate the economic benefits of statistical sampling. Nevertheless, we may infer, based on a single sample from a given population, that there is a 95 percent probability that the unknown *population mean* lies between *A* and *C*. In other words, if we were to take 100

[2] Ibid., p. 147.

samples, 95 of the sample means would be expected to fall between A and C. There is a 95 percent probability, therefore, that the sample we do take is one of the 95 that would fall between A and C. There is, concurrently, a five percent risk that the population mean will not fall between A and C. A lower or higher risk may be specified in designing the sample and this will increase or decrease the sample size accordingly to maintain the same monetary or numeric precision represented by the distance between A and C.

Easy to Use

The principal advantage of the mean estimate is that it is easy to understand and fairly simple to calculate. No prior knowledge is required. The sample is selected; the sample items are counted, priced, and extended; and the physical inventory is estimated. Where a book inventory or other suitable record from which to select does not exist, the mean estimate may be the only possible choice of estimate.

Unfortunately, mean estimates of accounting data are usually not nearly as precise as other types of estimates, so that, where precision is required, mean estimates are likely to be found wanting for accounting purposes. There are many situations in other areas of business, such as the typical market or political survey, where mean estimates may be useful and where close precision may not be too important.

Mean Estimate of Differences

A popular method of overcoming some of the deficiencies of a simple mean estimate, when dealing with accounting data, is to make a mean estimate of the differences by using the following formula:

$$\hat{Y} = X + \frac{N}{n}(y - x) \qquad (2.3)$$

In using this procedure, the differences between the physical and book values of the inventory are determined for each of the sample items. If the differences are distributed normally, half of these differences $(y_i - x_i)$ would be negative. From the algebraic sum of these differences $(y - x)$ between the physical value and the book value of the sample, an estimate of the total difference $(Y - X)$ is made. For example, let us say that the sum of the extended actual values in a sample of 250 items is $125,000 and the sum of the extended book values for the same items is $124,000. We then have a difference $(y - x)$ of $1000 for the sample items and a mean difference of $4 ($1000 ÷ 250) for each sample item. If there is an average difference of $4 for each item in the random sample, a total difference of $80,000 would be expected, on the average, for all 20,000 items. If the total book value is known to be $10,000,000, then the mean estimate of differences will yield an estimate of $10,080,000 for the actual value.

The advantage of a mean estimate of differences over a simple mean estimate is easy to understand. The simple estimate uses only knowledge about the physical values of inventory items that are selected for the sample. The mean estimate of differences uses information about the book value of each item in the sample and also about the total book value (X) of the population that would otherwise be disregarded. In all types of estimation it is desirable to make use of all the information that is available to improve the estimating procedure. When this is done, it is known as a *sufficient* estimate.

Monetary Selection

In dealing with accounting populations such as a physical inventory, the technique of monetary selection is a more sophisticated approach than either a simple mean estimate or a mean estimate of differences.

Most estimation sampling is done in numerical units wherein the unit is an account or part number and one unit would be selected out of every 20 or 30 units, for example. Where units are unequal in dollar size, and this is true of most accounting populations, the classical approach has been to stratify the population by dollar value and select at higher rates from the strata with the units of higher dollar value. This tends to increase the probability of selecting units with larger amounts.

More or less the same effect can be accomplished by selecting sampling units with probability proportional to size.[3] What this means is that a $100 item will have 10 times as great a chance of being selected as a $10 item. This substitutes monetary sampling for numerical sampling as now every $1 in the population has an equal probability of selection rather than every unit. This monetary selection technique is often useful where computerized records are not available for selection purposes. The evaluation may still be done on the computer.

In this sampling technique the determinable probability of selecting any particular inventory item is proportional to its amount except for top stratum items above a given cutoff which are sampled completely. The formula for a mean estimate with probabilities proportional to size is

$$\hat{Y} = \frac{N}{n} \sum_{i=1}^{n} \left[y_i \cdot \frac{\mu(X)}{x_i} \right] \qquad (2.4)$$

The relative probability of selecting each item in the population is the book value of the item divided by the mean of the book values. In the sample

[3] William G. Cochran, *Sampling Techniques*, 2nd ed., Wiley, New York, 1963, p. 251.

evaluation, each individual physical value, including those that agree with the corresponding book value, is weighted by the reciprocal of this selection probability. In the cases where the book population contains minus values that need to be sampled, the minus signs should be ignored. Selections and weightings are thereby determined on absolute values.

For an estimate to be statistically valid, it is not necessary that each item in the population have an equal probability of being selected. On a monetary sampling basis, therefore, more of the large-value items are going to be in the sample.

Given a book population of $10,000,000 with 2500 items and a sample size of 125, monetary selection will take approximately one item out of each $80,000. Assuming that one $80,000 segment consisted of eighty $1000 items, the chance of selecting any one of those items is clearly one out of 80. If the next segment were to consist of eight hundred $100 items, the chance of selection is now one out of 800. Similarly, if there were eighty thousand $1 items in the following segment, the probabilities change to one out of 80,000.

Obviously the data will not be so neatly arrayed but we do know that the average item, or expected value of any one item selected, is $4000 ($10,000,000 ÷ 2500). Quite clearly, the probability of selecting a $4000 item is one out of twenty (125 ÷ 2500), or the same as if the sample were selected with equal probabilities. In the case of the $1000 item, we concluded that the chances were one out of 80. This may be thought of as being made up of two parts, both of which are visible in the formula; one, the chance of selection (1 out of 20) if all items equaled the average item ($4000), and the other, the ratio of the item value ($1000) to the mean value ($4000) or a selection probability of one out of four, the two parts giving a product of one out of 80. This would hold equally true for the $100 item or the $1 item cited above and the formula (2.4) includes the necessary weighting to correct for the unequal probabilities of selection.

RATIO ESTIMATE

A ratio estimate may be used when, as is usually the case, additional information, such as a book inventory, is available. While the ratio estimate is somewhat more difficult to calculate than a mean estimate, it is still possible to calculate it manually. Thus it has become an acceptable and useful form of statistical estimation. The formula for a ratio estimate is:

$$\hat{Y} = \frac{\bar{y}}{\bar{x}} X \qquad (2.5)$$

The assumption that is made in using a ratio estimate of a physical inventory is that the ratio of the physical values to the book values in the total population is also likely to occur in the sample. Accordingly, the sums of the inventory physical values and of the corresponding book values are determined for a sample. The ratio of these sums, or of their means (which would be the same), is then multiplied by the total book value to estimate the physical value.

If one were to make a graph of the physical values and book values for each individual item, and if a line passing more or less through all these values would also pass through the origin of the graph, then a ratio estimate would be a satisfactory estimate for this purpose. As a practical matter, however, this relationship hardly ever seems to hold, although it does appear to be a reasonable assumption about the relationship between the book and physical values.

A ratio estimate of a physical inventory will generally have considerably tighter precision surrounding the estimate than a simple mean estimate. It would not be unreasonable to expect, for most accounting data, that a sample evaluated as an unstratified ratio estimate might have monetary precision of $150,000 as against $250,000 for the same sample evaluated as an unstratified mean estimate.

The difference in precision between a ratio estimate and a mean estimate of differences, or a mean estimate with probability proportional to size, is not likely to be significant.

A mean estimate of differences is very similar to a ratio estimate in that the formulas are very much alike and the results are apt to be much alike. A basic assumption of any mean estimate is that the mean of the sample will equal the mean of the population. Extending this assumption, we would also assume that the sampling interval is equal to the relationship between total book value and the sample book value. By substitution, as shown in Appendix 4, the formula for a mean estimate of differences will simplify to the formula for a ratio estimate.

In obtaining a random sample from a population, it is quite unlikely that the book sample mean will equal the book population mean, both of which would be known. We would expect, however, that they would be close to each other. If they should happen to be exactly the same, then there would be no difference between a ratio estimate and a mean estimate of differences.

A mean estimate with selection probabilities proportional to size is also similar to a ratio estimate, the difference being only in the summation of the ratios, as set forth in Appendix 4. In the one case the ratios are determined for each item in the sample and the ratios are averaged over the whole sample. This will not produce the same result as a ratio determined from the sample totals, but the likelihood is that it will be very close. In many situations monetary sampling may have an advantage over a ratio estimate in that the emphasis of the selection is on monetary amount rather than on equal probabilities of selecting the items.

Ratio estimates of differences have also been used with some success. In certain cases, negative ratios can produce somewhat disastrous results. For this reason they are not recommended.

REGRESSION ESTIMATE

Regression estimates have been used 35 years or more but have not been used widely. Regression analysis has long been acknowledged as the best way to determine a relationship that exists between two sets of paired data. It follows logically that the same technique should be used when, as in most accounting situations, the feature of sampling interest becomes the relationship between a book value and a physical value. It is also likely that more applications for regression estimates exist in accounting than anywhere else as the relationship between recorded values and actual values is close to unity. Even further, it may be shown that the regression estimate will produce better results than any other form of estimate in those situations where its use is feasible. Why then has there been a lack of acceptance?

The principal reason that regression estimates have not been used more often in those places where they are applicable is that the necessary calculations are time-consuming and tedious. With a computer available, however, the burden of computation is easily handled.

When the perpetual inventory record is maintained on a computer, the feature of sampling interest becomes the relationship between the physical inventory and the perpetual record. We want to know how accurate the perpetual record is. The sample is taken for the purpose of determining what the relationship might be and a regression estimate is ideal for this purpose. The formula for a regression estimate is

$$\hat{Y} = \frac{N}{n}\, y + Nb\,[\mu(X) - \bar{x}] \tag{2.6}$$

where b is the usual least squares estimate of the slope of the regression line as determined from the sample.

Parent Form

What may not be evident from looking at the various formulas used as estimators is that the specific formulas for (1) a mean estimate, (2) a mean estimate of differences, and (3) a ratio estimate may all be included in the general class of regression estimates. In other words, the regression estimate is the parent form of all the estimators and uses all the available information.

The other estimators have fewer parameters or ignore some of those that are available.

This does not mean that these other estimators do not have their place, for they do, but in an accounting environment, where computer records are more the rule than the exception and data are usually highly correlated, regression estimates will provide the most precise estimates obtainable. This may be demonstrated both algebraically and geometrically.

Algebraic Discussion

The regression estimate is not too closely related to the mean estimate. If we compare the formula for a regression estimate (2.6) to the simple mean estimate formula (2.2) we see that the last term in (2.6) is omitted in the latter. If we set $b = 0$ in (2.6), then the last term disappears. Thus as a special form of the regression estimate, the mean estimate disregards knowledge about the relationship of physical values to book values or any knowledge about the book values, and assumes that the sample mean will be equal to the population mean. It is the least desirable estimator for accounting purposes and should not be used where better estimators could be used at reasonable cost.

The regression estimate is closely related to the ratio estimate as shown in Appendix 4. If we substitute the ratio of the means of the sample items $(\bar{y} \div \bar{x})$ for the b in the regression estimate formula (2.6) and simplify the formula, it will then become (2.5) for a ratio estimate. In the basic regression equation for the line of best fit as shown in (2.1), the symbol b is an estimate of the slope of the line and the symbol a is an estimate of the constant or intercept of the y axis as shown in Figure 2.2. Using the ratio of the means as

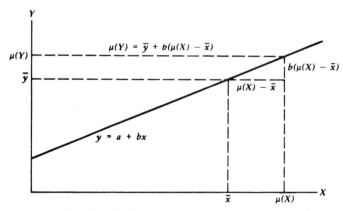

Figure 2.2 Graph of a regression estimate.

an estimator for b is the mathematical equivalent of setting the constant at zero ($a = 0$). The effect of this may or may not be significant depending on the true value of a. As a practical matter, it is unlikely that the value of a will ever be zero, and therefore the regression estimate will always be somewhat better than a ratio estimate and significantly better in some cases.

The regression estimate is also closely related to the mean estimate of differences. If we set $\hat{b}$ equal to one in the regression estimate formula (2.6) and simplify, we obtain the formula for a mean estimate of differences (2.3). This implies that we are setting two parameters arbitrarily ($a = 0$; $b = 1$) and ignoring their true values. If we assume that there is no difference between the book population mean and the book sample mean, we can substitute $N\bar{x}$ for X in the formula for the ratio estimate (2.5) and obtain the formula for the mean estimate of differences (2.3). This, in a roundabout way, points out that the mean estimate of differences disregards any difference between the sample and population mean book values. This deficiency in the mean estimate of differences is not readily apparent from looking at the formula nor is it always understood by those who advocate the use of this form for accounting purposes. The significance of this will depend on the circumstances, but the parent regression estimator would have to be better than a mean estimate of differences.

Geometric Discussion

In taking a sample from the book values of a population, we are interested in the relationship of the book values to the physical values item by item and overall. It is a reasonable assumption to expect this relationship to hold for the entire population. As stated previously, the accepted way of analyzing this relationship is by use of regression analysis. A regression line is calculated to best fit the sample values.

In the regression equation (2.1), two statistics, a and b, are developed which are estimators of similar parameters in the population. The first of these, a, is a constant value which may be plus or minus but is unlikely to be exactly zero. The second is the slope statistic, b, which is a measure of the relative increase in Y for a given increase in X. In a situation where we are testing the validity of an accounting population, the value of b is going to be close to unity. In other sampling situations, and particularly in non-accounting situations, this may not hold true.

The difference between a regression estimator and the other forms of estimators may be seen geometrically by reference to Figure 2.2.

For a given sample from a population, the sample mean, $\bar{x}$, is unlikely to be exactly the same as the population mean, $\mu(X)$, and thus a difference is formed $[\mu(X) - \bar{x}]$. By reference to (2.6), it may be seen that this is part of the last term $Nb [\mu(X) - \bar{x}]$. It is this last term that distinguishes a regression estimate from a mean estimate and by reference to Figure 2.2 we can visualize what this difference signifies.

If, from the two points on the X axis representing the sample mean and the population mean, lines are drawn vertically up to the regression line, the horizontal distance between them represents the difference in means $[\mu(X) - \bar{x}]$. If the sample mean of the y values, $\bar{y}$, is drawn horizontally until it meets the X population mean line, the part of the line beyond the regression line is, by construction, equal to $[\mu(X) - \bar{x}]$, the difference in means.

A specific characteristic of any regression analysis is that the means of each set of variables will be on the regression line as shown in Figure 2.2 for the sample means, $\bar{x}$ and $\bar{y}$. To the extent that we have a difference between the sample mean and population mean of the book values, it is reasonable to expect that a similar difference would occur between the sample mean and population mean of the physical values. In a sampling situation, the unknown population mean of the physical values is what we are estimating. Given that there is a difference between the population means of the physical values and the book values, we would expect that the same relationship would hold between these population means as between the sample means. In other words,

$$\mu(Y) - \bar{y} = b[\mu(X) - \bar{x}] \qquad (2.7)$$

The triangle formed by the intersection of the four means and the line of regression proves this point quite clearly. By construction, the increase from $\bar{y}$ to $\mu(Y)$ must equal the increase from $\bar{x}$ to $\mu(X)$ multiplied by the slope parameter. Adding this term (2.7) in the regression formula (2.6) corrects the mean estimate for an obvious deficiency which, in this type of accounting estimate, is clearly avoidable.

Thus by logic, algebra, and geometry, one is forced to conclude that whenever an adequate sample has been taken, a regression estimator will be, in most cases, far superior to other types of estimators. There may be other factors such as cost or lack of information that will justify the use of other types of estimates but when the accounting records are computer-oriented, regression estimates will prove to be the best.

Development of Variance

Precision and reliability are mathematically interdependent and, on this account, are often referred to as statistically inseparable. The precision of an estimate indicates the range within which it is expected to be accurate, and the reliability (or confidence) is the probability of achieving this accuracy.

Precision and reliability often are expressed as goals in the design stage of a sample. We may say that we want $15,000 of monetary precision at 95 percent reliability. The evaluation of the actual sample will determine the precision obtained and whether the goals are met.

The precision of a sample depends upon several elements, the most important of which, the variance, is developed from the sample. The variance of the sample is the average of the sum of the squared deviations of each item in the sample from the regression line or mean, depending on the type of estimate. The square root of the variance gives us an unbiased estimate of the standard error of the unknown population.[4] The deviations are measured from the regression line, the ratio, or the mean of the sample items depending on the type of estimate. In view of the close correspondence between recorded and actual values in most accounting populations, measuring deviations from the regression line will reduce the variance more than 80 percent for a wide range of unstratified data. It is also interesting to note in passing that the standard deviation of the sampling procedure will be reduced if the sample size is increased.

Relation to Normal Theory

It was stated earlier, with reference to Figure 2.1, that we would expect 95 of the 100 sample means to fall between points A and C. From tables of the normal distribution we can measure certain distances along the base measured from B toward both A and C that cut off a given area of risk at the tails of the distribution. These measurements are called standard normal deviates and are usually referred to as t values which correspond to the degree of reliability specified. Some of the more commonly used t values for two-tailed reliability are:

t	Probability
1.00	.6826
1.65	.9010
1.96	.9500
2.97	.9970

In accounting applications of statistical sampling, precision is often used to express an upper and lower limit around the statistical estimate. At a two-tailed reliability of 95 percent, each precision limit is approximately two standard errors from the mean. A precision of three standard errors from the mean in both directions provides 99.7 percent two-tailed reliability and is often referred to as statistical certainty.

[4] Ibid., pp. 24–25.

In special situations we may be concerned with only one precision limit: either the upper or lower. For example, in a purchase investigation, we may be concerned only that the physical assets are no less than a stated book value. In such situations we can achieve 95 percent reliability as to the one limit with only 1.65 standard errors. This comes about because we are making only a one-tailed estimate. Our concern is that the true value is no less than a stated book value and we are not concerned that there is also a five percent risk that the true value is more than the stated value. Although 1.65 standard errors give about 90 percent two-tailed reliability, ignoring the 5 percent risk at one side of the distribution allows the same number (1.65) of standard errors to provide the same precision limit in the required direction at 95 percent one-tailed reliability. We want to be sure that we are getting at least what we are paying for and the seller assumes the risk that we may be getting more for our money.

Sampling without Replacement

Sampling probabilities differ depending upon whether the samples are from a finite population of numerically determinable size or from an infinite population. A population may not be infinite but it may still not be countable or determinable, such as the number of fish in the sea. Accounting populations, on the other hand, are usually finite but can become effectively infinite if each sample item selected is replaced before another selection is made, in which case the sample size could conceivably exceed the population size. When populations are finite for sampling purposes and sampling is without replacement, the sample size (n) clearly cannot exceed the population size (N) and often will be less than 10 percent of that amount.

One of the factors involved in calculating the precision of an estimate is the finite population correction. In many cases this correction is not a major adjustment, but there are times when it does become important. The correction is made necessary by the fact that most sampling of accounting populations is sampling without replacement. This means that as an item is selected for inclusion in the sample it is not replaced in the population and does not have a chance of being selected again.

The nature of accounting records is such that there is no advantage in selecting an item twice, and the nature of computer records is such that it is logical to select on a systematic basis starting at the beginning of the file and going through to the end of the file. Under such an approach, even though the item is still technically contained in the file, it would not become available for selection once again.

When sampling without replacement, the probabilities of selection change with every item selected. This change in selection probabilities is not particularly important if the population (N) is very large and the sampling fraction ($n \div N$) is less than one-tenth, but it can become important when the population is small and the sampling fraction is larger. As an illustration, if we are selecting two items out of five with replacement after each selection, the probability of selecting any one item is always 20 percent. If we sample without replacement, the probability of selecting any one item as the first sample item is still 20 percent but the probability of selecting any one of the remaining four items as the second selection is 25 percent.

The correction for sampling without replacement is made by multiplying the variance by

$$\frac{N - n}{N - 1} \qquad (2.8)$$

When n is very small in relation to N, the value of this formula will be close to one and such value will have little effect on the variance. It has even less effect on the standard deviation because the effect will be the square root of this value. The square root of any decimal fraction is always closer to unity than the fraction itself. On the other hand, as n approaches N the value comes closer to zero and reduces the variance substantially. The calculation can be approximated for large N by subtracting the sampling fraction ($n \div N$) from 1.[5] Thus if we are selecting 1 out of 20, the finite population correction would be approximately .95.

Abnormal Data

The hope of every statistician is that all the population data are representative of the population and normally distributed, and that the items selected in the sample will also be normally distributed, but this is rarely the case. Accounting data usually tend to a large number of small-value items and a decreasingly lesser number of large-value items. Occasionally the one or two items at the large-value end of the spectrum may be so extreme in size that the random selection of one of these items in the sample will influence the estimate far beyond the bounds of normality.

A similar problem of sample bias may occur when a book inventory item is small but the corresponding physical value turns out to be very large. This might come about through improper recording of a recently received shipment. These types of items will have an upsetting effect on the estimate and particularly on the variance. To prevent this, it is helpful to draw on the knowledge and experience of those who have been handling the inventory.

[5] W. Edwards Deming, *Sample Design and Business Research*, Wiley, New York, 1960, p. 385.

In every inventory there are certain attractive items that, unless kept under lock and key, will tend to disappear. There are items that, for one reason or another, may be sold under two or more different part numbers. These may be confused in the records or in the shipping process so that offsetting errors might develop. Other items may look similar, causing shipping clerks to ship wrong parts and thus create sizable differences between the book records and physical inventory quantities. If such items are known about in advance, they can be handled easily by stratification, as will be discussed later. When they turn up as surprises in the sample, their causes are usually fairly obvious but considerably more effort is required to compensate for their effects.

Reduction in Variance

The only way that the reliability can be strengthened, or the precision tightened, is by a reduction in the variance. Any steps that will lead to a reduction in variance are therefore appropriate and desirable. One of the principal ways of reducing a variance is by choosing an appropriate type of estimate.

Choice of Estimate. The choice of estimate depends on a number of different things such as the cost of obtaining the data and the burden of computation. In a situation such as a physical inventory, where a high degree of correspondence is expected between the book and physical values, the regression estimate will be far superior to that of a mean estimate. Where there is a reasonable expectation that the correlation between book and physical inventory is better than 90 percent, the reduction in variance may well be 80 percent or better. A greater understanding of the variance calculations may be gained from Figure 2.3.

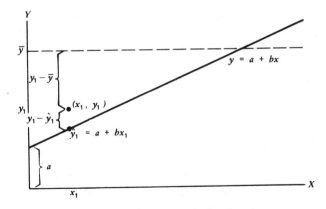

Figure 2.3 Measurement of variance.

For a given x value in the sample, a predicted y value may be determined. This predicted y value will fall on the line of regression. The squared deviation of this predicted value from the actual y value is summed, along with other such squared deviations, to produce the total variance of the sample. For a specific point, y_1, the deviation from the line of regression ($y_1 - \hat{y}_1$), as shown in Figure 2.3, is considerably less than the deviation from the mean ($y_1 - \bar{y}$). This is to be expected where there is a high correlation of x and y values.

In calculating the variance for a sample taken from a physical inventory it is unlikely that any item will equal the mean, and so each item will have a deviation from the mean and thus produce a relatively sizable variance. On the other hand, it is fairly normal to find complete agreement between book and physical values on perhaps 60 percent of the inventory items and fairly close agreement on most of the remainder. Thus the deviation between the actual physical value and the predicted physical value based on the book value may be virtually negligible on most of the items, and the resulting total variance will be relatively much smaller.

Stratification.   Another way in which the variance can be reduced considerably is through stratification, as will be discussed below. The variance may be reduced by the way in which the strata are chosen and also by the way in which the sample is allocated to the various strata.

In one company, the change over a period of several years from stratified mean estimates to stratified regression estimates has resulted in a reduction of the precision, expressed as a percentage of the estimate, from nearly 3 percent to something less than 1 percent. Stratified regression estimates are a powerful tool in inventory estimation because of the expected close correspondence between the book and physical values.

The gain in precision through the use of stratified regression estimates over other types of estimates may not always be so large, but there is always likely to be some gain in precision. If computed on a manual basis, it could be argued that the additional gain might not be worth the effort required to make the necessary calculations. When computed electronically, however, even a small gain could be worthwhile, as there is no incremental cost for more complex calculations.

STRATIFICATION

In stratified sampling, the inventory items are first grouped into a given number of classes, and then each is treated as a subgroup. A random sample is drawn from each group, usually with a different sampling rate for each. An estimate is obtained from each group, and the results are combined into a single overall estimate.

Inventory populations lend themselves readily to stratified sampling. The logical variate for stratification is the physical value itself. Unfortunately, this is not known at the time that the sample is selected. The book value, however, should be a reasonable approximation of this value and consequently is a logical proxy for stratification purposes.

Reason for Use

The principal reason for stratification is to reduce the variance for a given sample size and thus tighten the precision surrounding an estimate. A stratified estimate based on inventory values will have to be better than an unstratified estimate. An analysis of the propagation of variance will show that the unstratified estimate contains variances between strata that are eliminated from the stratified estimate.[6] The stratified variance must therefore be lower and, in most cases, will be considerably lower.

The purpose of stratification is to take advantage of existing knowledge regarding the accounting population so as to reduce the variance. In the case of a physical inventory, the recorded monetary values provide the best basis for stratification. It should be pointed out, however, that there may be other ways in which an accounting population may be stratified, such as by geographical location. For example, separate estimates might be obtained at various locations by stratifying on monetary value, and these separate estimates combined into an overall estimate which would be stratified by geographical location. Another possible way to stratify might be by types of parts such as engine parts, electrical parts, small parts, and so on, or by characteristics such as current, slow moving, and obsolete. As the likelihood of error would be small where obsolete parts are concerned, the sampling fraction could be much lower without having too large an effect on the overall variance.

Number of Strata

The number of strata may vary from two to virtually as many items as there are in the population. If the population is divided into two strata, each stratum will have its own mean and the squared mean errors will be measured from their respective means. This minimizes the variance within each stratum and thus minimizes the total variance. For example, let us consider the variance for a sample of four items: 2, 4, 6, and 8. If the sample is not

[6] Ibid., pp. 285–294.

stratified, the mean or average value is 5 and the variance from the mean is computed as follows:

$$
\begin{aligned}
(2 - 5)^2 &= 9 \\
(4 - 5)^2 &= 1 \\
(6 - 5)^2 &= 1 \\
(8 - 5)^2 &= 9 \\
\hline
&\ \ 20
\end{aligned}
$$

Now, if the sample is divided into two strata, consisting of (2, 4) and (6, 8), the means of each stratum are 3 and 7 respectively. The variance of each stratum is computed in the following manner:

$$
\begin{array}{ll}
(2 - 3)^2 = 1 & (6 - 7)^2 = 1 \\
(4 - 3)^2 = 1 & (8 - 7)^2 = 1 \\
\hline
\quad\quad\quad\ 2 & \quad\quad\quad\ 2
\end{array}
$$

What has happened here is that a substantial part of the variance, generally referred to as the variance between strata, has been removed by stratification. In this simple illustration, the larger variance of 20 consists of the variances within each strata of 4, (2 + 2) and the variance between strata of 16. This latter value may be developed by squaring the difference between the stratum mean and the unstratified mean for each item as follows:

$$
\begin{aligned}
(3 - 5)^2 &= 4 \\
(3 - 5)^2 &= 4 \\
(7 - 5)^2 &= 4 \\
(7 - 5)^2 &= 4 \\
\hline
&\ \ 16
\end{aligned}
$$

The significance of this variance reduction is that it will enable the financial manager to make estimates with greater precision than could be made with an unstratified estimate. In the case of the unstratified estimate we divide the total variance of 20 by the four items to get an average variance of 5. The standard deviation is $\sqrt{5}$ or approximately 2.24. To obtain 95 percent reliability for an estimate of a population of 100 we would require about two standard deviations. The precision associated with the unstratified estimate would be twice 2.24 multiplied by the 100 items in the population, or 448.

In the case of the stratified estimate we could obtain much lower precision with the same 95 percent reliability. The average variance in each stratum is now 1, and the standard deviation in each stratum is 1. The resulting precision would be twice the standard deviation multiplied by 100 items, or 200. If we can expect the estimate to be within plus or minus 200 instead of plus or minus 448 with the same degree of reliability, there are obvious advantages to stratification as this simple example shows.

When stratification is by value, the greater the stratification, the more reduction there will be in the overall variance. Unlimited stratification should theoretically result in the greatest reduction in the variance, but most of the reduction can be achieved with a reasonable number of strata and more precise positioning of the strata limits.

When a narrow range of monetary precision is required, it has been determined, by process of trial and error, that a useful number of strata is 20. This number may be excessive where the precision requirement is relaxed, but any such excess can be removed by collapsing the strata, or putting two adjacent strata together, when the indicated sample in any one stratum would be too small. The procedure that will be described later (Appendix 5), automatically adjusts to 20 strata or less as may be required. A lesser number of strata may be specified as an option.

Stratum Limits

The variance of a stratified estimate may be reduced even further by selecting the upper limit of each stratum in such a way that the variance in that stratum is minimized. The statistical theory for optimum stratification has been available for many years.[7] While the goal of all optimization procedures is to reduce the variance to a minimum, the optimum state can never be achieved absolutely, and a near minimum is ordinarily good enough.

In a two-stratum design, the upper cutoff of the bottom stratum would lie between, and would approximate, the average of the two stratum means. Moving the stratum cutoff up or down would change both the stratum means and, as a consequence, would also change the sum of the squared mean errors of each stratum. As we move the cutoff point up or down, there will be one cutoff point at which the sum of the squared mean errors of both strata would be at a minimum. Taking our previous example of variance calculation, we effectively placed the upper cutoff at 5, so that 2 and 4 fell in the bottom stratum and 6 and 8 were included in the top stratum. Placing the cutoff at that point reduced the total variance to a minimum. If we moved the cutoff down to 3 the variance calculation would change as follows:

[7] Tore Dalenius and Joseph L. Hodges, Jr., "Minimum Variance Stratification," *American Statistical Association Journal*, March 1959, p. 94.

$$(2 - 2)^2 = 0 \qquad (4 - 6)^2 = 4$$
$$(6 - 6)^2 = 0$$
$$(8 - 6)^2 = \underline{4}$$
$$\underline{\underline{8}}$$

Instead of 4 the total variance now is 8. The same total variance would result from moving the cutoff up to 7. The location of this minimum cutoff point depends on the nature of the distribution, but, given knowledge of the distribution, it is relatively easy to approximate this point. The same procedure can be extended to any number of strata so that the sum of the squared deviations will be a minimum.

It has been shown that the optimum solution to minimizing the total variance will be obtained when the expected contribution from each stratum to the total aggregate variance is made equal for each stratum.[8] This is the way in which optimum stratification was achieved in the simple example shown above.

Exponential Distribution.   Most physical inventories, and for that matter most accounting populations, follow an exponential distribution in that they contain a large number of items of small value and a decreasing number of items as the value increases. This distribution describes a pattern found quite often in business, engineering, and nature as, for example, the life of equipment, length of telephone calls, or decay rate of radioactive material.

The usual portrayal of the exponential distribution is as a cumulative frequency distribution with the total number of items on the vertical axis and the item dollar value, or other features of interest, on the horizontal axis. The steadily decreasing slope, a characteristic of the exponential distribution, indicates the number of items that exceed a given dollar value or, in the case of equipment, have a useful life exceeding so many months. Using our previous inventory example of 2500 items, with a total value of $10,000,000, the cumulative frequency distribution would appear as shown in Figure 2.4.

Figure 2.4 shows that approximately 1500 items would have a dollar value of $2000 or more and about 500 items would have a value of $6400 or more. We know that the mean value is $4000, and about 900 items will be more than and 1600 items less than, this mean value. The characteristics of the exponential distribution are sufficiently well known that a close approximation to optimum stratification is relatively easy to obtain.

The graph in Figure 2.4 shows an exponential distribution with dollar values being on the X or horizontal axis, and the number of items greater

[8] P. C. Mahalanobis, "Some Aspects of the Design of Sample Surveys," *Sankhya*, 1952, Vol. 12, Part 1–2, p. 4, footnote.

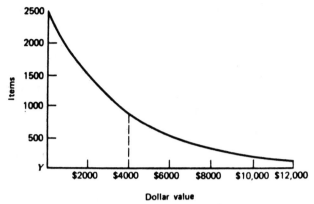

Figure 2.4 Exponential distribution.

than each dollar value being on the Y or vertical axis. Plotting the number greater than each dollar value defines the shape of the distribution.

In contrast to Figure 2.4, the usual approach to expressing an exponential population graphically is to set forth the X axis in terms of dollar values related to the mean and to set forth the Y axis in terms of decimal frequency. Thus a new X scale is developed with each X value being divided by the mean and for this purpose, the mean may be approximate. This scaling results in the mean value of this new distribution being one. The Y axis is likewise scaled down by dividing the number of items for each dollar value by the total number of items so that the axis is expressed as a frequency. Figure 2.5 shows how Figure 2.4 appears after these changes in scale.

By the use of natural logarithms, or through reference to a table of the negative exponential function, the exponents may be found that will divide the area under the curve equally. If vertical lines are drawn at these cutoff

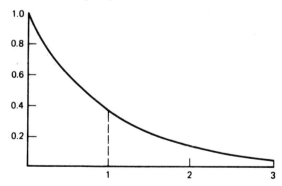

Figure 2.5 Standard exponential distribution.

points, the appearance of the distribution will resemble a series of near rectangles gradually decreasing in height and increasing in width, as shown in Figure 2.6 where the distribution has been divided into five equal strata with 500 items in each stratum. The extended values associated with these strata would become larger as we move toward the higher unit dollar values. Since the variance would not increase nearly as rapidly as we move to the right, we are coming fairly close to the optimum goal of an equal variance for each stratum. One further adjustment is required.

Optimum Stratification.   We know from the nature of an exponential distribution that the mean of each of these rectangles in Figure 2.6 would lie slightly to the left of the midpoint. It would seem, intuitively, that this would produce a larger variance than if the mean were located at the midpoint. This situation can be accomplished conceptually by constructing alongside the bottom stratum, another stratum of equal width with its height equal to the ordinate at the original first cutoff point, as shown in Figure 2.7. Considering these two rectangles as depicting one bottom stratum, the mean is now located at the midpoint and the variance is near to a minimum. If the second and subsequent strata are constructed in a like manner, it seems reasonable to assume that the cutoff points will closely approximate the stratification needed to minimize the variance. Although this approach has been set forth in mathematical terms and proved to be only a first approximation, nearly all the advantage to be gained from optimum stratification is obtained as a practical matter by using this first approximation.

All that is then required to determine any cutoff point is to multiply the exponential value for a given area in units of the mean by twice the value of the mean. By reference to a table of the negative exponential distribution, or as shown below, we find that 20 percent of the area is to the left of 0.2231.

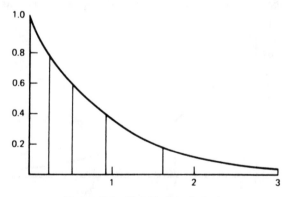

Figure 2.6 Division into 5 strata.

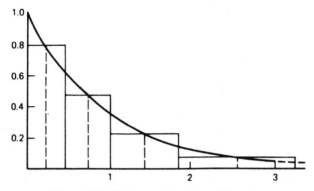

Figure 2.7 Optimum allocation of 5 strata.

Thus for a population whose mean value is $4000, the first cutoff in a five-stratum design would be at $1785 ($0.223 \times 2 \times 4000$). By a similar procedure, the second cutoff would be located at $4086, the third at $7330, and the fourth at $12,875.

Stratum Number	Area to Right	X Value
1	0.95	0.0513
2	0.90	0.1054
3	0.85	0.1625
4	0.80	0.2231
5	0.75	0.2877
6	0.70	0.3567
7	0.65	0.4308
8	0.60	0.5108
9	0.55	0.5978
10	0.50	0.6931
11	0.45	0.7985
12	0.40	0.9163
13	0.35	1.0498
14	0.30	1.2040
15	0.25	1.3863
16	0.20	1.6094
17	0.15	1.8971
18	0.10	2.3026
19	0.05	2.9957
20	0.00	∞

Allocation of Sample to Strata

Once the strata limits have been determined and the size of the overall sample is known, a further reduction in variance may be achieved by the proper allocation of the sample size to each stratum. There is one allocation of the sample items for which the variance is a minimum. The problem is to determine this allocation before the variance is known.

Arbitrary Allocation.   The allocation of the sample items to strata could be arbitrary, particularly where prior knowledge of certain situations exists. For instance, as discussed earlier, a very low sampling fraction might be used on obsolete items where it is unlikely that there has been any change from the previous physical inventory. The reverse might be true where certain items are susceptible to damage or pilferage, in which case every such item might be included in the sample and the group of items treated as a separate stratum to be sampled completely. It is desirable to include all items falling in the top stratum in the sample so that a sampling fraction of one is also arbitrary.

Proportional Allocation.   A proportional allocation is often used, particularly when a sample is selected manually. If the sample items are allocated in proportion to the number of items in the population in each stratum, this can be achieved by applying a single sampling fraction throughout the whole population. The ease with which the sample may be selected manually may overcome any advantage from further minimizing the variance.

If the sample size is allocated to strata in proportion to the dollar values in each stratum, the variance is more likely to be near a minimum, and this allocation procedure is relatively easy to apply when the sample is to be selected manually.[9] It would require as a prerequisite, however, a distribution of numbers and dollar book values by strata. As an example of how that might work in practice, let us assume that a sample of 250 is required from an inventory of $10,000,000.

The stratification of this inventory and the allocation by strata might be as follows:

Stratum Number	Cutoff	Dollar Amount	Dollar Percent	Sample Size
1	$1000	$ 900,000	9.0	23
2	2000	1,750,000	17.5	44
3	4000	3,300,000	33.0	82
4	7500	2,750,000	27.5	68
5	∞	1,300,000	13.0	33
		$10,000,000	100.0	250

[9] Des Raj, *Sampling Theory*, McGraw-Hill, New York, 1968, pp. 67–68.

Although such an allocation of the sample would probably not produce a minimum variance, it might be sufficiently close when manual selection methods are required. When a computer is not available for selection purposes, it may be much easier to classify by strata and select proportionately. Minimum variance obviously is desirable, but there are also time and cost factors to be considered.

Optimum Allocation. The principle of optimum allocation is that the total sample will be allocated to strata in accordance with the weighted standard deviation within each stratum.[10] The weighted standard deviation is computed for each stratum by multiplying the stratum standard deviation by the number of items in that stratum. The ratio of each computation to the sum of such computations for all strata not sampled completely is used to allocate the total sample size to strata. This requires prior knowledge that may not be available when selection is made manually but can be obtained with a computer.

As these factors are easy to calculate by computer and are necessary to determine the overall sample size, it is a simple computation to allocate the total sample to each stratum on the basis of the weighted standard deviations. Some adjustments will be required so that the sample will not exceed the number in the stratum. It is also desirable to increase the number of sample items in each stratum to at least one out of 1000 items. As the allocation factor may produce a fractional number, the sample size is always rounded upwards to the nearest whole number. The coding required for optimum allocation is shown in Appendix 5.

Collapsing Strata. The formula for calculation of the variance of a regression estimate[11] requires that no one stratum have less than three sample items to be evaluated. This means either that a minimum of three items must be selected in each stratum or that two or more strata must be combined to ensure that three or more items are selected.

A programmed procedure shown in Appendix 5 examines the intervals in each stratum successively, and determines the size of the sample that would be taken and whether the sample size is sufficient for the type of estimate to be made. If it is insufficient, this stratum would be added to the next stratum, and the calculations repeated. The process is continued until all strata have been examined. If the indicated sample in the next to last stratum should be insufficient, this stratum would be combined with the previous one.

Zeros and Minus Values. One of the seeming characteristics of a computer inventory population is a fairly large number of zero book balances for which physical quantities are unlikely to exist. These may be out of stock or

---

[10] Deming, *Sample Design*, p. 318.
[11] Cochran, *Sampling Techniques*, p. 195.

new parts not yet received. There may be no variance for these items, and as a consequence no part of the sample would be allocated to them based on the weighted standard deviation. As a matter of convenience, therefore, these items will be stratified in the lowest stratum for which the upper cutoff will be zero.

Similarly, and for various reasons, minus values will occur in the book inventory. These also pose a particular problem in that the physical value, if any, must be positive. Generallly speaking, small minus values are errors that occur from breakage in pricing out pieces individually or in different quantities, that were purchased or manufactured at a cost per dozen, per gross, or per gallon. Preliminary procedures can eliminate such minus values, but if they remain in the inventory, they will be included in the lowest stratum. In order to have some of these items in the sample, they are sampled along with the zero value items at the same rate as in the next lowest stratum.

Precautions

In sampling data for the first time, it is well to be cautious so that one is not surprised later. The wariness with which many people approach statistical sampling is undoubtedly due to publicized blunders that have occurred in sample surveys in the past. These errors of the past were usually operational blunders or were due to structural limitations of the data. The use of computer programs avoids the possibility of many operational blunders. Some foresight in gaining an understanding of the data limitations prior to taking the sample can avoid other problems.

Large Items.   When there are a few very large items in the population, it is possible that the sample may not include one of them and therefore may give a distorted estimate. This can usually be avoided by including all the items in the top stratum in the sample.

Unrecorded Items.   When selection is made from book values, there is also the possibility that certain items of physical inventory may not have a chance to get into the sample because they are not recorded in the books. This may be avoided by a careful check, in advance of taking the inventory, between the locations and those shown on the computer records. For example, if cards are punched for all locations showing greater than zero quantities on the computer records and if these cards are matched to the physical locations on a "one for one" basis, stock not recorded properly by location will be discovered. The computer records can then be corrected before the sample is taken.

Large Differences.   Sometimes there are large differences between the book values and the physical values. If the physical values are less than the book values, the problem is not too severe, as most such items would be included in the top stratum by book value and would accordingly be counted in the sample. Where the book value is low and the physical value is high, however, there is a possibility that including such an item in the sample will distort the estimate and enlarge the variance substantially. If such a condition is known or thought to exist for a particular reason, all items that might fall within this category should be included in the top stratum of the sample.

A problem may also arise in the choice of estimate. Under certain circumstances, a ratio estimate will be unsatisfactory because the values in a stratum ratio may be of opposite sign. Nearly all problems arising from the choice of an estimate disappear when regression estimates are used.

DEVELOPMENT OF COMPUTER PROGRAMS

The development of the computer programs (described more fully in Chapter 11) was a direct response to the need for samples in the accounting area. Where the inventories of parts and supplies were particularly large, the high cost of taking such an inventory to determine income indicated a need for a sampling procedure. The first samples that were taken were rather crude by today's standards, although samples are still being taken by accountants on that basis every day.

The stratification was performed by the use of data processing equipment, and sample sizes were calculated manually from such data. The actual selection of the samples was done either manually or on a mechanical basis, given the sampling interval in each stratum. To evaluate the estimate and the related precision, control totals from the data processing equipment were obtained from each stratum giving the necessary sums of squares and sums of cross products. The rest of the evaluation was performed manually. The first computer program that was developed in this area was one that evaluated the sample results directly from the sample input. Many improvements have been made in the original program, but the procedure remains essentially the same.

Need for Programs

One need perform only a few of these evaluations manually to appreciate the value of a computer program in this area. The complexity of the calculations and the repetitiveness of the procedure are such that use of the computer is desirable; furthermore, it assures the accuracy of the computations. At an early stage in the progress, there were few staff accountants with the requisite statistical knowledge to make these calculations manually, and so the development of computer programs was a useful way of imparting this statistical knowledge.

Some years earlier, a general-purpose computer program, the Auditape system, had been developed by Deloitte Haskins & Sells and widely used within the firm for auditing purposes. This system freed auditors from the need for specialized programs to obtain necessary information from client computer records. It introduced auditors to computer techniques merely through use of these programs, and helped them overcome any inhibitions they might have had resulting from a lack of computer knowledge. It was a fairly simple step to include statistical programs in the Auditape system for the design, selection, and evaluation of sample estimates. Users of these programs would not necessarily require a high degree of statistical knowledge, as the programs would make the necessary calculations for them.

In 1966, Deloitte Haskins & Sells made the Auditape system, including these statistical programs, available to its clients and others who were interested in using these programs.[12] Although there is a nominal charge to cover the necessary cost of providing such a service, this cost has been waived in the case of schools and other not-for-profit institutions using the programs for academic or research purposes.

---

[12] Inquiries should be addressed to Deloitte Haskins & Sells, Computer Services Department, One World Trade Center, New York, NY 10048.

CHAPTER 3

ACCOUNTING POPULATIONS

STATISTICAL REQUIREMENTS

There are certain basic statistical requirements for any sampling operation, but these are apt to be somewhat different for accounting populations. Accounting populations generally are much better defined than other types of populations with which statisticians might have gained their sampling experience. It is well to consider the ways in which accounting populations differ, for they may indicate that statistical methods different from those in science and the social sciences should be employed.

Target Population

A primary statistical sampling requirement is to define a universe or target population about which information is to be estimated and from which the sample may be drawn. The target population would encompass all the items that we wish to study, such as people in a country, accounts in an accounts receivable ledger, or parts in an inventory. We may know, in general, the boundaries of the population, such as all the parts in Warehouse A or all the people in the United States, but as we get more specific, it is not always possible to get a list or record of all the items comprising the target population. The U.S. Census Bureau makes a determined effort to count all the people in the United States once every 10 years but not everyone gets counted. In many similar situations it may be quite difficult to obtain a satisfactory list of all items encompassed by a defined target population, as, for instance, when attempting to estimate the number of fish in a pond or the number of trees in a forest. This tends to make statistical estimation of such target populations quite difficult.

On the other hand, the accounting populations about which information is likely to be estimated and from which samples can be taken are much more precisely definable. The population is often represented by a complete record of everything that might be included in the sample. Thus there is a marked difference between accounting populations and the target population commonly referred to as the universe by statisticians sampling in other areas.

Statistical Frame

Statisticians often refer to the listing or record from which a sample is selected as a frame, simply because they have no assurance that the frame includes all the items in the target population from which they would like to draw the sample. A record compiled a year or so ago may be the best frame available for a defined population despite the fact that some changes have occurred. From a statistical standpoint, however, the only valid inferences that can be made from a sample apply to the frame from which the sample is drawn. Any inference about the target population, if it exceeds the frame, is beyond the limits of statistical inference.

Internal Control.   Most frames from which accounting samples are to be drawn are likely to be reasonably complete representations of the population because the system of internal control is designed to keep the records up to date and under accounting control. Some types of records, such as perpetual inventory records, may not include some items that are in the warehouse and that are defined as being included in the population. In these cases, as discussed later, a little preliminary checking can clear up such differences so that it is reasonable to assume that the statistical frame and the universe, as these terms are used generally by statisticians, are one and the same for most accounting populations. If for any reason they are not, it is quite likely that they can be made the same with a minimum amount of effort.

This coincidence of universe and frame in the case of accounting populations permits the extension of valid statistical inference to the entire accounting population. Generalizations beyond the frame to the universe are otherwise a matter of judgment, as statistical theory does not provide any basis for such generalizations. Further references in this book to accounting populations may be regarded as synonymous with statistical frame.

The accounting population from which a sample is to be drawn is more often than not a computer record of substantial size from which a printout may be obtained in complete detail showing extensive characteristics of each item. The principal advantage of these records in a statistical situation is not so much that they show the complete detail of each item, as that these records are capable of being manipulated in the computer to obtain and investigate certain statistical characteristics that might otherwise not be available.

Nature of Population Distribution.   One useful statistical characteristic is the nature of the population distribution. If the shape of this distribution is not known from a previous analysis, it is relatively easy to gain an understanding of the distribution through computer analysis. The items in the population may be classified according to various dollar limits so that anyone making a statistical estimate will understand the nature of the distribution from which the sampling will be done. This information enables one to set strata limits and decide on the type of estimate that would be most satisfactory for the purpose.

Sampling Units.   Each individual item within the population constitutes a sampling unit. Thus there is a need to define what a sampling unit consists of, and these definitions are sometimes adjustable and often not too clear.

Accounting records maintained on an computer meet these requirements for definition and clarity in all respects. The size of the population in dollars is often indicated by control totals, and the detailed records building up to those totals constitute the sampling units. Even if some characteristic other than dollars is being sampled, the dollar amounts can still serve to represent the sampling units in the frame. Accounting records not maintained on a computer will usually meet these statistical requirements for well defined sampling units, but seldom as conveniently.

Serialization.   Every sampling unit in the frame should have a serial number and, if this is not the case, some means must be developed for assigning a number for sampling purposes in such a way that random numbers may be used to select the units to be sampled. In the absence of an adequate frame in the form of a listing, one fairly common method is to fasten or stick prenumbered tags or labels to all the sampling units that exist physically. Where sampling units are listed as lines on a page, the numbers may be assigned according to page and line number so that the tenth line on page eight would be 810.

Accounting records usually bear an account number, part number, or serial number by which the specific units may be identified. In the event, however, that this is not so, and where there is some logical sequence to the records, they may be assigned numbers in sequence without the number being actually recorded on the item. The twenty-fifth item would be the twenty-fifth item from the beginning of the file. A computer file is either sequential or may be arranged in sequence quickly so that an implied sequence number may be developed and used for random selection.

Variability.   If every item in the population had exactly the same dollar value or attribute, any size sample, even a sample of one, would give a precise estimate of the value or attribute in the population. Unfortunately, this is rarely, if ever, the case and so we have a degree of variability in every population. As long as we have variability, repeated samples from the same population will produce different results. The parameters of repeated samples from the same frame will form a distribution of their own, and this distribution will approach a normal distribution as the number of samples increases.

The variability within the population, measured by the standard deviation, is one of the determinants of sample size, but this characteristic is difficult to measure accurately until the sample has been taken. Variability may be estimated from samples taken previously or by taking small pilot samples from current data. Familiarity with similar populations may help in estimating variability, but anyone making a statistical estimate is always faced with the possibility that the variability within this particular population may be different than expected.

Accounting populations have certain advantages in estimating variability, as will be discussed later in more detail. In many cases, computer files may be available from prior years from which fairly precise calculations may be made of the standard deviation of the population. In most cases, accounting data will not change greatly from one year to the next unless some major change has occurred, such as a merger or acquisition. In cases where prior data are not available, reasonable estimates may be made from the current records. Accounting records are usually updated at least once a month so that a standard deviation may be calculated from the most recent monthly record.

ACCOUNTING RECORDS

Accounting records in most large companies contain numerous individual items, necessitating the use of large-scale data processing equipment. An inventory record may contain 2000–3000 items in a small company and 200,000–300,000 items in a large company. Specific variables such as the dollar amount for any given part in inventory are expected to conform more and more to an underlying pattern as the number of items in the population tend toward infinity. A statistical sample of 100 items should conform rather closely to the characteristics of the parent population.

Frequency Distribution

It is difficult for even a trained mind to grasp fully the significance of a large accounting population without some degree of classification. For example, we age accounts receivable in order to judge the collectibility of the individual accounts that make up the accounts receivable total. A classification useful for statistical sampling purposes is called a frequency distribution.

If we set up dollar intervals and classify the number of specific parts in an inventory by those intervals we would arrive at a frequency distribution similar to that shown in Figure 3.1

By narrowing the dollar intervals and reclassifying the items, the frequency distribution would approximate a smooth curve. The larger the number of items in the inventory, the smoother the curve would be, until we think of it as a continuous distribution. Whether or not we ever choose to make such a distribution, and such distributions are easily made with a computer, we should realize that such an underlying frequency distribution exists. This is a useful method of classification regardless of the statistical attributes of the population.

In a mathematical sense, a continuous distribution may be represented by a function that describes the size and shape of the distribution. The shape of a distribution is also described by the moments of the distribution. For any given value along the horizontal axis, the corresponding value on the vertical axis may be determined from the mathematical function. Plotting successive values will trace the pattern of the distribution. Moment is a term borrowed from mathematical physics. The first moment is analogous to the center of gravity and the second moment to the moment of inertia.

The principal moments of the distribution, the mean and standard deviation, determine the location and scale of the distribution. Two distributions may be similar and have approximately the same mathematical function but the underlying values may have a different mean, as shown in Figure 3.2.

If we subtract the mean value of 100 in Figure 3.2a from every value in that distribution and the mean value of 250 in Figure 3.2b from every value in that distribution, each distribution would be centered at zero and would be identical. Thus we could have the same mathematical function for two

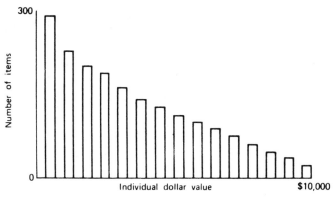

Figure 3.1 Frequency distribution.

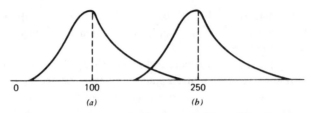

Figure 3.2   Similar distributions at different locations.

different distributions even though the means or first moments of the distributions are different.

Similarly we may have two distributions with the same mathematical function and the same mean but with different standard deviations as shown in Figure 3.3.

It may be shown that if we divide each value in each distribution by the standard deviation of its own distribution, both distributions would again be identical. Thus all four distributions shown in Figures 3.2 and 3.3 have the same shape and mathematical function, or standardized distribution, but differ in one or more parameters. Distributions can be generalized by their shape or function and specified by their parameters. Location and scale are determined by the moments which become parameters of the distribution and part of the mathematical function. If the scales are chosen so that the area under the curve and the number of observations are both equal to one, we have what is known as a probability distribution.

The principal point to be made from this discussion is that if we have some general idea of the shape of an accounting distribution, and can determine or approximate the important parameters such as the mean and the standard deviation, then we have sufficient knowledge with which to design an effective sample with tight precision.

Exponential Distribution.   For many years some accountants have used a rule of thumb for accounting populations which states that 80 percent of the

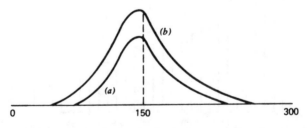

Figure 3.3   Dissimilar distributions at same location.

items represent 20 percent of the value, and the remaining 20 percent of the items represent 80 percent of the value. In recent years, as accountants have become more acquainted with statistical theory, this rule has been recognized as a paraphrase of the exponential distribution that has the characteristic shape shown in Figure 3.4.

Many, if not most, accounting populations follow an exponential distribution, and experience has shown that inventories of parts and supplies are likely to be so distributed.

The exponential distribution plays an important part in statistical theory[1] and its mathematical function is as follows:

$$e^{-x} \quad \text{where } e = 2.71828 \tag{3.1}$$

where e is the exponential value (2.71828) or the natural antilogarithm of 1. The properties of the exponential distribution are tabulated extensively, and its relation to the exponential integral that forms the base for natural logarithms makes a calculation of any specific value for the exponential distribution relatively easy.

One of the characteristics of the exponential distribution is that it has a steadily decreasing slope, as may be seen in Figure 3.4, and the slope of the function at any given point is equal to the corresponding value of the function on the vertical axis. The slope is measured by a tangent to the point on the curve and is equal to the ordinate value at all points on the curve. For a

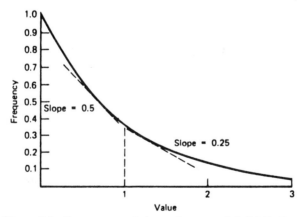

Figure 3.4   Frequency and slope of exponential distribution.

[1] John E. Freund, *Mathematical Statistics*, Prentice-Hall, Englewood Cliffs, NJ, 1962, p. 126.

value of approximately 0.7 on the horizontal axis, the corresponding function on the vertical axis is 0.5, and the slope at the intersection of 0.7 and 0.5 is also 0.5 as indicated in Figure 3.4. If we double the value on the horizontal axis to approximately 1.4, we halve both the corresponding function on the vertical axis and the slope at that point, both now being 0.25 as may be seen in Figure 3.4.

Another important characteristic of the exponential distribution is that the mean and variance are the same. For the standardized exponential distribution where the variance is 1, the mean and the standard deviation are the same. Also, about 63 percent of the total number of items in an exponential distribution will fall below the mean, and nearly 37 percent will fall above the mean. As a consequence we may find, for any value along the horizontal axis, the applicable percentage of the number of items falling to the right or higher than that value.

X	Percent
0.5	61
1.0	37
1.5	22
2.0	14
2.5	8
3.0	5

To facilitate calculations in terms of cumulative percentage the formula given above may be restated to the following form:

$$X = -\text{Ln } (\%) \cdot \bar{x} \cdot 2 \tag{3.2}$$

where X is the cutoff value on the horizontal axis, Ln is the natural logarithm, $\bar{x}$ is the mean, and % is the cumulative percentage. Calculations can thus be made to determine the cutoffs for 25 percent, 50 percent, 75 percent or any desired cumulative percentage of the number of items as shown below:

Percent	X	Cutoff ($\bar{x}$ = $4,000)
75	0.2876	$ 2,301
50	0.6931	5,545
25	1.3863	11,090
5	2.9957	23,965

While the calculations to support the distribution of the cumulative dollar value are not quite as simple, it can be shown that in terms of total dollar value, about 26 percent of the total dollar value in an exponential distribution will be below and about 74 percent above the mean dollar value. Therefore, if the items in an accounting population are distributed exponentially, approximately 37 percent of the items will constitute approximately 74 percent of the dollar value of the population.

When the perpetual inventory records are maintained on a computer, a magnetic tape or file can be drawn off at any point and used to make a number of statistical calculations and analyses in a short period of time. As stated above, if we know the general shape of the distribution and the key parameters we have sufficient knowledge with which to design an effective sample. The inventory values may be stratified by dollar classification quickly to provide a good understanding of the shape of the distribution. Thus there is satisfactory knowledge available of the frame from which the sample is to be taken to a degree not always the case in other types of statistical estimation. The type of analysis that can be made by computer is more comprehensive and efficient than anything that could be done manually. From an inventory of 10,000 parts, for example, it is possible to obtain the number of items within each stratum, the mean value for each stratum, and the standard deviation for each stratum in less time than it would take to compute the standard deviation of 25 items manually.

Aggregate Data.   Although accounting data at the transaction level will usually follow an exponential distribution, when such accounting data are summarized for postings to journals or ledgers, the populations formed by these totals are likely to tend toward a normal distribution. The more that data are aggregated, the more likely it is that they will follow the normal distribution.

The normal curve, as shown in Figure 3.5, is perfectly symmetrical about the mean value, at which point the number of items is at a maximum. The normal distribution may be specified completely by the mean and the standard deviation, both of which can be derived readily from any set of data.

Sample Means.   As discussed previously, if we were to take 100 samples from the same population and determine the means of these respective samples, the distribution of the 100 means would closely approximate a normal distribution. The point is that even though the sample may be drawn from an exponentially distributed population, such as an inventory of parts, the inference that we will draw from the sample can be based on a normal distribution defined by the sample mean and the sample standard error. Thus we can rely on mathematical statistics and the laws of probability to be 95 percent certain that the true but unknown population mean lies within a range of the

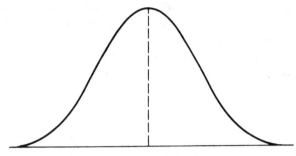

Figure 3.5 Normal distribution.

sample mean plus or minus two standard errors, with the number of standard errors determining the percentage of certainty. We need knowledge of the underlying distribution of the population only as an aid in designing a sample. We draw statistical inferences from the sample based upon the normal distribution.

Correspondence of Values

In order to stratify an inventory population, it is necessary to determine the lower and upper dollar limits of the items falling in each stratum. The lower limit of the bottom stratum must necessarily be negative infinity, unless specifically set otherwise, and the upper limit of the top stratum is positive infinity. As used in this connection, the bottom stratum would contain the lowest values. By setting the upper limit of the bottom stratum at zero, the problem then is to determine the upper limits of the intervening strata; the upper limit of one stratum automatically defines the lower limit for the next stratum.

When the perpetual inventory records are maintained on a computer, those records often are a reasonable proxy for the physical inventory population. In fact, the true feature of sampling interest is the degree to which the book inventory is representative of the physical inventory. The number of items in the book inventory and the total dollar value of the population will usually be known, at least approximately, so that all the necessary values are known with which to compute the strata limits.

When the strata limits have been determined, the book population may be classified according to these limits. An illustrative classification is shown below and the totals thus obtained will clarify the nature of the distribution.

Stratum	Upper Cutoff	Items	Book Value
1	$ 2,301	1,086	$ 1,101,476
2	5,545	764	2,835,505
3	11,090	468	3,606,933
4	23,965	157	2,300,613
5	∞	25	155,473
		2,500	$10,000,000

In this illustrative distribution, the number of items decreases with each succeeding stratum and thus generally conforms to the exponential pattern. In the event that the upper cutoffs set on the basis of an exponential distribution are not adequate for the purpose, these may be adjusted so that a more reasonable distribution of dollar values in the various strata will be obtained. A distribution of items that results in a fairly even dollar value in each stratum will be approximately correct although the bottom and top strata need not conform.

The expected correspondence of book and physical values provides the setting for the use of regression estimates. Regression estimates place emphasis on the relationship of the physical value to the book value, and are useful to the accountant in determining how closely the physical values correspond to the book records. The regression estimate utilizes all the information contained in the sample and is therefore, in a statistical sense, a sufficient estimate.

Let us consider a sample of 6 taken from a population of 100 items with a book value of $1250, disregarding small sample theory for the sake of simple explanation. The sample items are as follows:

	Book Value (X)	Physical Value (Y)
	15	15
	11	11
	15	16
	12	12
	10	10
	13	14
	76	78
Means	12.67	13

If we make a mean estimate based solely on the Y values and disregard the information contained in the X values, we arrive at the following:

$$\hat{Y} = \frac{N}{n} y$$

$$= \frac{100}{6} (78) \qquad (2.2)$$

$$= 1300$$

Thus our estimate of the population physical value is $1300 but it is an insufficient estimate as we have not made use of all the information available.

On the other hand, if we run a regression analysis of the above data we come up with a regression equation as follows:

$$\bar{y} = 1.13\bar{x} - 1.25 \qquad (2.1)$$

This gives us a value for b, the slope, of 1.13. We also know that the population book value is $1250 and thus the mean value is $12.50 for the population. The fact that it is not the same as the sample mean of $12.67 is an indication that some adjustment needs to be made. The regression estimate produces the following answer:

$$\hat{Y} = \frac{N}{n} y + Nb(\mu(X) - \bar{x})$$

$$= \frac{100}{6} (78) + (100 \cdot 1.13) \cdot (12.5 - 12.67) \qquad (2.6)$$

$$= 1281$$

This estimate is a sufficient estimate in that it uses all available information in arriving at the result.

Accounting Procedures

A clear understanding of the accounting procedures that are to be followed in the taking of the physical inventory and of the coordination of these procedures with the data processing division is essential if a statistical sample is to be taken properly. Among the necessary procedures are the choice of the selection and count dates, adherence to proper cutoffs, reduction of any processing lag and a check for units that may be missing from the computer records that serve as the statistical frame.

Processing Lag. There is usually a paperwork lag between the time when quantities are physically added to or withdrawn from inventory and the time when these transactions are recorded. This lag may be anywhere from several days to several weeks, so that, for example, it may be near the end of June by the calendar before the records are posted through June 15. As a consequence, the computer record from which the sample is drawn is not likely to have the same record date as the items that are to be counted.

A definite effort should be made to minimize the elapsed paperwork processing time during inventory taking. Part of the difficulty in this connection arises from the fact that many data processing departments may work on a weekly or semimonthly schedule in updating inventory. If updating is performed weekly, this will introduce a lag of a week, and if updating is semimonthly, a 15-day lag will occur. This lag may be avoided completely for smaller inventories that are all at one location; but where the operations are widespread, some processing lag will almost always be found.

By choosing a selection date near the end of the week or before a holiday weekend, it may be possible to bring the records sufficiently up to date so that the counts may be made on the next working day without having to adjust for any unrecorded receipts or withdrawls of inventory items in the intervening period. With some prior thought and planning, a good deal can be done to minimize the problems associated with the normal paperwork lag. On the incoming side, the purchasing department can plan so that shipments into the warehouse will be at a low point in the few days before the inventory is taken. Goods received at the last moment can perhaps be separated from the rest of the stock. On the outgoing side, shipments can be expedited during the earlier days of the week so that a final cutoff can be made on Thursday or Friday allowing enough time for the paperwork to catch up. While there may be situations where, even with the best planning, the lag cannot be eliminated, some very large and complicated inventory situations have been resolved by these methods.

Selection Date. It is customary to count the physical inventory as of the close of business at the end of a week or month, and it is important that this count date be chosen carefully both to facilitate the physical count and ensure that a satisfactory book record will be available as of that date. Although the actual count may be made on the first, second or third of the following month, the record count date is the end of the preceding month.

At the time that the sample items are selected, the recorded book value will be as of the selection date. At the time the physical count is made, the physical count will be as of the count date. Where these two dates are not the same because of the processing lag, and where inventory movement occurs after the selection date but before the count date, the difference between the book record at the selection date and the book record as of the count date represents the recorded transactions in and out during the intervening period. It has to be assumed that the same transactions have occurred in the physical quantities.

It is necessary, therefore, to adjust the physical quantity at the count date back to the physical quantity on the selection date in order to make an adequate comparison to the book value at the selection date. This adjustment is made by adding algebraically to the physical count quantity the difference between the book records on the selection date and on the count date. It must be clearly understood by all parties, and particularly by data processing personnel, that this adjustment has to be made. Furthermore, accurate cutoffs must be made at both the selection date and the count date; otherwise the adjustment may be a futile exercise. The shorter the lag between selection date and count date, the easier and more accurate this adjustment will be. If it can be avoided entirely, so much the better. At a minimum, it is essential that the selection date files and count date files be preserved on magnetic tape or disk so that this adjustment may be determined.

Cutoff.   During any accounting period, the paper work flow from various departments or outlying branches is apt to be sporadic. It is not uncommon for a particular day's work from one location to be processed ahead of or behind the main paperwork stream. This may be caused by a slow mail delivery, bad weather conditions, or the pressure of business at a particular location. It would be a normal operating procedure, however, to ensure that this did not happen at the end of an accounting period, or at such time as a physical inventory might be counted. While accounting departments are alert to this possibility at the end of a period, they may not be so careful at an intermediate date that may be used for selection purposes. It is necessary, however, that accurate cutoffs be made at both the selection date and the count date in order to obtain a satisfactory estimate. It is very difficult at a later time to adjust for any failure to make accurate cutoffs at the selection date.

Missing records.   In sampling from a perpetual inventory record, any item in the record should have an equal or determinable probability of being selected. One way in which a physical inventory item might not be open to selection is if some quantity or value is not recorded in the perpetual inventory record. Our universe is the physical inventory, and our frame, or means of access to the universe, is the book inventory. We usually think of these as containing the same items, but some care needs to be exercised to make sure that this is so.

A useful procedure to follow in this regard is to punch cards for each inventory item that shows a quantity by each location and sort these cards by location. At times when activity is at a low ebb, the warehousemen can match them to the actual parts locations and note the quantities at unmatched locations. If this procedure is followed several weeks in advance of actually selecting and counting the physical inventory, any records missing at that time can be included in the perpetual record and be subject to being sampled.

Inventory Records

Inventory records are maintained for locating parts, for inventory and accounting control, and for purchasing. These reasons often determine whether the records are simple or complicated. An example of a simple inventory record is the stock cards or bin records that may be maintained in a stockroom or warehouse. These cards will often contain nothing more than a part number, the quantity of the item on hand, and the location. They are used by the stockroom clerk for his or her own convenience in ascertaining if these parts are in stock and where they are located. Since these records show no dollar values, they are not likely to be maintained under accounting control where individual records can be summed to agree with control totals, and errors and misposting are likely to occur from time to time as stock movement is recorded. Nevertheless, such records are usually sufficiently accurate for the purpose of determining quantity and location.

Perpetual Inventory Record. A perpetual inventory record in a finished goods warehouse may require considerably more information to determine whether an order can be filled immediately or whether some or all parts on the order must be backordered. In addition to quantity and location, the record may be subdivided by color and size. Such a record may also contain unit cost or unit selling price. When such a perpetual record is well maintained, an invoice might be written immediately, before the stock is pulled, with the knowledge that the order is likely to be filled correctly when it is sent out to the warehouse.

A record of this type requires a higher degree of accuracy than may be sufficient for a bin record. Supplemental procedures may be applied to see that postings are made correctly. For example, fast moving items may be counted periodically and checked against the perpetual records to see that they are in proper balance or to provide for correcting the records. The quantities on hand may be checked at the time that a production or purchase order is issued for a new supply of these goods.

Perpetual records of this type are often maintained under accounting control whereby general ledger accounts establish what the monetary total of the records should be. This improves the likelihood of agreement between the perpetual records and the physical quantities on hand by reducing such possibilities as misposting to these records, or failing to record returned goods. Losses or pilferage, however, still go undetected.

Computer Record. Perpetual inventory records that are maintained on a computer are likely to be quite complicated. The record for each part number may be extensive and contain information for purchasing purposes as well as information for marketing and control purposes. The additional information may include the extended values of the quantities on hand at cost and at sales price. It may also include an historical record of sales by months for several years, together with the unit cost over such a period. Information may be included as to primary sources for purchased parts. A single record of this type may be of considerable length, and the length may vary from one record to another.

Clean File. Considerable difficulty may be avoided in the estimation of a physical inventory by starting with a "clean" inventory file, one that contains all the essential information but no information that is irrelevant to the purpose of estimation. Extracting only the essential information will require the development of a new file by a separate operation which can be performed by a utility program or a program designed especially for the purpose.

From an accounting standpoint, the development of a new file ensures agreement between the detailed inventory records and the accounting control over these records. From a computer processing standpoint, it ensures that the new file contains only the specific data required and no extraneous or unreadable records. From a statistical standpoint, it provides a firm foundation for sampling purposes. If all the records are readable and proved to the control totals, this file provides a satisfactory statistical frame from which the sample may be drawn.

The only information that is absolutely essential is the part number or some other means of identification and the extended cost of the book inventory. Quantity and unit cost may be brought forward on each part so that the extended value can be computed. The location or locations of the part can be useful information, as well as information on category or type which may be helpful in making meaningful segregations of the book inventory. For example, a separate category for parts especially susceptible to pilferage can improve the overall statistical results.

Another useful step in the preparatory stage is to clear out of the inventory old part numbers that have no quantity balances and all obsolete parts that have been written down to zero values. In some cases, these may form as much as 50 percent of the inventory so that elimination of these items will improve the statistical procedure. It will also be helpful to exclude from the tape very small minus or plus values that correspond to zero quantities. These values sometimes accumulate from pricing breakage and are not always cleared out of the inventory when they should be by adequate programming.

Sequence. The sequence in which items are placed in the computer file may or may not have significance. This should be determined at an early stage, for if the sequence is to be changed, it may be changed in the editing stage. The data may be in part number sequence with a group of numbers being assigned to certain categories of parts or supplies. Alternatively, a separate category code could be used for sequencing, so that the data are in order by part number within category for each location. A printout of the first hundred records from the file will often help in understanding the way in which the data are collated and in arriving at necessary decisions before too much computer time is wasted.

When the inventory contains only a few thousand items, all of which are in one basic location, there are no particular problems in estimating the total inventory and the natural order of the computer file may be preserved. From this frame, a sample of a few hundred items may be selected, counted, priced, extended, and evaluated in a relatively short period of time.

Separate Inventories. In a situation where the inventory may consist of some 100,000 different parts which may be subdivided readily into four or five identifiable categories, it may be more practical to treat these as separate inventories and to make estimates of the separate inventories at different times. This may be feasible even when the parts are maintained in the same warehouse. It is easier to do, however, if the parts are segregated in the warehouse or maintained at different locations. As weekends are popular times for taking inventory, the division of the whole procedure into several segments would permit the inventories to be estimated over several weekends without interrupting the normal business activity.

Different Locations. Many situations will be encountered where similar parts and supplies are stored at a number of different geographical locations. It is not uncommon to find the same part numbers stored at 25 or even 50 locations. The same items are not necessarily stored in the same quantities at every location, nor are all the parts likely to be found at all locations.

A decision needs to be made as to whether to estimate the inventory separately at each location or to disregard location and estimate the inventory as a whole. The latter approach may be preferable if it is feasible, but distance may impose special problems. When the inventory is to be estimated as a whole, the quantities at each location should be aggregated for each part number in the preparatory stage. Random selection of a part number for sampling would mean that the same part number would be counted at every location and the resulting counts aggregated for evaluation purposes. An alternative to this approach, which might require a somewhat larger sample, is to select from a combined file that has not been aggregated by location. In this way different parts would be counted at each location and combined into a single estimate for evaluation.

Time and distance limitations may make it more practical to estimate inventories at each location separately, and possibly at different times. When this is to be done, it will be necessary to create a separate file for each location. Categories within each location may also be treated as separate inventories for estimation purposes and counted at different times. The degree of subdivision of the total inventory is at the discretion of management. Where the proper cutoffs can be made, breaking the inventory down into categories or locations may prove advantageous for control purposes. A smaller and better trained group can work more effectively if time and distance limitations are removed. The number of sample items counted in this manner would have to be larger to obtain the same degree of precision and reliability at each location. As these sample items would be counted at different places, the fact that more items would be counted overall would not, perhaps, be a major disadvantage. Furthermore, the combined precision of all locations at the specified reliability could be considerably reduced.

VARIABILITY

Knowledge of Variability

One statistic that is not available from a stratification of the book inventory values is the relationship that exists between the book values and the unknown physical inventory values. It is unrealistic to expect a complete correspondence in all items in the physical inventory, but one would not expect a wide diversity. This statistic will be developed in the evaluation stage of the sample as the standard deviation of regression but some advance knowledge is helpful for design purposes. This information can come from previous samples of the physical inventory, or it may be estimated in other ways, such as from the known variation in similar inventories.

Previous Physical Count.   When a sampling procedure is first used for the purpose of estimating a physical inventory, the previous full count will provide the best available information on the degree of correspondence. It is unfortunately a common practice in many companies to reuse computer tapes for other purposes or erase older files, and information from a previous inventory may not be available. When it is anticipated that the company may use sampling in taking a physical inventory for the following year, the computer files containing the book values and physical values for each part should be transferred to magnetic tape and saved for future use.

When this prior information is available, it becomes possible to compute standard deviations around the regression line for each stratum and to design the sample using these as a base. As this relationship is not likely to change radically from year to year, it may provide the best available basis for future sample design.

Simulation. A better understanding of the sampling procedure may also be gained by simulating a sample from the prior year's book and physical records. This is particularly helpful to the computer personnel who will be given an opportunity to become familiar with the sampling procedures on a trial run basis. The simulation will be the same from the processing point of view as the regular sampling procedure, except that no processing cutoffs will be required and the selected sample items will not have to be physically counted.

In a simulated procedure, the file from which the sample is to be selected contains both book values and physical values for all sampling units. The sample design will be based on the variability between those values together with the monetary precision and reliability specified. Since book and physical values for the items selected for the sample would be available on the output file, the sample taken is ready immediately for evaluation. When this sample is evaluated, it may be used to show interested parties just how the procedure will work. It will also help to reassure those who are somewhat dubious of statistical sampling.

Pilot Sample. Taking a small pilot sample of 50–100 items is another way of gaining knowledge of the variability between book and physical inventory. This sample would be evaluated, and the results of the evaluation used to design the larger sample.

Prior Sample. When sampling has been used in prior years, information obtained in the evaluation of that prior sample may be used as the design factors. Any sample can be redesigned after the fact on the basis of information developed during the evaluation to show what, in effect, the correct sample design should have been to obtain the precision desired under the present circumstances. After several years of experience with sampling, it may hardly be necessary to correct the sample design for the following year.

Unknown Variability

Situations may exist where there is inadequate prior knowledge on which to base the sample design. In other cases the inventory may be so large that processing the file to obtain this knowledge may not improve the sample design sufficiently to justify the additional processing time and cost. Since the basic requirement of the design procedure is that the file be passed through once for design purposes and a second time for selection, elimination of the first pass through the computer will cut the processing time in half, and this could be a substantial time reduction. In such cases, assumptions such as those listed below may necessarily have to be made.

Assumption of Standard Deviation.   One approach would be to stratify the file in the usual manner and determine the standard deviation of the mean based on the book values. This calculation will usually underestimate the standard deviation of the mean based on the unknown physical values considerably, because the physical values are likely to be more widely dispersed. This can be corrected, however, by assuming a standard deviation either based on prior knowledge of comparable inventories or by a more simple expedient, empirically suggested, such as doubling the standard deviation of the mean based on book values.

Exponential Assumption.   A satisfactory way to avoid the design stage altogether is to proceed on the assumption that the particular distribution is an exponential distribution. As stated earlier, the mean and the standard deviation of an exponential distribution are the same, and the approximate mean book value is readily calculated from independent data that would normally be available. Strata limits, sample size, and sample allocations may be determined solely on the basis of an assumed exponential distribution. The results obtained from this procedure are sufficiently good, as compared with the more lengthy procedure of running the file through twice, so that it could become standard practice.

Rule of Thumb.   When all else fails, it is possible to proceed on the basis of stratifying the book values and reducing the design precision by some factor so as to obtain the necessary sample size to produce the required precision in the subsequent evaluation. If a precision range of $50,000 is required in the final evaluation, a safe approximation for design purposes may be obtained by using a factor of five. Thus a precision of $10,000 for a design based on book values will, in most cases, produce a final evaluation close to the desired $50,000. It should be stressed that this is a last resort and should only be used if none of the other methods previously described can be used. It has been used in a sufficient number of cases, however, to provide empirical support for its use as a rule of thumb approach to sample design in accounting populations.

CHAPTER 4

SAMPLE DESIGN

STATEMENT OF PROBLEM

In Statistical Terms

The estimate from a statistical sample is simply an extrapolation or projection of the results obtained from a sample and is similar to the estimates that would ordinarily be made intuitively from a nonstatistical sample. The unique feature of statistical sampling is that it provides a means for measuring the degree of assurance, or, conversely, of uncertainty, associated with the sample estimate. These measurements are based on the mathematical concepts of probability and are expressed in terms of reliability and precision.

The precision for making a sampling application consists of the three stages of design, selection, and evaluation of the sample. To design a sample, it is necessary to:

1. Identify the population to be sampled and the statistical frame representing it.
2. Define the sampling units.
3. Define the related feature of sampling interest.
4. Decide on the type of estimate.
5. Specify the desired statistical assurance in terms of reliability and monetary precision.
6. Determine the basis for stratification.
7. Compute, or specify approximately, the standard deviation.
8. Compute the approximate sample size.

In Accounting Terms

To make some of these statistical concepts more understandable in an accounting framework, let us be more specific and talk in terms of an inventory of 2500 different part numbers having a total book value of $10,000,000. The inventory is maintained as a perpetual inventory record by computer.

Population To Be Sampled.   This computer record is the statistical frame from which the sample is to be selected and should be reasonably similar to the physical inventory that is to be estimated. Associated with each part number would be a quantity on hand and a unit cost. Multiplying the quantity on hand by the unit cost would provide the extended book value for each part number. The sum of these extended book values, by part number, would constitute the total book inventory of $10,000,000.

Sampling Units.   The part numbers thus become the sampling units. The sample will be obtained by selecting from these sampling units in some prescribed manner such as systematic selection with a random start. The accounting question then is whether the perpetual inventory record is a reliable indicator of the condition of the physical inventory maintained in the stockroom or warehouse.

Feature of Sampling Interest.   The related feature of sampling interest thus becomes the relationship between the physical inventory and the perpetual inventory record. We are interested not so much in the sample itself as in the relationship of the sample items in the physical inventory to the corresponding items on the book inventory records. We are going to count a certain number of part numbers in the physical inventory to determine whether the quantities thus counted agree or disagree with the quantities shown on the book record. To the extent that there is disagreement, and there always will be, we will measure statistically the degree of disagreement and expect the same rate of disagreement to apply to the book record as a whole.

Type of Estimate.   As discussed previously, the best type of estimate for this purpose would be a stratified regression estimate. The regression estimate measures the relationship between the book and physical items in the sample more satisfactorily than any other type of estimate and should be used for this purpose. The stratification provides a more precise estimate than could otherwise be obtained by any other type of estimate for a given sample size.

Other Specifications.   The reliability and monetary precision to be used in designing the sample are matters for management decision based on consideration of the relative degree of assurance required and the related cost. Some indication of these relationships may be obtained by a simulation based on previous computer records. To complete the specifications we shall require monetary precision of $150,000 at 95 percent reliability and stratification will be by monetary value. An example of the specifications required to develop the sample size is given in Exhibit 2 in Appendix 1.

DESIGN INPUT

Population To Be Stratified

The statistical frame on which the sample design is to be based should be made available as a computer file. The inventory record from which this file is to be drawn can date from the day on which the sample is to be selected, but is likely to have a previous date, such as the end of the preceding month. The statistical characteristics of an inventory will seldom change noticeably from month to month, so that availability is the principal determinant of the record to be used for design purposes.

Book Inventory. This file should be extracted from the perpetual inventory record so as to provide part number and extended inventory cost for each different part number in the inventory. It becomes relatively easy to process this file of the book inventory and obtain the necessary data to design a sample, making due allowance for the expected relationship between the book and physical inventory. The advance information from the book inventory permits more careful design of the sample than would otherwise be the case. The type of analysis that can be made from the computer file is more comprehensive than anything that could be done on a manual basis.

Prior Inventory Record. One statistic not available from a stratification of the book inventory values is the relationship that exists between the book values and the as yet unknown physical inventory values. It is unrealistic to expect correspondence with all items in the physical inventory, but one does not expect a wide diversity. Experience has shown that about 60 percent of the part numbers will match and the remainder will differ in some degree.

When a sampling procedure is first used for the purpose of estimating a physical inventory, the previous full count will provide the best available information on this matter of correspondence. Unfortunately, information from a previous inventory may not always be available as the files on which the data were resident may have been reused for work tapes in the meanwhile.

With such prior information, it becomes possible to compute standard deviations around the regression line for each stratum and to design the sample using these as a base. Since this relationship usually does not change greatly from year to year, it may provide the best available basis for sample design. When sampling has been used in prior years, information obtained in the evaluation of the sample may be used to assist in the design stage.

When the previous physical inventory values are available, they should be included in the input file together with the book values by part number. Such files are useful not only for design purposes, but for instruction as well. Samples may be taken from this file and evaluated so that all those concerned with the actual taking of the sample may gain experience in how the sample is to be taken and evaluated. Such simulation does much to reassure those with no prior statistical experience that these estimation sampling procedures will lead to satisfactory results.

Stratification

The purpose of stratifying the population in advance of selecting a sample is to determine the number of items that fall in each stratum by the extended monetary book value of each part number. Let us suppose that we are classifying items by every $500 of value up to $2000 and a top stratum including everything over that amount. We would end up with five groups of items; one would contain all items of $500 or under, another would contain items of $501 to $1000, and so on. In effect, the population would be divided into five smaller populations of varying sizes and total values. Each stratum would be sampled separately at varying rates with the top stratum being sampled completely.

As a byproduct of the stratification run, the total monetary value of each stratum is determined and printed as shown in Appendix 1 (Exhibit 3). The visual display of items and total dollars by stratum will confirm that the population is distributed exponentially as we would normally expect it to be. A further step in the stratification stage is to determine the important population parameters, such as the mean and standard deviation, for each stratum and for the entire population.

Population Mean.   Two of the necessary inputs to the design stage are the total number of items in the book population and the total amount of the book population. These totals are generally available from control totals, or they can be obtained in the editing stage during which the computer file of the book population is prepared for stratification. In the event that these data are not available, an approximation of the amounts is satisfactory. The purpose of entering these specifications into the design stage is to be able to determine, either exactly or approximately, the mean of the population that is being stratified. This would normally be the book inventory, but there might be an occasion when it would be desirable, for information purposes, to stratify the previous physical inventory.

Number of Strata. Before stratifying the population, the number of strata must be determined. This could be any number from two up to the number of items in the population. Very little added efficiency is gained, in a statistical sense, from extreme stratification, and from a computer programming standpoint, it is desirable to have some reasonable number as a limit to the number of strata. It has been found empirically that, in dealing with accounting populations, 20 strata are usually adequate and in some cases even more than adequate. Consequently, the Estimation Sampling Program uses 20 strata, plus one stratum to include the zero and minus values that are often present in accounting populations. These strata are numbered from 1 to 21, with the zeros and minus values in the bottom stratum or Stratum 1 and all the highest value items in the top stratum or Stratum 21.

The Program also makes it possible to specify the number of strata when an exact number is required. This feature is likely to be used when it is desirable to have a uniform design at a number of different sampling locations with reasonably comparable populations.

Stratum Cutoffs. In addition to the number of strata, the upper cutoff of each stratum must be determined by the program or specified by the user. Given the number of strata and the total population value, the upper cutoffs can be determined on the basis of an exponential distribution.

As discussed earlier, the exponential distribution can be fully described by its mean. For example, by determining the mean of the population, we are able to create a model framework of the exponential distribution on which to stratify the population. Thus to make a 21-stratum exponential model of a population with a mean value of $4000, the calculations of the stratum cutoffs would be made by dividing the area into 20 equal parts, finding the natural logarithm of this area, changing the sign of the logarithm, and then multiplying this logarithmic value by twice the mean value, or $8000, as shown on the following page and in Appendix 1 (Exhibit 3).

The upper cutoff of the next to last stratum will be approximately six times the mean of the population, so that if the population mean is $4000 ($10,000,000 ÷ 2500) the upper cutoff would be $23,965 and all items above that would fall into the top stratum. The selection of this upper cutoff has much to do with the reduction of the variance.

The Program has a provision for specification of stratum cutoffs, since there may be situations in which this would be desirable. One such situation, as mentioned before, would be when the same design seemed to be desirable for a number of different locations. For example, if individual samples are designed for five different locations, the mean value at each location would not likely be the same and the stratum cutoffs would be different. This would make comparison between locations more difficult. On the other hand, if the

Stratum	Area	−(Ln Area)	Cutoff
1	1.00	0.0000	$ 0
2	0.95	0.0513	410
3	0.90	0.1053	842
4	0.85	0.1625	1300
5	0.80	0.2231	1785
6	0.75	0.2877	2301
7	0.70	0.3567	2853
8	0.65	0.4308	3446
9	0.60	0.5108	4086
10	0.55	0.5978	4782
11	0.50	0.6931	5545
12	0.45	0.7984	6387
13	0.40	0.9163	7330
14	0.35	1.0498	8398
15	0.30	1.2040	9631
16	0.25	1.3863	11090
17	0.20	1.6094	12875
18	0.15	1.8971	15176
19	0.10	2.3026	18420
20	0.05	2.9957	23965
21			∞

stratum cutoffs were determined for the largest of the five inventories and these cutoffs were specified for the other four locations, the samples and the sample results would be comparable.

There might be times when it would be desirable to stratify the population based on cutoffs in, say, even-numbered hundreds of dollars. This might be useful for information purposes even when a sample is not required. Also, this might be done as a preliminary to sample design, or might serve an entirely different purpose such as inventory control. Furthermore, there will be some accounting populations that just do not follow an exponential distribution, and where some modification of the stratum cutoffs may be necessary to get a useful stratification for sampling purposes. If the desired cutoffs are specified, the Estimation Sampling Program will stratify according to these values.

Stratification.   The stratification procedure (Appendix 5) is simple. Each item is taken as it appears in the input file and measured against the strata boundaries to determine the stratum to which it applies. The item is counted as an item in that particular stratum and the monetary value is accumulated in a total for that stratum.

In situations where the actual number of items that fall into a stratum are insufficient to provide an adequate sample, that stratum is combined with the next higher stratum. The Program thus provides automatically for a reasonable number of strata and an adequate sample in each stratum.

Statistical Assurance

Two other specifications that are necessary in the design stage are precision and reliability. These values have a considerable effect on the sample size required. It is often said that precision and reliability are statistically inseparable. This means that we cannot use one without the other. We cannot say that we have 95 percent reliability for an estimate unless we specify the range of precision surrounding the estimate. Similarly, we cannot say that we can rely on an estimate being within a $100,000 range either way without stating a percentage of reliability to go with it. We can, however, discuss them separately.

Monetary Precision. The monetary precision that is specified in the design stage is a plus or minus range around the estimate. This is the range in which we would expect the inventory value to fall if we made a complete count and used identical procedures. The monetary precision specified is the amount of error that we can tolerate in the sampling procedure at the specified reliability.

In specifying the monetary precision required, particularly where there is no information on the relationship between the book and the physical inventory, some conservatism may be indicated. The specification of the monetary precision is a management function and, in percentages, usually ranges from 2 to 5 percent of the total book inventory, with 3 percent being the median choice.

Reliability. If we specify a reliability of 95 percent, we are saying that, if we sample from the same frame a large number of times, we can expect a normal distribution of the sample means and that 95 percent of these sample means will be no more than about two standard errors from the unknown population mean. On this premise, a statistical inference is made from a single sample that the population value falls within the range of that sample estimate, plus or minus the precision achieved and not the precision specified.

What must be realized is that for every 20 samples taken, at 95 percent reliability, one of the individual sample means may fall outside the range of two standard errors from the population mean. Consequently, if the inference is made from that particular sample that the population value falls within the specified range, the inference may well be wrong. For this reason, some statisticians advocate the use of three standard deviations around the mean. This reduces the chances of an incorrect inference to only 3 in 1000. This is referred to as statistical certainty but requires a considerably larger sample size. On the other hand, really bad estimates are fairly noticeable in an accounting environment, so that a 5 percent risk is probably a reasonable one to take.

In all cases, the expected standard error is the result of dividing the desired monetary precision by the normal deviate for the specified reliability. Thus if we specify monetary precision of $100,000 at 95 percent reliability, we are stating, in effect, that the achieved standard error of the estimate must not be greater than $50,000. The size of the expected standard error of the estimate can be raised or lowered but doing so will decrease or increase the sample size.

Optional Procedures

In addition to what might be considered a standard or usual approach to designing an estimation sample, a number of optional procedures may be used concurrently with, or in place of, certain aspects of the design stage. None of these are necessary in any given situation, but these options may prove useful in particular cases.

Pilot Sample. Some book inventories of parts and supplies may contain several hundred thousand separate items, in which case the stratification procedures might require a considerable amount of computer time. A satisfactory sample design can then be obtained by stratifying a sample from the population rather than by stratifying every item in the population. A sampling rate, such as one in ten, can be specified, in which case the computer, with a random start, will select every tenth item thereafter and stratify in the usual way. When this sampling stratification procedure is completed, the results in turn are multiplied by the sampling interval of 10 to approximate the result that would be obtained by stratifying the entire population. The s andard deviations of each stratum are increased by two of their own standard errors[1] so that there is not likely to be an underestimate of sample size through use of this procedure. As long as the population is of reasonably large size, the results from using this pilot sampling approach to stratification appear to produce approximately the same sample design as would be obtained with a complete stratification.

[1] W. Edwards Deming, *Sample Design in Business Research*, Wiley, New York, 1960, p. 439.

Assumed Exponential Distribution. The stratification stage may be bypassed completely, thus saving approximately one-half the computer time required in the design and selection stage. This may be done by making an assumption that the inventory is distributed exponentially. As discussed earlier, this is not an unreasonable assumption, for most accounting populations tend to be distributed exponentially. With this assumption, further assumptions can be made in regard to the distribution to each stratum of the total number of items and the total dollar value of the population. The overall mean and standard deviation of a standardized exponential distribution are one and the same. The means and the standard deviations from the mean in each stratum may also be assumed.

Based on these assumed data and the other specifications, the sample size can be determined as if a complete or partial stratification procedure had been followed. A sample selected on the basis of the exponential assumption would in most cases approximate the results otherwise obtained and eliminate the time required to pass a long file through the stratification procedure.

Approximate Standard Deviation. Some preliminary estimates as to the extent of variability to be expected in the sample of the physical inventory need to be made in order to compute the approximate sample size required. This preliminary estimate of variability could be based on the results of a previous complete physical inventory if a prior inventory is available, or on the results of a previous sample. In situations where the prior physical inventory is available, the standard deviation can be computed around the regression line, which ordinarily will be very close to the same value that will ultimately be developed for the current physical inventory. For example, if the analysis of the last year's inventory showed a standard deviation from the line of regression of $685.51, it is reasonable to expect that this year's inventory would produce similar results. Accounting populations are sufficiently consistent from one year to another so that the variability of the data will not change radically. Since the effect of year-to-year inflation should be considered, an estimated standard deviation of $700 would be suitable for design purposes.

The next best thing is to make an analysis of the most recently available perpetual record and to introduce some conservatism into the precision desired so as to provide for the unknown, and perhaps unexpected, relationship between the book inventory and the physical inventory. In this connection, general experience with other inventories believed to be roughly comparable to this one can be helpful in the design stage.

Where the prior physical inventory is not available, and stratification is based solely on the book inventory, the standard deviation from the mean of the book inventory that will be developed is likely to be much lower than the standard deviation from the regression line. The question is, how much lower. It may be possible to approximate the unknown standard deviation with information from other sources such as a small pilot sample or similar inventories. If an approximate standard deviation from the regression line can be determined or assumed, it may be substituted for the standard deviation developed in the design stage and thus greatly improve the sample design. In situations where this has been done, the results obtained from stratifying only the book inventory were nearly as good as if the prior physical inventory had been available.

Specified Upper Cutoff. The upper cutoff below infinity is set automatically at approximately six times the mean of the population, unless another cutoff is specified. There may be situations in which it would be desirable to raise or lower this cutoff or to set some arbitrary dollar amount as the point above which all items would be included in the sample. For instance, a company might want to count all items with a value over $1000, in which case $1000 would be specified as this upper cutoff. Unless the cutoffs for other strata are also specified, the program will automatically scale all those cutoffs according to the percentage amount by which the upper cutoff below infinity has been changed.

Specified Lower Cutoff for Stratum 1. The bottom stratum is reserved for zero values and small minus values that need to be sampled, but at a fairly low rate. Zero values usually occur because parts that are normally stocked are now out of stock. If there are more than 10 percent zero values in the book inventory, it may be better to separate them from the rest of the inventory. Zero values in the physical inventory add nothing to its estimated value or to the estimation procedure. This leaves only the situation where there is an actual quantity in the physical inventory but a zero quantity in the perpetual record. If this occurs frequently, checking procedures should be instituted to correct the condition before taking the physical inventory.

Small minus values in the book inventory may be shipping errors, posting errors, or may come about as the result of pricing errors or changes. If a dozen parts with part no. 957 are mistakenly shipped and billed in place of part no. 956 because there were no parts numbered 956, the subsequent reduction of the perpetual record would show part no. 956 with a quantity balance of minus 12. A similar result could ensue if part no. 957 is correctly shipped but posted to the perpetual record for part no. 956. Many computer programs are not designed to flag minus values resulting from such errors and they continue in the record until some adjustment is made. In a similar manner, parts may be bought for $5.79 per dozen and costed out at $0.483 per piece, which is equivalent to a credit of $5.796 per dozen. The accumulation of these six-tenths of a cent over several dozen will produce small minus values which often go unheeded until physical inventory time.

In addition, there is the question of large minus errors and how we define large. For the purposes of the Program, this lower cutoff for Stratum 1 has been set arbitrarily at minus \$100 although a different lower cutoff can be specified. This means that all items that have minus values larger than \$100 will be included in the top stratum to be sampled completely.

Specified Interval for Zero Sampling. The zeros and small minus values that fall in the bottom stratum will be sampled at the same rate as the next higher stratum unless a different sampling rate is specified. In deciding whether a higher or lower rate needs to be used, much depends on the nature of the situation that produces the zero balances. The sampling of zero book balances adds little to the process of estimating the physical inventory, but as long as these zero balances exist in the inventory, they must be sampled at some arbitrary rate.

DETERMINATION OF SAMPLE SIZE

In the process of stratification, totals are developed for both items and values in each stratum, and also for the entire population without regard to stratum. In addition, all individual values are squared. If two individual values, representing book and physical, are available as input to the computer, the additional squares and cross-products are obtained for each stratum to assist in the subsequent determination of the standard deviations from the regression line in each stratum. If any physical value exceeds the upper cutoff below infinity and is four times greater than the corresponding book value, that item will be included in the top stratum for design purposes. This is a precaution to prevent a few huge or unusual differences from distorting the standard deviation and upsetting the sample design.

Preliminary Calculation

When the necessary sums of squares and sums of cross products have been obtained at the end of the stratification run, the mean and standard deviation for each stratum are determined.

Weighted Standard Deviation. The first step in the determination of the sample size is to find the weighted average of the stratum standard deviations. This average is obtained by multiplying the standard deviation in each stratum, except for the top and bottom strata, by the number of items in the stratum and summing those products over all strata. This sum is then divided by the total number of items in all but the first and last strata, to arrive at a weighted average standard deviation. The bottom stratum is omitted because it often contains only zeros, and therefore no standard deviation, or contains small minus values which would have no useful influence on the sample design. The top stratum is omitted because it will be counted in its entirety and consequently will have no associated standard deviation of sampling.

Standard Normal Deviate.   The percentage of reliability, or confidence, that is specified for the sample design has to be translated into standard normal deviates. Tables of those deviates are available for areas of the normal curve so that 95 percent may be readily translated to 1.96 deviates for use in the formula. These tables express areas of the curve usually in terms of one direction from the mean, so that those areas must be doubled to obtain the reliability for both directions that is generally wanted for most types of estimation sampling. By use of a subroutine (Appendix 5) that contains the necessary mathematical function, the Program automatically translates the specified percentage reliability to the corresponding standard normal deviate.

Formula for Sample Size.   A first approximation[2] to the sample size is obtained from the following formula:

$$n_0 = \left(\frac{NtS}{P} \right)^2 \tag{4.1}$$

where N is the number of items in Strata 2–20, t is the standard deviate, S is the weighted average standard deviation, and P is the specified monetary precision. It is easy to see from studying the formula why precision and reliability affect sample size. A change in either t or P will affect sample size and vice versa.

Given a population of 2500 items, a standard deviation of $500, monetary precision $250,000 (2.5 percent of $10,000,000 population total) at 95 percent reliability, or a t value of approximately 2, we can solve for a preliminary sample size as follows:

$$n_0 = \left(\frac{2500 \cdot 2 \cdot 500}{250,000} \right)^2$$

$$= 100$$

---

[2] William G. Cochran, *Sampling Techniques,* 2nd ed., Wiley, New York, 1963, p. 76.

If we use 99.7 percent reliability or 3 standard deviations with the above data, notice how the sample size changes:

$$n_0 = \left(\frac{2500 \cdot 3 \cdot 500}{250,000} \right)^2$$

$$= 225$$

Thus we can gain the additional assurance of statistical certainty by more than doubling the sample size. It is doubtful that there are many situations in accounting where such a high degree of reliability as 99.7 percent would be required but it is important to understand that it is available at the price of substantial additional work.

If we also reduce the monetary precision to $100,000 at 99.7 percent reliability, notice the further effect:

$$n_0 = \left(\frac{2500 \cdot 3 \cdot 500}{100,000} \right)^2$$

$$= 1406$$

Thus it can be seen that the total effect both of reducing monetary precision from $250,000 to $100,000 and increasing the reliability from 95 percent to 99.7 percent is to increase the preliminary sample size over 14 times. Obviously, careful consideration should be given to the degree of accuracy desired because a requirement for tighter precision and increased reliability can be costly in terms of the work performed. These hypothetical calculations illustrate the wasted effort in a full complete count of 2500 items where reasonable accuracy could be obtained with small samples.

Finite Population Correction

When the monetary precision is set at quite a low amount, the desired reliability is set very high, or when the weighted standard deviation of the data is quite large, the preliminary sample size, as determined from the above formula, may be large relative to the population size (N). When the sample size as a proportion of the population is 20 percent or greater, the effect of sampling from a finite population without replacement is significant and suggests an adjustment to the sample size. This adjustment is made by means of the finite population correction[3] as reflected in the following additional formula:

$$n = \frac{n_0}{1 + [(n_0 - 1)/N]} \tag{4.2}$$

where n is the final sample size, n_0 is the preliminary sample size, and N is the number of items in Strata 2–20. The finite population correction is theoretically justified in all cases where a finite population is sampled without replacement. Since this is the typical case, the finite population correction is included in the Estimation Sampling Program for those situations where a larger sample is required. Its effect will be minimal when the sample proportion is low.

As an example of the significance of the adjustment for sampling without replacement, consider the effect on the previous preliminary sample size calculations shown below:

$$n = \frac{100}{1 + (99/2500)}$$

$$= 97$$

$$n = \frac{225}{1 + (224/2500)}$$

$$= 207$$

$$n = \frac{1406}{1 + (1405/2500)}$$

$$= 901$$

In the first two cases, the adjustment is not significant. In the last case it is substantial, because the sample size changes from 14 times the first case to only nine times. The smaller the population size, the more likely it is that the finite population correction will be substantial.

Allocation of Sample Size to Strata

Once the overall sample size has been determined by use of the formulas shown above, the sample must be allocated to the various strata on some

[3] Ibid., p. 75.

basis. Diverse bases could be used, but the principle of optimum allocation is logical in this situation.

The principle of optimum (Neyman) allocation[4] states that the variance will be at a minimum if the total sample is allocated to strata in accordance with the weighted standard deviation within each stratum. As these factors have already been calculated to determine the overall sample size, it is not too difficult to allocate the total sample to each stratum according to this principle. The Program (Appendix 5) makes adjustments to the allocated sample size in each stratum so that the sample size will not exceed the population size in any stratum, and in no case will exceed 1000 items. As the allocation may produce a fractional number, the sample size in each stratum is rounded to the nearest whole number.

The sampling interval is determined by dividing the total number of population items in each stratum by the sample required. This interval is computed to two decimal places and truncated. For instance, if the allocation indicated a sample of 9.31 items out of a total of 188 in that stratum, the sampling interval, to five decimal places, would be 20.19334. This would be truncated to 20.19 and the indicated sample would be rounded to nine items. The actual sample would be either 9 or 10 depending on the random start. This interval is limited as an arbitrary rule to no less than one and to no more than 1000. The sampling interval for the top stratum is set at one, so that each item in that stratum will be selected. The interval for the bottom stratum, as stated before, is set at the same interval as the second stratum, or at such other rate as may be specified by the user. If it is known or expected that a large number of the zero book balances will actually have physical values, it may be necessary to use a smaller sampling interval to get a larger sample.

Due to the inclusion of an $(n - 2)$ term in the formula for calculation of the variance of a regression estimate, it is necessary that no one stratum have less than three sample items to be evaluated. This either means that a minimum number of three items must be selected in each stratum, or that two or more strata must be combined to ensure that three or more items are selected. One way to do this would be to increase the reliability, or reduce the monetary precision, or both. If the design specifications cannot be changed so that three or more items will be selected in each stratum, the situation will be corrected automatically by the collapsing strata feature (Appendix 5) built into the Program.

The collapsing strata feature examines the intervals in each stratum successively, determines the size of the sample that is to be taken, and decides whether the sample is sufficient for the type of estimate to be made. If it is

---

[4] Ibid., p. 97.

insufficient in any stratum, this stratum will be added to the next stratum and the calculations repeated. The process is continued until all strata have been examined. If the indicated sample in the next to last stratum is insufficient, this stratum will be combined with the previous one. The top and bottom strata are not considered in this process, so that the full 20 strata can be reduced to no fewer than three by this procedure. Usually, this type of reduction will affect only one or two strata at most.

OUTPUT OF DESIGN STAGE

At this point in the Program, the design stage is completed and the results are printed for each stratum, and in total, as shown in Appendix 1 (Exhibit 3). Many people have found this report useful simply for the information it contains about the distribution of items in the inventory. In one case, an inventory reduction program was started on the basis of the large monetary value contained in a very few inventory items. It was determined that the cost of airlifting parts from the factory was outweighed, in many cases, by the cost of maintaining expensive parts at distant inventory locations.

Upper Cutoffs

The first column on the printed report from the design stage shows the stratum numbers; next to it are the upper cutoffs for each stratum. These cutoffs would normally have been computed automatically by the Program, but could have been specified by the user in the design stage. Each item on the input file has been compared to these boundaries and dropped accordingly into one stratum or another. The totals for each stratum, both by number of items and by monetary value, are shown in the next two columns for the population that is being stratified. In this illustrative case, the primary population is the book value.

The corresponding physical values, by item and dollar value, will be shown in the next two columns if they are present on the input file, and are indicated for stratification. Stratification in this case is by the same stratum into which the primary, or book, value has been classified. It is necessary to bear in mind that if the primary stratification were by physical values rather than book values, the various items could well fall into other strata according to their physical values.

Selection Intervals

Under the broad heading of "indicated sample" are shown the selection interval and the indicated sample size. The total sample is arrived at first, by the methods described above, and then allocated to the strata on the principle of optimum allocation. The selection intervals are obtained, as also described above, by dividing the number of population items in each stratum by the sample size.

In the event that the indicated sample size in any one stratum is insufficient for the particular type of estimate, the collapsing feature will be employed automatically to reduce the number of strata. A footnote will be included at the bottom of the design printout to show that this feature has been used and to indicate the final number of required strata.

Specification for Selection Stage

If the specifications indicate that the program is to be used for design only, the program output will terminate at this point. The necessary specifications for the selection stage will be punched into cards so that the selection procedure may be continued at another time, perhaps with another accounting record. For large inventories, it is highly desirable to design the sample at some time prior to the actual selection. This will minimize the computer time required at the selection date when time is likely to be at a premium.

If the program specifications indicate "design and selection," the program will automatically move into the selection stage and use the data developed in the design stage for this purpose. In this case, an option may be exercised to print and punch the design data shown in Appendix 1 (Exhibit 4). Normally this information would not be needed.

CHAPTER 5

SAMPLE SELECTION

The sample selection phase of the program may be initiated in one of the following ways. First, it can be a continuation of the design procedure, in which case no separate input specifications are necessary. Second, it can be based on a sample design made at some previous time, in which case the separate input specifications would have been stored in a file or punched out into cards in the design process for the selection stage. In this case, however, the population file from which the selection is to be made may differ from the file used in the design process, and it is therefore also possible to change the separate input specifications as a result of information gained in the design stage. The third way in which the selection phase of the program can be initiated is to introduce entirely new selection specifications. These specifications could be based on experience gained from a previous sample.

SELECTION INPUT SPECIFICATIONS

Since separate input specifications may have to be changed or created for the second and third uses cited above, some understanding of the selection specifications is helpful. The important specifications are the population to be sampled, a random number, the output specifications, and the stratum cards.

Population To Be Sampled

When the design and selection phases are combined, the file will be restarted after the stratification stage and the sample will be selected from the same file. This procedure is well suited to inventories of less than 10,000 different part numbers. It can also be effective for larger inventories if used with either the pilot sample approach or the assumed exponential approach. When the inventories contain more than 10,000 different part numbers, it is usually better to accomplish the design stage at some early date and run only the selection phase at the last minute, when time is a critical factor.

Current Record Date. The record date of the file version used for selection purposes should be the latest that is possible to obtain. Although any prior date would probably be suitable for the design stage, ideally the selection date and count date should be the same. For example, if the inventory is to be taken as of June 30, all paper work should be processed through that date with proper cutoffs to ensure that no subsequent transactions are recorded, and a file as of June 30 should be used for selection. If the counts are to be made on the following business day, due care must be exercised that no stock additions or withdrawals are physically made before the actual counts. In this way, one can expect a correspondence between the book records and the physical quantities.

Earlier Record Date. On the other hand, if the paperwork processing is slow and a selection file as of June 30 cannot be prepared until July 14, it is obvious that some adjustment will have to be made. The selection program may be run on July 14, but the selection date will be June 30. The physical counts will be made as of July 14 or later and must be adjusted to what they would have been on June 30. This is done by algebraically adjusting the physical counts for the quantitative transactions that have taken place in the book record between June 30 and July 14. It should perhaps be emphasized that the correct procedure in such a case is to backdate the physical counts to the selection date. It is not correct to update the book records to July 14, as the stratification and selection intervals are all based on June 30.

Later Record Date. It is also possible to select from a file version as of an earlier date, count at the current or a later date, and use the later record date, but the procedure is far more complicated. During the period from the earlier record date used for selection to the later count date, any new part numbers must be both segregated from the physical inventory, and excluded from the perpetual inventory at the count date. Old part numbers must remain in the later perpetual record. If this can be done easily, the procedure is feasible. When a file is available for the actual count date, the part numbers and the sequence of parts on the file must be exactly the same as in the later selection version. This later file must then be stratified with the same cutoffs as for the previous selection and a new sample file created by matching it with the old sample file by line or sequence number. The new sample file would also have to be stratified. The number of parts selected and the part numbers would be the same, but the extended book values could be different for each of the sample items and could fall into different strata than they did originally. If all of this is done carefully, and new selection intervals are computed for evaluation purposes, the sample would be valid as of the count date. The entirely new part numbers excluded as above would be handled separately or could be added to the top stratum items and counted completely.

Random Number

The concept of randomness requires that every item in the stratum to which it is assigned have an equal or determinable probability of being selected. It is this known probability that enables us to be mathematically explicit about the degree of confidence that we may place in our sample estimates. Random numbers are the usual way in which statistical randomness is assured in the selection process.

There are many seemingly random processes in nature, in the physical sciences, and in the business world. Life and death, neutron collisions, electrical noise, or telephone directory numbers are illustrative of these processes.

A very considerable amount of time and effort has gone into developing tables of random numbers. Part of such a table is shown below:

382	112	685	949	496
652	778	282	272	195
446	530	335	138	050
494	175	076	786	401
556	617	822	332	716
801	157	604	055	683
141	379	825	951	470
840	122	403	866	372
394	305	048	336	345
791	471	573	089	693

There are many tables of random numbers available commercially that have been produced in a manner considered to provide randomness, and that have been subjected to various statistical tests for randomness.

With the advent of computers, and through the use of applied number theory, it has been possible to develop random numbers with a computer program (Appendix 5) by a recurrence relation. While these numbers are not truly random, as they are the result of a deterministic process, they can be considered to be random for selection purposes, provided that they are uniformly distributed, are statistically independent of one another, and meet the necessary statistical tests for randomness.

A random number is required to start the selection process. A table of random numbers may be used, but a simple way is to use the last six digits from any one dollar bill selected at random. This number will be the input to a random number program, which will produce additional random starting points for each stratum. This starting random number will be recorded on the output record of the specifications. One of the particular advantages of computer-generated random numbers is that they are reproducible and the results of earlier calculations can be duplicated for review purposes. A different starting random number, however, will produce an entirely different selection pattern so that the selection procedure can be considered to operate randomly without intervention or bias.

Output Specifications

Some specific decisions have to be made at selection time as to the nature and content of the output. The output may be on magnetic tape or disk, and there are good reasons in favor of each. It is also necessary to indicate whether information such as the stratum number or the sequence number are to be retained in the sample output file. Normally, these numbers should be saved, but there are occasionally restraints on the number of fields that are available for this purpose because of other information that may be more important to retain.

Stratum cards

The stratum cards or file produced during the design stage may be introduced without change as part of the selection specifications. If the specifications change, however, it will be necessary to change the cards. When only the selection phase is used, the cards can be punched directly.

SELECTION PROCEDURE

Whether the selection follows the design stage or begins at this point, the selection procedure is essentially the same. The population is classified by stratum, and sample items are selected systematically from each stratum with a random start in each stratum.

Stratification Against Cutoffs

If the selection procedure continues from the design stage, the stratum cutoffs will have been determined already and now will be available. If the selection procedure begins at this point, the stratum cutoffs must be specified. To some extent the stratification procedure is duplicated in the selection phase, but this is unavoidable as there is a possibility that the population or the stratum cutoffs may now be changed.

Systematic Selection

Statistical selection methods are prerequisite to valid statistical evaluation. Each item in the population must have an equal or otherwise determinable probability of being selected. There are two basic statistical selection methods: random selection and systematic selection with a random start. Systematic selection from accounting data is usually more efficient than random selection and is the selection method used by the Program.

Systematic selection ordinarily utilizes sampling intervals or sampling rates. In one technique of systematic selection, the first sample item in the first sampling interval for each stratum is selected at random and the remaining items are selected using the sampling interval. For example, if the random starting point were the third item in the stratum and if the sampling interval were 10, then the third, thirteenth, twenty-third, and so on, items would be selected in that stratum. As a computer file is sequential, this type of selection is readily adaptable to accounting populations maintained on a computer file.

Random Start

Beginning with a six-digit random number supplied at the start of the Program, a new six-digit random number is computed by a subroutine (Appendix 5) for each of the strata in turn. Each random number is divided by the sampling interval for that stratum, and the remainder to two decimal places is used as the random start within that particular stratum. As the random numbers and the intervals are calculated in a completely different way, nonrandom selection is not likely to occur. The first item on the file may or may not be selected depending on the stratum in which it falls and on the random start within that stratum. The same holds true for the second, third, fourth, and all subsequent items. Thus stratification tends to do away with the nonrandomness that occasionally might occur with systematic selection.

Sampling Interval.   Given the random start within each stratum, the Program systematically selects items within each stratum. The first item in the file is matched to the stratum limits, and its number and dollar value are accumulated in totals for that stratum. When the number of items in each stratum equals, or first exceeds because of the decimal places, the random start for that stratum, that item is selected and passed to the output file. The counter for the corresponding stratum is then reset so that another item will be selected when the number of items equals or exceeds the sampling interval, and so on.

All items in the top stratum are selected without reference to counters or random numbers. The Program proceeds sequentially through the file, using 20 separate counters to keep track of the random starts, and selection intervals for each stratum. Thus each item is selected or rejected in a completely random fashion. The computer is effectively selecting 20 different samples at the same time, each sample from a stratum by systematic selection with a different random start and a different selection interval.

As a practical matter, the indicated sample may not be selected exactly in each stratum. In some cases it may be one more or one less due to the incidence of the random start. In cases where the designed selection procedure is based on a certain population and used to select from another population, the sample sizes in each stratum may differ more widely.

Sample Output

As each item is selected from the input file, an output file is created of only the items selected. At the time of selection, the stratum number into which the item has been classified is carried to the output file so that it will be available at a later date for evaluation purposes. The selected items will be carried to the sample output file in the same order in which they appeared on the population input file. An option is available to carry a sequence number to the output file. This is the sequential number or line number of the item as it appears on the input file. The Program counts the items as they enter, which is useful for tracing the sample back to the input file if necessary.

Other information that is contained in the original input record can be carried over to the sample output file, provided that it does not conflict with the fields specified for the sample information. Fields that are designated to contain the sample value, the stratum number, or the sequence number will override any information contained in the same fields in the input file. Data such as part number, description or unit price are the kinds of information that may be usefully carried forward.

SELECTION OUTPUT

At the end of the selection procedure, a printout, as given in Appendix 1 (Exhibit 5), establishes the control over each stratum and shows the stratum cutoff, the population data, the selection interval, and the sample data. The sample output file would normally be printed, as shown in Appendix 1 (Exhibit 6), as a record of the sample to be taken. This guards against unintentional destruction or erasure of the sample output file before the evaluation is completed.

To facilitate evaluation of the sample at a later date, the essential control and stratum information is retained in a computer file or is punched into cards (Appendix 1, Exhibit 7). It is also printed in the event that the punched cards are lost or mislaid. The use of the file or punched cards not only simplifies the evaluation but also protects against errors that might otherwise creep into the procedure.

SAMPLE VALUES

Obtaining Sample Values

Cards may be punched from the sample output file to provide a unit record for each item to be sampled. These cards would contain at a minimum the part number, or other identification, the book value of the item selected, and the stratum number. Cards may be reproduced and interpreted to provide a basis for the actual count in the stockroom or warehouse when the actual counting is done. Accounting information such as book quantity, unit price, and the book value would probably not be reproduced in the cards used for the actual count.

For each of the items selected in the sample, an actual value corresponding to the book value must be determined. In the case of a physical inventory, this would be done by counting, pricing, and extending to determine the physical value. In the case of reserves, the actual reserve needed for the particular class would be determined. These procedures are essentially the same whether the determination is made completely or by sample. The workload is sufficiently reduced with a sample, however, so that more care can be exercised in determining these values properly the first time. Reliable results will be obtained at low cost and with reasonable speed. The stresses and irritations that are usually present when a lot of work must be done in a very short period of time will virtually disappear when the workload is reduced to a sample.

Sample Controls

Two types of sampling controls are needed in taking a sample. One is to guard against nonsampling errors, and the other is to investigate, and thereby eliminate, huge and unusual differences.

Nonsampling Errors.   Nonsampling errors are the type of errors that could occur even if a complete count were made. For example, if a certain part is packaged six to a box, a count of boxes might be used in place of the number of parts and this mistake is a counting error rather than a sampling error. A number of different types of control can be exercised. One useful approach is to use double teams on the counts or, in effect, have two separate teams counting the same inventory at different times. In this way, the results can be compared, and any unusual differences can be reconciled quickly.

Another useful approach is to establish some kind of tolerance test based on either the quantity or the value. If an inventory count does not fall within the tolerance set for that particular item, the count must be made again by a different team.

At the end of the inventory count, but before the parts or supplies are released, some form of reconciliation to the perpetual records should be made either in manual or computer form so that glaring errors may be investigated immediately and missing or incomplete counts can be followed up.

Large Differences.   The precision surrounding the estimate will not be satisfactory if the sample contains a number of huge and unusual differences. If the difference is small enough for the physical value to remain in the same stratum as the book value, the effect on the overall precision will be small. If the physical value moves to an adjacent stratum, the effect on the overall precision will still not be too large. It is when the physical value jumps more than one stratum in either direction that the effect on the precision becomes considerable. Some of these huge differences may be eliminated on closer inspection. Perhaps the wrong items are being counted, in which case a recount is necessary. Sometimes a misposting is discovered in the book records that should be adjusted. In any event, the sample data should be reviewed as carefully as possible before proceeding with the evaluation.

CHAPTER 6

SAMPLE EVALUATION

As stated earlier, there must be a determination of an actual value corresponding to the book value for each item selected in the sample. The values are determined in exactly the same way for a sample as for a complete examination. In a physical inventory it is by counting, pricing, and extending that the physical value, or, in the case of liabilities or reserves, the applicable liability or reserve for that particular class is established. It needs to be emphasized that more care is usually exercised in determining these values properly as the workload is sufficiently reduced by the sample. It follows that reliable results can be obtained more quickly and easily by sample than by complete examination.

EVALUATION SPECIFICATIONS

When the sample data have been reviewed carefully, the evaluation can proceed. The Program requires as input the specification cards that are punched out in the selection procedure together with the sample data cards. Given these data, the entire evaluation can be accomplished within a few minutes.

Punched Output During Selection

The specification cards that are punched out at the end of the selection procedure as shown in Exhibit 7 (Appendix 1) contain all data necessary to make the evaluation and include data on the number of sample cards in each stratum. A comparison of the summary data on the sample selected as contained in Exhibit 5 with the specification card data given in Exhibit 7 shows the data that are necessary for evaluation purposes. These specification cards are checked for input errors and the specifications are printed as illustrated in Exhibit 8 before proceeding with the evaluation.

The specification cards that are punched out at the end of the selection process in most cases can be used without any change. This avoids the transcription errors that might be made if these data were punched by hand.

If it is necessary to change the specification cards, the existing card should be duplicated to the extent possible with changes being made at that time. At times it may be desirable to evaluate the sample using a sampling method different from that anticipated at the time of selection. As doing this requires only a single-column code change in the card, it is obviously better to duplicate the remainder of the card and simply punch the single-column change.

The primary specification card (EE02 card in Exhibit 7) contains such information as company name and description of the data being estimated together with the fields used for the book value, the physical value, and the stratum number. Other codes specify the type of estimate, the percentage of reliability to be used, and whether the test for unusual differences is to be bypassed. The secondary specification card (EE03 card) contains information required for the various options that may be used in the evaluation, such as a reduction in the number of strata, and for design of the next year's sample. These two cards are followed by up to 11 stratum cards (EE04 cards), each of which contains information on two strata, such as the number of items in the population, the number of items in the sample, the upper limit of that particular stratum and the monetary value of the book population in that stratum. These totals in the stratum card must be in agreement with the sample cards and the values as shown in Exhibit 5.

Sample Cards

The cards that were punched from the sample output file provide a unit record for each item to be sampled and should now contain the information on the sample values as shown in Exhibit 6. These sample cards should follow the specification cards into the card reader. It may be more efficient in some installations to enter the sample cards separately and set them up as a file on one of the work disks. In this way the file may be called for as needed, but, except for the necessary changes in job control language, the procedure would be exactly the same.

Unusual Differences

If erroneous data are entered into the evaluation program it is clear that the results will also be erroneous. It is not uncommon for the data representing the sample values to be punched into the wrong columns of the sample cards or at times into the wrong cards. Also, counts may be wrong or the wrong items may be counted. The test for unusual differences is an option that should be used to guard against the evaluation results being erroneous because of errors in recording or counting.

Next Sample

Another option that is available during the evaluation is to develop information for the next sample. This allows the Program to determine, as shown in Exhibit 10, the exact type and size sample required to obtain the desired precision at the given level of reliability based on information in the current sample. In other words, this corrects the sample size to what it should have been given perfect knowledge in the design stage.

This option also comes into play if a small pilot sample is taken and evaluated as a guide to taking a larger sample. In this situation, the specification cards (Exhibit 11) that are developed as a result of this next sample procedure may be used to enter the selection phase of the Design and Selection Program without further modification.

Manual Selection

There will undoubtedly be some situations in which selection may have to be made manually rather than by computer. The Evaluation Program may still be used when the selection is made manually. This has the advantage of making available more sophisticated types of estimates, for example, stratified regression estimates, in many situations where they might not otherwise be used because of the complexity of the calculations.

In manual selection, specification cards will be required for the evaluation program. Considerable care must be exercised in making up the specification cards. In most cases, practicalities will limit manual selection to one or two strata. Selection is usually made on a numerical basis when it is done manually, but it also may be performed by cumulative monetary amount sampling. In the latter case, the corresponding basis for evaluation must then be specified accordingly. If any stratification is used, the stratum cutoffs will have to be specified. Control totals for each stratum, giving the total number of items in each stratum and the dollar book amounts in each stratum, will also be required.

CHECKING PROCEDURES

A fairly large number of checks and controls have been built into the Evaluation Program to promote high quality performance.

Specification Cards

All the data entered on the specification cards, whether produced manually or by a previous computer run, are checked to see that alphabetic information is utilized only where it is called for, and that the numbers used are valid. Codes that exceed the possible range of choices will not be accepted. When all necessary specifications have been met satisfactorily, and no specifications are used illegally, the process will continue with the printing of the specification card data (Exhibit 8).

Card Counts

The stratum cards that are contained in the specifications indicate the number of sample cards that are expected in each stratum. Accordingly, as the sample cards are introduced into the computer, either physically or from a tape or disk file, the cards are stratified and counted. These card counts are compared to the counts indicated in the stratum cards and, if there is a difference in any one stratum, the evaluation procedure is terminated so that correction can be made. This precludes an evaluation being made with a card missing.

Unusual Differences

When the option to test for unusual differences is used, the book value is compared with the physical value (Appendix 5). If the physical value differs from the book value by more than 250 and more than fourfold, an unusual difference is indicated and the unusual-difference indicators will be set.

When all the cards have been processed, a notice that a certain number of unusual differences are contained in the sample data will be printed out. This notice will warn anyone using the evaluation that the results may be subject to error. If a review of these unusual differences indicates that they do not seem to be nonsampling errors, the Evaluation Program may be rerun without the test for unusual differences, so that the evaluation will not be labeled with the warning message.

Printed Totals

When the book values and population values contained in the stratum cards and specification cards are printed out as part of the evaluation (Exhibit 9), these may be checked against the totals obtained when the sample was selected, as shown in Exhibit 3. These amounts may be checked not only in total but stratum by stratum as further assurance that the correct sample data cards were used in the evaluation process.

Collapsing Strata

It was indicated earlier that a proper estimate cannot be made unless there are sufficient items in each stratum to permit such an estimate. This will be resolved in the selection process by combining several strata as required. In the event that the sample is selected manually or the combining is not done during the selection process, a similar procedure (Appendix 5) is used in the evaluation program so that there will be no difficulty with the final estimates.

CALCULATION OF ESTIMATES

The statistical calculations required to produce an estimate are composed of the preliminary analyses of the data by stratum, the preliminary calculations for each stratum, and the specific calculations required for the six possible types of estimates listed below.

Preliminary Analyses by Stratum

The preliminary analyses by stratum (Appendix 5) are concerned with classifying the data by stratum and obtaining the necessary totals for further calculations. As each sample item feeds into the computer, 23 separate counters are maintained as the items are classified by stratum. There are 21 separate stratum counts, one total count, and one count on any items that may for some reason be rejected. When all the sample cards have been read into the computer, the separate stratum counts are compared to the stratum counts contained in the stratum cards. As stated earlier, the program will terminate at this point if these stratum counts do not agree.

At the same time, the book value and the sample value in each card are each squared and cross-multiplied to provide the value described in statistical terms as X^2, XY, and Y^2, each with its own subscript from 1 to n. If cumulative monetary sampling has been used, so that the selection probabilities are unequal, the sample values are adjusted by these unequal probabilities.

The end result of these preliminary analyses by stratum is to obtain, for each stratum in the sample, the necessary sums of squares and sums of cross-products required to make the estimate. These are referred to in statistical terms as ΣX^2, ΣXY, ΣY^2. The Greek capital letter sigma indicates a summation.

Preliminary Calculations by Stratum

When these sums have been obtained for each stratum, the average values or sample means $(\bar{x}, \bar{y})$ may be calculated. In addition, the population book values, by stratum, are contained in the stratum cards and the population means $\mu(X)$ are also calculated (Appendix 5) for each stratum in the population. These three separate means are calculated for each of the up to 21 strata and in total, each of which carries a subscript indicating the appropriate stratum number.

Corrected Values

Up to this point, all the calculations have been made with reference to a zero origin, as is common in accounting practice. Most statistical references, however, with the exception of the mean, are made from the mean rather than from a zero reference point. A further calculation (Appendix 5) is therefore required to correct the various values so that they will reflect measurement from the mean. The values that have to be corrected to measurement from the mean are the sums of squares and cross-products. The formulas for these calculations, and the derivation of the formulas, may be found in almost any standard statistical textbook.[1]

Regression Estimate

The user has the choice of specifying one of the following types of evaluations to arrive at an estimate:

1. Combined regression estimate.
2. Separate regression estimate.
3. Combined ratio estimate.
4. Separate ratio estimate.
5. Mean estimate.
6. Mean estimate with selection proportional to size.

The evaluation procedure takes advantage of the fact stated earlier that ratio estimates and mean estimates are special forms of regression estimates. In this way a single procedure (Appendix 5) is used for all types of estimates. The estimate is made for each stratum independently, and these estimates are summed to arrive at the total estimate. The basic formula for a regression

[1] For example Ernest Kurnow, Gerald J. Glasser, and Frederick A. Ottman, *Statistics for Business Decisions*, R. D. Irwin, Homewood, Illinois, 1959, pp. 316–317.

estimate of the unknown mean of the physical population values as given earlier in (2.6) and (2.7) may be rearranged as follows:

$$\mu(\hat{Y}) = \bar{y} + b[\mu(X) - \bar{x}] \tag{6.1}$$

where x represents the book value and y the physical value; $(\bar{x}, \bar{y})$ indicate the sample means, and $[\mu(X), \mu(Y)]$ indicate the population means.

The regression estimate takes all the available information into consideration. The book population mean is known or determinable. If the book sample mean does not equal the known book population mean, as it rarely will, then the physical sample mean is not likely to equal the unknown physical population mean. The regression estimate adjusts the physical sample mean for this relative difference between the means of the book population and the book sample.

Experience shows that the combined estimate is more useful in most accounting situations, even though a separate estimate will often yield slightly tighter precision. In an inventory, for example, the population items will usually be stratified by monetary value. The fact that one part number falls in one stratum rather than another is a function of its quantity and price rather than of a discernible similarity between the part numbers that fall in one stratum. Thus we are more interested in the overall relationship of the book values to the physical values rather than in a relationship within any one stratum.

The value of b changes depending on the type of estimate. In the regression estimate, the value is computed for the sample from the standard formula for the slope of any regression line. This formula is

$$b = \frac{\sum xy}{\sum x^2} \tag{6.2}$$

where x^2 and xy are the sample squares and cross-products, corrected to the mean. The slope statistic, b, is a measure of the relative increase in Y for a given value of X. The essential difference between a combined estimate and a separate estimate is whether the slope is determined as a combined slope over the entire sample or separately for each stratum.

Ratio Estimate

A ratio estimate has many of the same properties as a regression estimate in that it takes into consideration available information about the book population. It has been a popular form of estimate because it is relatively simple to calculate manually and usually gives very good results. These results, however, can never be better than a regression estimate, which is difficult to compute manually. When a computer is available, therefore, there does not seem to be much point in using ratio estimates.

In a ratio estimate, the value of b in (6.1) above is the ratio of the mean of the physical values in the sample to the mean of the book values in the sample. For a separate ratio estimate, this calculation would be made separately for each stratum.

A ratio estimate will be as good as a regression estimate only when the regression coefficient b equals the ratio of the means of the two values under consideration. This situation will occur when the relation between the two variables is a straight line through the origin if the values are plotted on graph paper. As a practical matter, this relationship is hardly ever likely to hold for any large number of items, although it would appear to be a reasonable assumption about the relation between the physical and book values.

In Figure 6.1, the sums of the paired plotted points shown are equal to each other and thus the ratio of the mean values of x and y is equal to one. This equivalence is represented by the dashed line and implies that for any given book value, say 10, the expected physical value would also be 10. As desirable as this theoretical relationship may be, it rarely occurs over an entire inventory. Instead, the true relationship can usually be expressed more closely by a regression line represented by the solid line in the figure. The two lines intersect only at the point of paired mean values (15, 15).

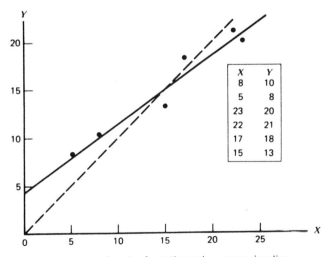

Figure 6.1 Graph of a ratio and a regression line.

Mean Estimate

A provision has been made in the Program to develop a mean estimate from the physical values. It is not recommended in any situation where a regression estimate could be made, because it is unwise to ignore available data and the results are likely to be considerably less precise when a mean estimate is used.

For a mean estimate, the value of b in (6.1) above is zero, so that the right-hand term disappears. Consequently, the best estimate of the mean of the physical population becomes the sample mean of the physical values, namely $\bar{y}$. As previously indicated, however, that sample mean will seldom coincide with the unknown population mean. This situation can be improved by using the mean estimate provision in the Program to make a mean estimate of differences.

Mean estimates are also used when selection is made with unequal probability, as in monetary selection, for certain technical reasons preclude the use of regression estimates in such a situation. The results are usually sufficiently precise because of the high degree of stratification involved in monetary selection.

CALCULATION OF PRECISION

The monetary precision is the range, plus or minus the estimate, into which we would expect the physical inventory value to fall if we sample from the same frame a large number of times. We would expect a normal distribution of these sample means, and that 95 percent of them would be no more than two standard errors from the unknown population mean.

Standard Deviate

In dealing with the normal distribution, we could look up, in tables of the standard normal distribution, a particular reliability percentage such as 95 percent and obtain the standard normal deviate of 1.96. Greater flexibility may be obtained, however, by using a subroutine (Appendix 5) that will convert from a given percentage to the standard deviate of the normal distribution. This not only saves time in looking up the tables, but also permits the use of percentages that would not be found readily in the tables and would necessarily involve interpolation.

Finite Population Correction

A second part of the precision calculation is the correction that must be made when sampling without replacement from a finite population. While this correction factor loses importance when the population from which the sample is being taken is very large, the correction can be important when the population is not too large or the sample required is relatively sizable as a proportion of the population.

Most of the sampling taught in elementary classes in statistics is likely to be sampling with replacement, which depends on the binomial theory for its probabilities. If we have 12 accounts receivable of which 1 is past due, and select 3 at random with replacement, there is a 21 percent probability that 1 of the 3 is the past due account. There is a very slight probability that the past due account would be picked each time and a slightly larger probability that the past due account would be picked 2 out of the 3 times. There is a much greater probability of about 77 percent that the single past due account will not be picked at all.

If we sample without replacement, it is not possible for all 3 items selected to be past due, or even for 2 of them to be past due, as there is only 1 past due account. The first time that we draw, we have 11 chances out of 12 of not finding it. On the second draw, assuming that we did not find it the first time, the chances of not getting it are now 10 out of 11. On the third draw, assuming no success on either of the previous two draws, the unfavorable odds are 9 out of 10. Thus the chances of not getting the one past due account out of three draws is as follows

$$\frac{11}{12} \cdot \frac{10}{11} \cdot \frac{9}{10} = .75$$

As a consequence, the chance of getting the past due account is 25 percent, the complement of the figure above. This is one way in which the probabilities are changed when sampling without replacement.

If we were to select 12 accounts at random from the same file with replacement after each selection, the probability of including the one past due account just once would increase to a little over 38 percent, whereas if these 12 were selected without replacement, this probability would become a certainty. This is another and more significant way in which the probabilities change when selecting without replacement. Each item selected changes the probability for the next item to be selected, and these probabilities may change considerably when a relatively large sample is selected. Sampling without replacement depends on hypergoemetric theory, and the probabilities are more difficult to calculate.

To put this in proper perspective, as far as sampling without replacement is concerned, the standard error that would be computed would be larger than it should be unless a correction is made. If all the items in the population are counted so that we have a 100 percent sample, there should be no standard error, as there would be no need for a range around the estimate. If no correction is made, however, the standard error of the population estimate would be close to the standard deviation of the book population. What is required is a correction factor that would gradually shade the standard error down to zero as the sample approaches 100 percent. To correct the variance of a sample, the formula for this factor is

$$\frac{N - n}{N - 1} \tag{6.3}$$

where N is the population size and n is the sample size. The square root of this factor could be applied directly to the standard error. The classical derivation of this formula is attributable to Gauss[2] in the year 1809. It should be understood that the above formula must be applied separately to each stratum variance using the total items in each stratum of the population and sample.

Variance by Stratum

The next step in the development of monetary precision is to obtain the variance by stratum. Stratification disposes of the variances between strata, but requires a more complicated calculation of the variances within each stratum. The purpose of developing a measure of precision is to estimate the degree of sampling variation that might be expected from repeated sample estimates. The calculation of variance is a well defined mathematical step that measures the dispersion of all sample items. Further steps may average this statistic to provide a measure of the variation between sampling units or may expand the total to obtain an estimate of the dispersion of all items in the population.

Variance of Mean Estimate. The basic calculation for the variance for each stratum in the sample will vary according to the type of estimate prescribed. The basic calculation for the variance of a mean estimate is the sum

[2] W. Edwards Deming, *Sample Design in Business Research*, Wiley, New York, 1960, pp. 392–393.

of the squared sample values measured from the mean, or, in statistical terms.

$$V(\hat{Y}) = \sum_{i=1}^{n} (y_i - \bar{y})^2 \tag{6.4}$$

Using the sample observations in Figure 6.1, and the sample mean ($\bar{y}$) of 15, the individual calculations required by (6.4) are as follows:

y_i	$\sum y = y_i - \bar{y}$	$\sum y^2 = (y_i - \bar{y})^2$
10	−5	25
8	−7	49
20	5	25
21	6	36
18	3	9
13	−2	4
90	0	148

The sum of the squares of the sample values corrected to the mean, or 148 in this case, is generally referred to as Σy^2. The formula (6.4) may be restated in a number of different ways such as

$$V(\hat{Y}) = \sum y^2 = \sum_{i=1}^{n} y_i^2 - n\bar{y}^2 \tag{6.5}$$

This formula is easier to use with a large number of sample values and gives identical results. Using the same data, the sum of the squares of the Y values is 1498, the mean, 15, squared and multiplied by 6 is 1350, and thus the result of (6.5) is also 148.

Variance of Ratio Estimate. The variance of a ratio estimate is more involved and the basic calculation is

$$V(\hat{Y}_R) = \sum (y_i - Rx_i)^2 \tag{6.6}$$

where R is the ratio of the sample means, or $\bar{y}$ divided by $\bar{x}$. Using the data shown in Figure 6.1, the ratio of the sample means equals 1.0 and the calculation follows

x_i	y_i	$y_i - Rx_i$	$(y_i - Rx_i)^2$
8	10	2	4
5	8	3	9
23	20	−3	9
22	21	−1	1
17	18	1	1
15	13	−2	4
90	90	0	28

The formula for the variance of a ratio estimate (6.6) may be expanded to (6.7) to simplify the calculations. Using this formula and the following data

$$\Sigma Y_i{}^2 = 1498$$

$$\Sigma X_i{}^2 = 1616$$

$$\Sigma X_i Y_i = 1543$$

$$V(\hat{Y}_R) = \sum_{i=1}^{n} y_i^2 - 2R \sum_{i=1}^{n} x_i y_i + R^2 \sum x_i^2 \qquad (6.7)$$

$$= 1498 - 2(1543) + 1616$$

$$= 28$$

(6.7) also reduces to the same result.

It is also interesting to note that the same formula (6.7) may be expressed in terms of corrected values. For purposes of illustration, the corrected values are obtained by subtracting the mean value of the x_i values from all the x_i values and the mean value of the y_i values from all y_i values. Then they may be squared and multiplied as follows:

$\Sigma x =$ $x_i - \bar{x}$	$\Sigma y =$ $y_i - \bar{y}$	$\Sigma x^2 =$ $(x_i - \bar{x})^2$	$\Sigma xy =$ $(x_i - \bar{x})(y_i - \bar{y})$	$\Sigma y^2 =$ $(y_i - \bar{y})^2$
−7	−5	49	35	25
−10	−7	100	70	49
8	−5	64	40	25
7	6	49	42	36

$\sum x =$ $x_i - \bar{x}$	$\sum y =$ $y_i - \bar{y}$	$\sum x^2 =$ $(x_i - \bar{x})^2$	$\sum xy =$ $(x_i - \bar{x})(y_i - \bar{y})$	$\sum y^2 =$ $(y_i - \bar{y})^2$
2	3	4	6	9
0	−2	0	0	4
0	0	266	193	148

By substituting the corrected values above in (6.8) it also produces identical results

$$V(\hat{Y}_R) = \sum y^2 - 2R\sum xy + R^2\sum x^2$$

$$= 148 - 2(193) + 266 \tag{6.8}$$

$$= 28$$

These calculations would be tedious if done manually and unnecessary if done by computer, for the formulas may be rearranged to get the results directly from the total values before correction.

As there is a tendency for the variance of a ratio estimate to be understated, the formula needs to be corrected whenever the sample sizes are small. To be conservative in the variance calculation, the variance formula is multiplied by another factor

$$1 + \frac{5}{n} \tag{6.9}$$

which closely approximates the degree of possible bias.[3]

Variance of regression estimate. The variance of a regression estimate is measured not from the mean but from the regression line and has the form

$$V(\hat{Y}_{reg}) = \sum_{i=1}^{n} (y_i - \hat{y}_i)^2 \tag{6.10}$$

where $\hat{y}_i = a + bx_i$ calculated from the sample data. Thus for any value of x there is an estimated value of y that is on the regression line. The variation in y corresponding to a given x is measured from that point.

[3] William G. Cochran, *Sampling Techniques*, 2nd ed., Wiley, New York, 1963, p. 160.

Using the data from Figure 6.1, the value of b is 0.7256 and the value of a is 4.1165. The calculations of the variance are as follows:

x_i	y_i	$\hat{y}_i = a + bx_i$	$y_i - \hat{y}_i$	$(y_i - \hat{y}_i)^2$
8	10	9.92	0.08	0.01
5	8	7.75	0.25	0.06
23	20	20.80	−0.80	0.64
22	21	20.08	0.92	0.85
17	18	16.45	1.55	2.40
15	13	15.00	−2.00	4.00
90	90	90.00	−0.00	7.96

Once again these rather complex calculations can be simplified to a formula based on corrected values in the following form

$$V(\hat{Y}_{reg}) = \sum y^2 - b \sum xy$$

$$= 148 - 0.7256(193) \qquad (6.11)$$

$$= 7.96$$

Using the corrected values given above, the formula reduces to the same result more quickly. The formula (6.11) is identical to the formula used for the residual variance in regression analysis. It is also worth noting that if b is set to zero in (6.11), the variance would be the same as that for a mean estimate. In other words, a mean estimate ignores any knowledge of the relationship between the known value X and the unknown corresponding value of Y.

Sum of Variances

The variances obtained for each stratum in the sample are each multiplied by the applicable finite population correction and expanded to provide an estimate of the total variance for each stratum. The expansion factor for the variance is the square of the ratio of the population size to the sample size in each stratum. These variances for each stratum are then added together to provide the total estimated population variance. The various program steps to calculate the variance are given in Appendix 5.

Precision

The standard deviation for the population is obtained by taking the square root of this total population variance. This in turn is multiplied by the standard deviate for the required percentage of reliability. A standard deviation of $100,000 would mean that an estimate would have approximately $200,000 monetary precision at 95 percent reliability and could be relied upon as being within $200,000 of the true population value.

In determining the overall variance and thus the monetary precision, it is important to recognize the interplay of the various factors, such as the percentage of reliability, the degree of variation in the data, the finite population correction, and the type of stratification. The principal factor affecting the variance and thus the precision is the sample size. Increasing the sample size will decrease the variance proportionately, but not decrease the precision likewise. Doubling the sample will halve the variance, but to halve the precision, the sample size must be increased fourfold.

Use of Results

The evaluation will result in a combined regression estimate as shown in Exhibit 9. Whether it is a good estimate depends on the total physical value, which is usually unknown. In this case, however, it is not unknown as it is shown in Exhibit 3 to be $10,019,849.50. The estimated value of $10,035,509.96 is the best estimate that can be made on the basis of the sample that was taken. This happens to be a rather good estimate, as it is within $16,000 or a small fraction of 1 percent of the population value. It is not likely that all the samples taken would be this good, yet a few might be better.

The precision of $132,832.16 is somewhat better than the desired precision as set in the sample specification. When sampling data for the first time, this would have to be considered to be reasonably good. One would normally scale down the specified precision on a first attempt so as to improve the likelihood of achieving the desired precision.

Inference and Risk.   Normally, we would not know the true population value, but we can proceed rationally on the assumption that if the whole frame is covered 100 percent with the same care, the population value would fall between $9,902,678 and $10,168,342. The statistical risk that the population value would not fall within this range is 5 percent, or 1 out of 20 such experiences, and is a reasonable risk to take under these circumstances.

Other Forms of Evaluation

While the combined regression estimate is recommended in this type of situation, it is interesting to note the results achieved when the same sample is evaluated using other estimators (Exhibits 12 to 15). For purpose of comparison the estimate and limits for each are given below:

Estimator	Estimate	Upper Limit	Lower Limit
Combined regression	$10,035,510	$10,168,342	$9,902,678
Separate regression	10,039,585	10,166,136	9,913,033
Combined ratio	10,036,216	10,182,589	9,889,844
Separate ratio	10,036,731	10,183,133	9,890,329
Mean	10,018,771	10,174,895	9,862,647

Accounting for Sample Results

The unresolved differences between the perpetual records and the physical counts for the sample items should be recorded in the accounting records. As to the remaining difference between the sample estimate and the perpetual records for the entire population, two possible approaches might be taken.

Preferable Approach. Under the first approach, the sample estimate of the total inventory would be used exactly as if a complete physical inventory had been taken. The inventory control account would be adjusted accordingly. The portion of such difference that could be identified with specific items would also be adjusted within the perpetual inventory records. The remaining difference that could not be so identified would be carried in the perpetual inventory records as an unallocated inventory adjustment account. After the first sampling application this account would be increased or decreased as necessary to reflect the results of subsequent samples. Inventory differences found as a result of subsequent cyclical counts would be considered part of this unallocated inventory adjustment account and corrected accordingly.

Test Approach. Under the second approach, the inventory sample would be regarded primarily as a test of the acceptability of the existing records rather than as a substitute for a complete physical inventory. Accordingly, the inventory records would be considered acceptable if the balance in the inventory control account were between the upper and lower precision limits for the sample estimate. The identified differences relating to specific sample items would be adjusted, but no unallocated adjustment would be recorded.

Test of Hypothesis

In this second approach, we are making a statistical test of a hypothesis that the perpetual inventory records as adjusted for identified differences found in the sample counts are correct. Accordingly, we will accept the adjusted book value if it falls within the limits determined for the sample estimate. It is implied, obviously, that the hypothesis would be rejected otherwise and this could lead to a larger sample or a complete count.

When a statistical hypothesis is rejected based on a sample at 95 percent reliability, there is 1 chance out of 20 that this is a wrong decision. When accounting data are being sampled, this statistical generality becomes modified by other factors and the risk, in most cases, would be substantially less than 5 percent. The system of internal control imposes restraints on the degree of error in accounting records, and other analytical measures provide an indication as to whether a sample is obviously incorrect. For these reasons, it is quite unlikely that this type of error, known statistically as a Type I error[4] or alpha (α) risk, will occur or go unrecognized with accounting data. The likelihood of this type of error would be mitigated by use of the first approach of adjusting the book inventory value to the best estimate.

A wrong decision can also be made, under this second approach, by accepting the hypothesis that the perpetual inventory records, as adjusted, are correct when the unknown true value is substantially different from the adjusted book value. There is a very, very small statistical risk that the book value could be near one limit, such as C in Figure 2.1, and the true value might be near the other limit, or A in the same figure. The difference in such a situation, as rare as it might be, is a possible difference of four standard errors. This is known statistically as a Type II error[5] or beta (β) risk. This risk would also be modified substantially by the system of internal control and other analytical measures. It would be minimized also by use of the recommended approach of adjusting the book inventory control to the best estimate developed from the sample.

---

[4] John E. Freund, *Mathematical Statistics*, Prentice-Hall, Englewood Cliffs, NJ, 1962, p. 239.
[5] Ibid.

Pilot Sample

In situations where little is known about the data being sampled, it may be desirable to take a small sample and evaluate it as a basis for the design and selection of the larger sample. The results given in Appendix 1, Exhibit 10 show the tentative design for the next sample which can be based on the pilot sample. The file of cards that is produced as indicated in Exhibit 11 would be used for the selection of the larger sample.

In other cases, where a pilot sample is not being used, these data merely provide information for the design of the sample the next time around. It is interesting to note that in this particular situation a smaller sample might conceivably have produced the desired results. Different samples will produce different results, so that it is difficult to make any hard and fast decisions based on any one sample. Samples taken over several years will give a much clearer pattern of what may be achieved.

Summary

A sampling estimate taken on the basis described above is a reliable and acceptable alternative to the complete count for financial statement purposes. More and more companies are likely to want to follow this approach in the future.

It is evident that there can be substantial savings in nonproductive labor through a sampling approach as the speed with which the samples can be taken could reduce downtime in manufacturing or processing operations. It is also evident that customer service can be improved where shipping operations might otherwise be delayed by a complete shutdown for several days to take inventory. Furthermore, there is good reason to believe that statistical estimates of this nature may in fact be closer to the true value than even some complete counts have been in the past.

CHAPTER 7

ESTIMATION OF ASSET VALUES

So far we have dealt with estimation sampling techniques as they are applied to the particular situation of estimating the values of physical inventories. This should enable the reader to apply estimation sampling in other situations that may develp in the financial or accounting area. Many of these situations are known, some may be conjectured, and a great many have yet to be discovered. The next few chapters are devoted to the uses of estimation sampling, such as the estimation of asset values, liabilities, and income or expense accounts, and in meeting regulatory or other business requirements. Some of these applications may be useful immediately in a given environment and others may stimulate further thought.

ACCOUNTS RECEIVABLE

There are several classification procedures—such as aging accounts receivable, determining sales characteristics, or making maturity spreads—and several accounting procedures—such as confirming accounts receivable, estimating collectibility, or determining the current portion of long-term receivables—that can be carried out by estimation sampling.

Aging of Accounts Receivable

At some time or another almost every company prepares an aging of accounts receivable, either as part of the collection procedure or perhaps to determine the requirements for a reserve for uncollected accounts. When there are a large number of accounts receivable the process can be shortened by the use of estimation sampling.

In most cases a computer record of the accounts receivable balances would exist so that a sample could be selected directly from this record.

The feature of sampling interest would be amounts overdue in a particular category, such as 30-day accounts. There would be a separate estimate for each uncollected category. In the absence of better information, it is suggested, for this type of estimation sampling, that reliability be specified at 95 percent and that monetary precision be set at approximately 1 percent of the population from which the sample is to be taken. After more experience is gained, the precision can be adjusted accordingly.

Once the sample has been selected, each account in the sample would be reviewed as to the amount that was current and the amount that belonged in various overdue categories such as 30, 60, 90, or 120 days and over. Separate fields in the sample tape or disk files could be used to record the amounts in each of these overdue categories. Where punched cards are used for the sample items, a more appropriate method would be to use a different set of sample cards for each uncollected category.

When this classification has been established and recorded in the sample file, the several evaluations are ready to be run. The sample items would be processed using all the items in the sample, whether past due or not, for the independent, or X value, and the 30-day past due amounts for the dependent, or Y value; an estimate would be made of the total amount of 30-day overdue accounts in the population. A similar process would be followed for the 60-day accounts, the 90-day accounts, and for the 120-day or longer accounts.

Many companies have this type of information available as part of the computer processing, obviating the need for estimation sampling in this connection. The same procedure could, however, be followed for estimating any characteristic of accounts receivable, such as the dollar sales to accounts in certain specified states, or for estimating sales to wholesalers or distributors where such information would not normally be available in the regular processing runs.

Confirmation of Accounts Receivable

It may be necessary to confirm the accounts receivable as of a certain date for a variety of reasons. This confirmation may be part of the annual audit, part of a review by the internal auditors, or it might be made by another company in connection with a purchase investigation. The purpose of such a procedure, which may well be conducted on a surprise basis, is to detect any material errors or irregularities in the accounts and to be sure that the accounts are not very much overstated. For the first time that sampling is used in this procedure, the design could be based on monetary precision of 2 percent of the accounts receivable at a reliability level of 95 percent. Whether this suggested 2 percent will provide a satisfactory evaluation depends on the degree of internal control in the recordkeeping, on general business conditions at the time of confirmation, and on the purpose for which confirmation is being made. More familiarity with this type of sampling will permit closer adjustment of the precision.

Assuming that a tape or disk file of accounts receivable would be available for this purpose, the sample can be selected directly and confirmations prepared and mailed out for each sample item. When the confirmations are returned, the confirmed amounts should be entered in a separate field in sample cards and the evaluation then made. As the amounts confirmed would, in most cases, be correct, and thus the correlation high, a stratified regression estimate would provide very satisfactory results in the confirmation of accounts receivable.

As the accounts receivable record often may be only an open invoice file, or a machine bookkeeping record, rather than a computer record, it is well to consider at this point other methods of selecting a sample that could be used in conjunction with computer evaluation. The following methods should be considered:

1. Create a computer file.
2. Take a monetary sample.
3. Take a numeric sample.

Computer File.   The first procedure is applicable particularly in a company that has computing capacity available but does not maintain these specific records on the computer. It is quite often easier to have cards punched for each account balance than to resort to the more cumbersome methods of manual selection. By creating a computer file for this purpose, computer selection could be used and the whole procedure would go more smoothly.

Monetary Amount Selection.   Where manual methods of selection must be used, the preferable way, in the case of accounts receivable, would be to use monetary amount selection. This procedure is a form of stratified sampling that will place more emphasis on the large dollar value items in selecting the sample. An upper cutoff should be established, based on experience, at approximately one-third the monetary precision specified for design purposes until more specific knowledge is acquired. If the desired monetary precision is 3 percent of the population dollars, the upper cutoff would then be set at approximately 1 percent of the population dollars. It is desirable from a selection standpoint to use a relatively even amount such as the nearest thousand dollars for this purpose. If the cutoff amount is $5000, all items of $5000 or more in the population would be selected in the sample and would constitute the second or upper stratum.

Sample items for the first or lower stratum would be selected on a systematic basis with a random start. A random number is selected between $1 and $5000 and the items in the population are added sequentially on an adding machine or using a hand calculator until this random number is reached or exceeded. The last item listed when the total reaches or exceeds the random number is selected as the first item in the sample. The target now becomes the random number plus $5000 and the listing continues until a new item is selected. The procedure continues in the same way until all items have been listed and the complete sample has been obtained.

An alternative monetary selection method, equally random, is to enter the random number in the adding machine and list items until the total equals or exceeds $5000, taking the last item into the sample. This would continue for $10,000, and so on, with the advantage being that items are selected by even values. A third method, described in Chapter 11, using negative complements, may also be used for monetary selection. This is the procedure (Appendix 5) used for numerical sampling in the selection phase of the Estimation Sampling Program.

Once the confirmations have been mailed out and returned, the evaluation proceeds as if the selection had been made by computer. As the items have been selected in relation to their proportional value, the evaluation must be made using probability proportional to size. When a computer is not available, the evaluation can be made by way of a time-sharing system.

Numeric Sample.   In the few cases where a numeric sample must be obtained for estimation sampling, a larger sample will be needed and the sample will often be unstratified because there is no easy way to separate the larger amounts into an upper stratum. A top stratum selected completely should be used where feasible. One common method in numeric sampling is some form of selection based on the numbers of the orders or invoices such as a terminal digit randomly selected. Thus all form numbers ending in seven could be selected for the sample, which would provide a 10 percent sample.

Formula 4.1 can be used to obtain a rough approximation of sample size. If the standard deviation is unknown, as it probably would be, it may be estimated by dividing the range of the accounts by 6.[1] If the highest dollar amount expected is $1200, the standard deviation would be estimated at $200 for use in the sample design formula. The sample selected in this manner may be evaluated as an unstratified sample either in the computer or by using a time-sharing terminal. Manual evaluation is possible if the sample

---

[1] W. Edwards Deming, *Sample Design in Business Research*, Wiley, New York, 1960, p. 260.

is relatively small but the calculations are usually extensive and could be subject to error. For this reason, manual evaluation is not recommended.

Uncollectible Accounts

Management is required periodically to estimate a reserve for uncollectible accounts. This may be a flat percentage, based on experience, or set based on a current aging of the accounts receivable. A satisfactory method would be to take a sample of the accounts receivable, analyze it for collectibility, and estimate the total uncollectible accounts. The selection would be made on the same basis as for aging accounts receivable and the sample items selected would be reviewed by the credit manager or others to obtain the anticipated loss, if any, on these accounts.

When this process is completed, the sample items could be evaluated and an estimate obtained of the total uncollectible accounts.

Current Portion of Installment Sales

Installment sales are made for long periods, up to eight or ten years in some cases, so that the expected cash flow in the following year, which could be classed as a current asset, is likely to be only a portion of the total installment sales. The usual way in which installment sales are recorded may make it difficult to determine the payments that will fall due in the following year, and some form of estimation will be required.

A satisfactory estimate of the current portion of the installment sales can be made by selecting a sample from the total population and analyzing these sample items. After this has been done for all the sample items, the current portion of installment sales may be reasonably estimated.

When these calculations are likely to enter into tax litigation, the company and its tax counsel should be familiar with Revenue Procedure 64-4 of the Internal Revenue Service and the appendix on "Standards of Probability Sampling for Legal Evidence." The sampling and evaluation procedures contained in the programs discussed herein conform, in all respects, to these standards. Revenue Procedure 64-4 prescribes, additionally, a coefficient of variation of the estimate of no more than 2 percent. In the terminology used in this book, this would be equivalent to precision of 4 percent of the estimate at 95 percent reliability.

Maturity Schedule

A somewhat similar type estimate is needed when a large number of loans, leases, or installment sales are spread over a sufficiently large period that a schedule of the amounts maturing each month or year may be required. The procedure would be essentially the same. The sample would be taken, the maturity of each sample item would be determined, and the evaluation would produce an estimate for each maturity. A separate evaluation would be required for each maturity. Precision should be set at no more than 1 percent until sufficient experience is available to make more precise adjustments.

INVENTORIES

The taking of a physical inventory is an area in which estimation sampling is widely used today. The considerable savings that can accrue from sampling, in place of full counts, has contributed much to its popularity. The first part of this book has laid considerable stress on its use in inventory, since almost everybody has an inventory-taking problem and can therefore more readily understand the explanation. The discussion here is limited to the differences by types of inventories and the different applications of estimation sampling to inventories.

Parts and Supplies

The use of estimation sampling in the taking of physical inventories of parts and supplies is fairly straightforward. The parts are usually in packages or boxes and thus are easy to distinguish and easy to count. Problems of measurement are rarely encountered in taking this kind of physical inventory.

Finished Goods

A physical inventory of finished goods is also relatively easy to take, in most situations, because the goods are readily identifiable, packaged, and clearly marked as to quantity so as to facilitate the counting of the units. Whenever a substantial amount of finished goods have to be counted, the use of estimation sampling should be considered.

Work-in-Process

Inventories of work-in-process are not so easily estimated. When the processing cycle is relatively short, the job is simple enough, but in work-in-process inventories that vary over a wide production period, it may not be too easy to use estimation sampling because the population is difficult to define. In many companies, the work-in-process ledger will be broken down into material, labor, and overhead components without further subdivision. It would then be quite difficult to use estimation sampling. If a job order system exists, and the work-in-process can be readily identified by job order, the taking of a sample may be easier to do.

Where the work-in-process flows through a number of divisions without inventory being taken at the end of each process, it would also be more difficult to sample, whereas inventories taken at the end of each process that can be readily identified as belonging to that process, take to sampling more easily. In summary, the population must be clearly identifiable by sampling units that may be found on the production floor for sampling to be effective in estimating work-in-process inventories.

Assembly Line

Successful applications have been made with assembly line operations that use standard cost systems with designated values at periodic points. Raw material items or parts to be assembled are grouped near the assembly line at points where they will be used. The number of items or parts to complete the assembly to the next standard cost point are segregated from the parts awaiting assembly and are counted as having been assembled at that cost point. A certain expertise and care is required to do this properly but production time saved is worthwhile.

Component Analysis

There are situations where the physical units are identifiable in the form of units finished at that particular stage of production, whereas the book inventory is still carried in labor, material, and overhead components. A problem arises in the conversion of the physical units at that stage of process to the corresponding book values for labor, material, and overhead in order to reconcile the book and physical inventories. There are other similar cases where one unit must be converted to another, and such a conversion is susceptible to estimation sampling.

There may be, for example, a complete record of all units finished in Department A and awaiting transfer to Department B. This record may be in units only, or in dollars only, or both. In any case, a selection may be made from this population and the sample units examined for their labor, material, and overhead components, When each unit in the sample has been converted into labor, material, and overhead costs, an estimate can be made, based on the sample units, of the labor, material, and overhead components of all units awaiting transfer to the next stage in production. After such an analysis has been made for all departments, the individual estimates can be added together and reconciled to the quantity shown on the general ledger for the individual components of work-in-process. As stated elsewhere, statistical variances are additive so that the precision for each component estimate should be squared and summed. The overall precision for the total estimate of work-in-process would be the square root of this sum.

Raw Materials

Estimation sampling is less likely to be required in taking physical inventories of raw materials as the number of raw materials is usually limited and the number of locations at which the raw material is available may also be limited.

There will be situations, however, where a single raw material may be stored at numerous locations so that an opportunity exists for selecting certain locations for the sample, visiting these locations to take the physical inventory of the raw material, and, based on the sample results, making an estimate of the entire physical inventory of that particular raw material.

There will also be some situations in which a company may have a sufficient number of different raw materials going into production to make estimation sampling worthwhile for the raw material inventory. Some companies that use a single raw material, such as steel, to make a great number of different finished parts may include all the work-in-process as raw material and relieve the raw material inventory solely on the basis of the finished goods. In such a case there would be an application of component analysis to the work-in-process inventory in order to reconcile the raw material inventory.

Retail Inventories

Department stores, as well as other retailers and distributors, generally carry their inventories at retail prices and take their physical inventories in the same way. In many cases, unit records will not exist so that the reconciliation must be made to total dollar value. This, of course, precludes the selection of sample units from the inventory population. In some cases, however, other populations may exist, or be created, to further the use of estimation sampling. Any record of units purchased or sold might be utilized for selection purposes and many retailers will maintain such records either by product or class of merchandise. A mean estimate could be made at retail value for reconciliation purposes and an additional mean estimate could be made at cost by pricing the sample units at cost.

Financial statement presentation requires that inventories be stated at cost or market, whichever is lower. Retail inventories that are on the accounting records at sales values must be reduced to cost or market accordingly. Historically, this is done by adjusting the inventory at retail price by some overall percentage gained from analysis of the relationship of purchase cost to sales price, and adjusted for markups and markdowns. This problem can also be solved by estimation sampling. After the retail inventory is compiled, a selection can be made from this population and the sample units priced at the lower of cost or market. When the sample units are evaluated this will provide an estimate of the entire inventory at the lower of cost or market.

LIFO Inventories

When inflationary trends are experienced, a significant number of companies change to the LIFO (last-in, first-out) method of determining inventory cost. Current interest in this method of accounting arises from the increased rate of inflation experienced in recent years and its effect on the nature and amount of earnings reported. The LIFO method has been acceptable for financial reporting and tax purposes since 1939, but if it is used for tax purposes, it must also be used for financial reporting, according to Federal Income Tax Regulations.

LIFO assumes that the cost of the first item used or sold is the cost of the last item received or produced. The two methods of computing the LIFO inventory value are specific item and dollar value. Although the specific item method is generally used in accounting textbooks as an illustration of the effects of using a LIFO basis for inventories, the more common method is the dollar value method. In the latter method, inventories are computed in terms of dollars without identification of specific items. The dollar value method measures the inventory level in terms of base year dollars. For this purpose the total dollar value may be divided into pools according to natural business units, by material content, or by cost components, such as material, labor, and overhead.

When calculating the LIFO inventory under the dollar value method, the closing inventory quantities must be priced at the current year cost and at the base year cost. This is known as the "double extension method." An index may be computed, however, by double extending a representative number of the inventory items in a pool or by using other sound and consistent statistical methods. The Internal Revenue Service considers an unbiased statistical sample superior to any other sampling method. The "index method" permits the double extension of a representative portion developed by estimation sampling. The index method is permitted by the Regulations only when complete double extension is impracticable because of technological change, extensive variety of items, or extreme fluctuation in the variety of items in the inventory.

The "link-chain method" differs from the index method only after the first year. In following years, an index is developed for the current year, in the same manner as for the first year, by double extending at the current year cost and at the beginning of the year cost, whereas the other methods refer to the base year. The newly generated index is multiplied by the beginning of the year cumulative index. The resulting cumulative index is then divided into the inventory at current cost to determine the base year cost of the inventory.

A combined regression estimate should be used with the Estimation Sampling Program to project the LIFO inventory at base year cost. This estimate takes advantage of all known information about the population being sampled. Monetary precision should be set at no more than one percent of the population at 95 percent reliability. This should result in an evaluation more than sufficient to meet the Internal Revenue Service requirements.

The items should be selected from the current year-end inventory and the year-end quantities should be extended at the beginning of the year costs. When these extensions have been made and entered into the file, the sample items may be evaluated to provide an estimate of the year-end quantities at the beginning of the year costs.

Many companies do not have computerized records and so a manual selection must be made. In such cases, a pilot sample of at least 50 items should be selected initially, using monetary amount sampling if possible. This sample should be evaluated, using the Estimation Evaluation Program to determine the actual sample size required.

Once the decision has been made to change to the LIFO method of accounting for inventories, it is not uncommon to find that the necessary work to obtain the LIFO inventory value is such that estimation sampling is the only logical answer.

Current Cost of Inventories

In March 1976, the Securities and Exchange Commission adopted an amendment to its Regulation S-X (ASR No. 190) which required registrants meeting certain criteria to disclose, in the footnotes to financial statements, the current cost at the end of the reporting period of replacing inventories. This disclosure was required for each fiscal year-end for which a balance sheet was presented. An excess of current replacement cost over net realizable value at that date had to be disclosed. The Commission noted that this requirement generally would necessitate the use of estimating and sampling techniques.

This requirement set off a chain reaction around the world as to better ways of disclosing the effects of inflation on financial statements. This culminated in the United States with Statement No. 33 issued by the Financial Accounting Standards Board on Financial Reporting and Changing Prices. Although the Commission still requires disclosure on inflation and changing prices, it has stated that data prepared according to SFAS 33 will be accepted. Foreign registrants may use their own country's version of SFAS 33 in order to meet the Commission requirements.

Major public enterprises are now required to report, among other things, the current cost amounts of inventory at the end of the fiscal year. Using estimation sampling and a combined regression estimate, it should be possible to obtain a fairly satisfactory estimate of replacement cost by taking a sample of a few hundred items. A separate sample would be required for each fiscal year for which a balance sheet is presented. The sample would be taken from the existing year-end inventory, with the sample items priced at current replacement cost. The procedure would be essentially the same as for estimating the LIFO value of an inventory except that replacement cost would be used in place of the LIFO value for the sample items.

In those cases where a sample has been taken to estimate the year-end inventory, the same sample may be used for estimating current cost, and there would be no need to take an additional sample. Two estimates would, of course, be required—one for current costs, and the other for cost or market, whichever is lower.

Quarterly Reporting

There have been cases in the past, and there are likely to be more in the future, where accountants are required to express opinions in connection with quarterly reports of listed companies. Often it is then necessary to take a physical inventory or at least test the adequacy of the perpetual records. Estimation sampling offers a convenient way to meet this need without incurring considerable costs in time and effort to take complete physical inventories. Where the sample is taken from a good perpetual inventory record, it is likely that the taking of quarterly physical inventories could be accomplished with a minimum of interruption to the normal operations of the company.

PROPERTY AND EQUIPMENT

As companies have expanded in size and the number of geographic locations, the recordkeeping for property and equipment has become more demanding. Most medium and large-size companies now have some form of continuing property record, either on computer or on a card file. There are a number of reasons why estimation sampling might be used in connection with these property records or, if such records do not exist, as a substitute for them, to obtain estimates of property and equipment values.

Identifiable Assets

The Financial Accounting Standards Board has issued Standard No. 14 which requires that the financial statements of a business enterprise shall include certain information about the industry segments of the enterprise. The purpose is to assist financial statement users in analyzing and understanding the financial statements of the enterprise by permitting better appraisals of past performance and future risks and prospects. Toward this end the FASB has proposed that identifiable assets, which would include property and equipment, shall be disclosed for each reportable segment. This requires a number of breakdowns of property and equipment that may not have been contemplated in the design of the existing property records. The property record may be difficult to rearrange for prior years and in some cases there may, of course, be no property records at all.

In order to arrive at a breakdown of the property and equipment amounts by industry segments, whether operational or geographical, the amounts allocable to each division could be determined by estimation sampling and would be satisfactory for the requirements of the accounting standard.

If property records exist, a sample of sufficient size to ensure the required precision and reliability could be drawn from them with the sample items identified by industry segment. These samples items could then be used to estimate the total dollar value of property and equipment in each segment. To the extent that the property records are available for prior fiscal year-ends, the estimates could also be made for those dates by selecting and evaluating a sample using the same procedure.

When property records for prior years are not available, samples taken from current records could be traced back through prior years, and estimates made for those years. Retirements in previous years would be added, for example. If many years need to be handled in this manner, the original sample should be larger than would normally be required for any one year to account for attrition in the number of sample items for items purchased in later years, so that this would not unduly compromise the estimates for earlier years.

In those situations where no property records exist, samples can be taken of the physical property and equipment in each division to provide estimates of the property and equipment committed to each division. This approach is, of course, not applicable to prior years.

Physical Inventory of Property and Equipment

A complete physical inventory of property and equipment is not required for financial statement purposes, so there is no compelling need for an annual physical inventory, particularly if adequate property records exist. Larger items of property and equipment cannot readily be removed and it is generally assumed that once purchased, the assets will always be there or will be missed. This may be an unwarranted assumption, however, in the case of smaller items which are easier to remove and are less likely to be missed, particularly small tools and other pieces of equipment that have a ready use elsewhere. For at least some of these items a periodic inventory is desirable, and estimation sampling is well suited for this purpose.

Where the property record is maintained on a computer, the procedure for taking the sample would be similar to a physical inventory of parts or supplies. The sample items would be selected and then verified by physical inspection of the property or equipment. Missing sample items would be recorded at zero value for sample purposes, and removed from the property record. Sample items in accord with the record would be carried at full value, and the estimate made from all the sample items. A combined regression estimate would be suitable for this purpose.

Lacking property records, use must be made of an alternate method of taking an inventory. One feasible approach is to tag by number every item sequentially by location. This, of course, needs to be done only once if the tags are affixed permanently and can serve as a control measure even if property records are maintained. As a larger sample will necessarily be required under such a situation it may be well to use a terminal digit approach and select a random number between 1 and 20. If this random number should turn out to be 16, then all items tagged with a number ending in 16, 36, 56, 76, or 96 would be recorded, their values ascertained, and a mean estimate of the property and equipment made from the sample items. The same sample could be used again for other purposes, such as identifying assets by division or for an independent audit.

Utility Rate Making

Rate applications in certain states customarily require that property and equipment be stated at fair value. This determination takes a great deal of effort and is usually done by applying an index to the total historical dollar cost of property and equipment. The index method is not always satisfactory as much depends on how the index is calculated. Estimation sampling would be a much sounder approach to a calculation of this nature. By taking a sample and then obtaining the fair value for each item in the sample, a combined regression estimate based on these sample items would provide a satisfactory estimate of the property and equipment at fair value.

Specific Price Index

In connection with Statement of Financial Accounting Standards No. 33, the Financial Accounting Standards Board discussed several possible approaches to developing current costs, such as externally generated price indexes, internally generated price indexes, and direct pricing. Direct pricing would offer the best approach but would require reference to large numbers of current invoices, vendor price lists, or the updating of standard cost sheets. On the other hand, indexes prepared by the government are usually not sufficiently specific to the industry or company in question.

Good results can be obtained, however, by estimation sampling for this is, in essence, an internally generated price index that is specific not only to the company but also to the assets in question. If we take a sample from inventory or property and equipment, price the sample at current cost, and make a regression estimate of the asset at current cost, we have developed as good an index as it is possible to have for the purpose. The relationship of the asset balances at historical cost and current cost is an internally generated price index applicable to that specific group of assets.

Current Cost

In March 1976, the Securities and Exchange Commission required disclosure of the estimated current cost of replacing productive capacity, together with the current net replacement cost represented by the depreciable, depletable, and amortizable assets. For those companies that fall under the provisions of SFAS 33, the Financial Accounting Standards Board requires disclosure of the current cost of property, plant, and equipment at the end of the current fiscal year and increases or decreases for the year net of inflation. These disclosures meet the SEC requirements. This information has to be shown as of the end of each fiscal year for which a balance sheet is presented. In many companies such a calculation, or series of calculations, would be virtually unmanageable if done completely, not only because of the number of items of property and equipment but because of the difficulty of obtaining current cost data on many of these items.

A better approach to this problem would be to determine the current cost of each of the items sampled from the property records. A combined regression estimate based on these sample items would be used to estimate the value of the property and equipment at current cost.

Leasehold Analysis

The development of lease financing techniques gave rise to a large number of off-balance sheet items that now have to be set up as capital assets, with contra liabilities offsetting them, under current interpretations of generally accepted accounting principles. In addition, reporting requirements call for analyses of current lease payments, and schedules of lease payments, for the next few years.

Where large numbers of these lease transactions have been entered into and property records have not been maintained, it may be necessary to take a sample of these leases, determine the property attached to each lease, and estimate the total value of leased property and equipment.

Similarly, an analysis of these payments could provide the current portion and the portion payable in later years, obviating the need to make a complete analysis of all rental payments.

SUMMARY

The principal applications of estimation sampling for asset values would be in the area of receivables, inventories, or property and equipment. There are situations where sampling could be used to estimate security values, particularly large quantities of bonds or registered securities. Occasionally, there may be an opportunity for the sampling of cash items but this will be rare, as most people expect cash to be counted completely.

The foregoing examples should provide sufficient illustration of the ways in which assets can be sampled to stimulate the readers' thinking about how estimation sampling might be applied to assets under their control or within their own environments.

CHAPTER 8

ESTIMATION OF LIABILITIES

Estimation sampling for liabilities is in most ways similar to the sampling of assets. A sample is taken from the existing record. The sample items are processed and then evaluated to obtain an estimate of the total liability outstanding. There is one important difference, however, in the sampling of liabilities that should be carefully considered in each situation—the risk of understatement. Certain asset records can, of course, be understated but usually the understatement is slight and in most cases unintentional. The major risk with asset records is one of overstatement. The maximum over-statement of any amount that is in the population is, in almost every case, the amount itself.

In sampling from liabilities, however, the principal risk is one of under-statement and there is no maximum limit on the amount of understatement, either of items included in the population or, more important, of those omitted from the population. In those situations where this risk could be considerable, extra care will be required to ensure that all the items are included in the population before the sample is taken.

ACCOUNTS PAYABLE

The use of estimation sampling in connection with accounts payable would be primarily in the confirmation, validation, and accrual of accounts payable where no record of accounts payable exists. A somewhat related application would be the confirmation of a bank's deposit liabilities.

Confirmation of Accounts Payable

The need to confirm accounts payable could arise from a regular audit, an internal audit, or management's wish to check the accuracy of clerical and accounting procedures. Where an accounts payable record or a voucher payable record is available as a statistical frame for the population, the sample would be selected and confirmations prepared. The confirmations would be· mailed to the suppliers and, upon their return, the evaluation would be made to produce an estimate of the accounts payable.

To the extent that all confirmations are returned properly confirmed, this estimate would be reliable for all the accounts payable shown in the balance sheet. In the case of non-response, a further effort should be made by mail or telephone to obtain confirmation of the amount payable. If this fails, or further follow-up is not feasible, an alternative procedure might be to check the disbursements for succeeding periods to determine whether the amounts shown as payable at the time were paid subsequently in those amounts, and were actual liabilities at the year-end.

If the company has either an approved or a controlled master list of vendors, these vendors should be included in the population to be sampled even though they might have zero balances. This would create greater assurance as to the reliability of the estimate, particularly in regard to possible understatement of accounts payable. If all possible vendors are included in the population from which the sample is drawn, the reliability and precision are extended to all the possible vendors and the likelihood of understatement is greatly reduced.

Validation of Accounts Payable

When the reason for confirming accounts payable is to look for evidence of understatement, and where a master file of vendors is not available to guard against accidental or intentional understatement, it may be necessary to supplement the sample confirmation of accounts payable with a sample taken from a related population, such as a later voucher record or cash disbursement register.

Normally, most amounts due and owing at the verification date would be paid within the next 30 days. An examination of the voucher record or cash disbursement record for the 30 or 60 days subsequent to the specified date and a comparison with the accounts payable record could indicate accounts payable that would have been owing but were not recorded as of that date. Such a complete examination could be very tedious in a large company, but a sample taken from a later voucher record or cash disbursement record could be used for this purpose. The sample items would be investigated to determine whether or not they were due and payable as of the verification date and, if so, whether they were then recorded. Based on these sample items, an estimate could be made of all accounts payable due but not recorded as of that date. If none were found, it would bolster the evidence supplied by the confirmation of accounts payable.

Accrual of Accounts Payable

Although not so common as in the past, a situation may arise in a governmental unit, or a not-for-profit institution that is on a cash basis, where there is no record of accounts payable as of a specific date. This accrual could be estimated by taking a sample from a related population, such as cash disbursements for several following periods, and determining the amounts due as of the year-end date. Based on these sample items, the evaluation would produce an estimate of the accounts payable at the fiscal year-end.

Confirmation of Deposit Liabilities

There has been an increasing trend, in recent years, toward confirmation of the deposit liabilities of banks. This is due, in part, to the increasing use of outside auditors but is also being promoted by examining authorities and by bonding companies which issue a blanket credit on the insurance premium to those banks that do send out confirmations periodically. In general, the confirmation of deposit liabilities is similar to the confirmation of accounts payable, particularly in regard to the problem of testing for understatement.

There are differences, however, that must be considered in designing a sampling plan to confirm deposit liabilities. For example, the average account payable will be liquidated within 30 to 60 days, whereas a bank deposit may not be drawn upon for many years. Corporate bank accounts may remain open indefinitely and even personal accounts are likely to exist for many years.

Another difference is that depositors may change addresses frequently or may request that their mail be held or delivered to places other than their residences while they are traveling or for reasons of convenience or confidence. Thus there is often less assurance that a letter being mailed will be received by the party to whom it is addressed. Fraud is more likely to be perpetrated by bank employees on dormant bank accounts where the control over changes of address may either be weak or nonexistent.

The population from which the sample is to be drawn should be carefully developed. It should include not only current accounts but all accounts closed during the year. The fact that it does include all such accounts should be tested separately, by comparison with independent records of the opening and closing of accounts. In addition, all the dormant accounts at the end of the previous year and all accounts transferred to a dormant ledger during the current year should be included not only in the population from which the sample is drawn but also in the sample. Similarly, the addresses of all accounts selected in the sample should be checked against the addresses shown at the end of the previous year. All address changes should be verified to ensure that the new address is valid.

The internal control over bank bookkeeping is usually thorough enough to keep errors in the customers' accounts at a minimum. For this reason the correlation between book records and confirmations would be high and the use of stratified regression estimates would greatly enhance the precision of an estimate at a specified reliability. As a consequence, a relatively small sample would usually be sufficient to provide satisfactory results.

In some cases, the regulatory authorities or the bonding company may specify that a bank must confirm some given percentage of the demand deposits. Though this may be four or five times the size of the sample normally needed for this purpose, the larger sample would not only meet the regulatory requirements but would also give very reliable results.

Payroll Taxes Withheld

One may want to gain assurance that the liability shown for various payroll taxes is reasonably stated. Since the amounts withheld for income taxes, social security, and other state and local taxes are based on the payroll, a sample selection can be made from the payroll and the various deductions can be determined for these sample items. Former employees who have worked during the period under review should be included in the population from which this sample is to be taken. As the correlation between the amounts withheld and the total payroll should be fairly stable, in a statistical sense, a satisfactory stratified regression estimate should be obtained with a reasonably small sample.

Accrued Vacation, Illness, and Holiday Pay

If accurate records are not being maintained on the amount of vacation, illness, and holiday time due to each employee less the amount that he has taken, it may be necessary to estimate the accrued vacation, illness, and holiday pay to comply with SASF 43. This can be done by taking a sample from the payroll and determining the amount of vacation, illness, and holiday pay due each employee in the sample.

This will provide the basis for an estimate of the total accrued vacation, illness, and holiday pay that can be used to either record or check the accrual.

UNEARNED REVENUE

Unearned revenue arises when money is received or amounts are billed in advance of goods being delivered or services being rendered. As the liability to deliver a magazine or to fly a person to Honolulu may not be fulfilled in the current accounting period, this revenue is unearned until the earning process is complete. It may be necessary, at the end of an accounting period, to determine the amount of revenue already received that is still unearned.

Airline Revenue

An extremely complicated calculation of unearned revenue occurs in connection with the sale of airline tickets. Sampling is useful in determining the amount of interline billings and of earned revenue for each airline based on the services provided.

Airlines, or travel agents acting for them, may sell tickets in the standard multipart forms for travel not only on their own airlines but often at least partly on other airlines as well. It is thus possible for a person to complete a flight on several airlines before any of the airlines have been paid for this travel. On the other hand, the money may be paid well in advance of the travel and the travel may take place at a much later time or may never take place. With many millions of airline tickets being sold and lifted in return for travel at thousands of places all over the country and the world, it is difficult to arrive at the amount of monthly earnings.

A number of years ago some of the major airlines mutually agreed upon sampling as a means of determining interline billings. Each airline takes a sample of all tickets that it has lifted during a given period for travel on its airline and computes the amounts paid for each item in the sample. It also determines, for each item in the sample, the amount of revenue due from each of the other airlines. An estimate is made of the total due and payments are made accordingly.

The amounts received for the sale of tickets less the amounts paid to the other airlines become part of the unearned revenue, at least temporarily. Similarly, the amounts received from other airlines also become part of the unearned revenue. Although, theoretically, each part of the ticket lifted for one leg of the trip may be matched against the original record of the ticket sale, this procedure becomes extremely cumbersome even when computers are available for this purpose. A common practice is to segregate the ticket revenue by month of sale and also to break down the tickets lifted by month of sale. With millions of tickets sold, even these procedures are cumbersome and usually an estimate is made, based on a sample of the ticket lifts, to determine the breakdown of the revenue by month of sale. Although most travel takes place within a few months after the ticket sale, some tickets will not be lifted or redeemed for perhaps 18–24 months. At some point in time, however, the unearned revenue for a particular month will either be earned, or the small remaining balances can be written off as earned. In the meantime, the relief of unearned revenue and the transfer to earnings will be made based on the sample estimate.

Unearned Discount

In many types of loans made by banks and finance companies, the interest on the loan is deducted in advance, or discounted, from the face amount of the loan. Some part of this discount will be earned during each month that the loan is in force until maturity. The income on each loan tends to diminish with the passage of time as the balance of the loan is reduced by monthly payments. The general accrual of this income is an orderly progression and can be predicted in advance except for those loans that do not run to maturity or whose installments are not paid when due.

Many different methods have been developed for the accrual of unearned discount and it is possible, with the aid of computers, to make individual monthly calculations on each loan each month. The cost may be justified when the calculation is part of the regular posting to the loan records, but may not be if it is made as a separate run, not on a computer. The correlation between interest earned and the outstanding balance of the loan is so high that a relatively small sample, evaluated as a stratified regression estimate, would give results approximately equal to those obtained by individual calculations, at a considerable reduction in computer running time.

LONG-TERM LIABILITIES

A number of accounting changes in recent years have emphasized the need to determine more accurately the long-term liabilities outstanding, particularly in such areas as insurance reserves for life and casualty companies, and the liability on employee pension funds.

Life Insurance Reserves

For over 50 years, life insurance reserves in many states have been prescribed by law. The purpose of these statutory reserves is to ensure that the life insurance companies are solvent and can pay their obligations many years in the future. The statutory formulas, though conservative and useful in ensuring solvency, do not take into consideration deferral of acquisition costs and make no allowance for the expected number of insured who will withdraw from the insurance plans before death or completion of the contract. The interest rates allowed by law on investments for the purpose of calculating statutory reserves are appreciably lower than those actually experienced in the last decade. Similarly, the mortality tables prescribed for use are extremely conservative and make no allowance for selection based on medical condition.

In 1972 the American Institute of Certified Public Accountants published an audit guide on stock life insurance companies which prescribed generally accepted accounting principles for life insurance companies and proposed several methods of calculating reserves. These calculations are based on expected interest rates, reasonable mortality tables, expected withdrawal tables, and the deferral of acquisition costs, with a sufficient provision for adverse deviations in any of these factors.

The calculation of insurance reserves on the basis of generally accepted accounting principles (GAAP) poses a significant problem for life insurance companies because of the large number of policies, and various simplified methods have been developed to obtain approximate answers. Inasmuch as insurance companies calculate statutory reserves, or obtain them from tables that have been prepared for this purpose, it is a relatively easy task to select a sample from the statutory reserves applicable to the insurance in force and to compute the GAAP reserves for each of the sample items. Although the correlation between the GAAP reserves and the statutory reserves is not likely to be as high as it might be for other accounting populations, a reasonably sized sample should provide an estimate of the GAAP reserves that would be adequate for this purpose.

Casualty Insurance Reserves

In casualty insurance and, to some extent, accident and health insurance, the ravages of inflation may be such that the estimates of claims cost based on past experience are insufficient to meet actual needs. Insurance of this type is often written for an annual period, and the claims for accidents occurring within that year are likely to be pressed within, at most, the next year or two. Consequently, there is a continuing need to test the adequacy of the reserves by relating them to the actual claims being processed and to the estimated loss experience.

If a sample is taken from all the insurance written during a given period such as a calendar year, it should be possible to determine, for each policy in the sample, whether or not a claim had been made under that policy. With reasonable effort, the probable liability for any claim made under that policy could be calculated. Based on the sample policies, an estimate could be made of the probable liability for all policies written during the year. This amount then could be compared to the reserves provided as a test of adequacy of the reserves. Such an analysis might be made monthly or quarterly to provide management with a means of detecting and correcting an unfavorable trend before it had too adverse an effect on the operations of the company.

Vested Retirement Benefits

Because the accounting for pension plans has changed considerably in recent years, and changes are made from time to time in the pension provisions and in the actuarial assumptions, it is necessary periodically to compare the present value of the vested benefits under a retirement plan with the total assets of the pension fund. If the pension plan is adequately funded, the present value of all future benefits is equal to, or exceeded by, the total assets of the pension fund.

The present value of the vested benefits could be approximated by taking a sample from all the individuals covered by the pension plan and making the necessary calculations for those individuals in the sample. Based on the sample, an estimate could be made of the present value of all future benefits to be paid under the plan based on the situation existing at that time.

CAPITAL STOCK

There are times when a company needs information about stockholders or about the capital structure. Although these needs are not likely to occur very often, they usually arise unexpectedly and it is well to keep in mind that sampling may be useful in this connection.

Analysis of Stockholdings

There have been instances in which company management was unaware of significant changes in stockholdings until confronted with a tender offer or a request for change in the composition of the board of directors. Regardless of whether management would or could have taken particular steps had it been aware of these changes in stockholdings at an earlier date, such knowledge nevertheless would have been desirable.

Although it is difficult to detect significant changes in stockholdings as the transfers take place daily, and are reported to the company, it should be possible to detect them over a monthly or quarterly period. This could be done by taking samples from the stockholder list at various dates and classifying the shares in the sample according to the information which seems to be of importance. For instance, the company might be interested in the percentage of its voting stock that is held in large units and which might conceivably affect the voting control of the company. It would be a relatively easy matter to estimate from a sample the percentage of the stock held in lots of, say, 1000 or over. Similar information might be developed on the amount of stock held by mutual funds, banks or trust companies, corporations, individuals, or in street name. Continued analysis of this type would reveal any major shifts before they might otherwise become apparent.

Tax Basis for Exchange of Stock

When a stockholder receives stock of one corporation in a tax-free exchange for stock that he holds in another corporation, the tax basis of the new stock is the same as the tax basis of the old stock. The tax basis would be different for different stockholders, depending on the prices that were paid when the stock was originally bought and on subsequent stock dividends or stock splits that may have occurred.

The tax basis to the corporation that has issued its own stock for the stock of a company acquired from individual stockholders is the sum of the tax bases of all the individual stockholders of the acquired company. This calculation may be rather difficult to make as the stockholders may not know their tax bases, and the mere collection of such information could be time consuming and costly. This is a case where a stratified sample would give excellent results with a minimum expenditure of time and effort. Furthermore, it is unlikely that a sample taken on this basis would be challenged by the tax authorities.

The selection could be made from stockholder lists in existence at the date of the exchange, and letters could be written to all stockholders selected for the sample to ascertain their tax basis. Special effort would probably be needed to follow up nonresponses to the first request for information. It is likely, however, that large blocks of stock can be isolated and information about them obtained rather quickly. A fair percentage of the stock might be in the hands of arbitragers at the date of exchange and their tax bases would be easy to determine, as their holding period would be very short and prices normally would vary in a narrow margin.

When all the sample items have been returned, one could estimate the tax basis to the corporation of the new stock issued in exchange.

CHAPTER 9

ESTIMATION OF
INCOME AND EXPENSE

In determining net income, the process of matching revenues with expenses requires a considerable amount of estimation. Although most of it traditionally has been judgmental, there is a potential for a more scientific approach to the recording of income and expense transactions. Many opportunities exist to estimate revenue, cost of sales, selling expenses, payroll costs, depreciation charges, and taxes based on samples. There are also possibilities for sampling in special studies such as sales analysis, payroll analysis, and various types of expense analyses.

One of the principal causes of nonsampling error in estimation sampling is measurement error. Measurement error is caused by incorrect counting, incorrect reading of a measuring instrument such as a ruler or barometer, or use of an improperly calibrated device such as a scale. For all practical purposes, measurement errors in the estimation of income and expense transactions are not likely to be of this type but rather the result of divergence between accounting theory and accounting practice. For example, items in common usage such as nuts, bolts, screws, and washers are often counted and expensed as purchased rather than as consumed. On a larger scale, costs of opening new market areas, developing data processing systems, and training personnel for new equipment are charged currently to cost of sales even though clearly they are intended to benefit future periods. A brief review of matching theory and the problems of measurement may be useful at this point.

MATCHING THEORY

Basic accounting theory holds that revenue and expenses should be included in the income statement in the fiscal year to which they relate. It is generally accepted that costs should be matched with the revenues that they produce. Expenditures made in one period to produce an expected future benefit should be deferred and charged against the income of such later periods if such benefits are measurable or reasonably certain.

As it became evident that the determination of income for a given period was an essential purpose of accounting, a theory of income measurement began to develop slowly in both professional and academic circles, based on the older concepts of accrual accounting and the entity concept. This has come to be generally known as the matching theory.

The matching process can more precisely be considered to be divided as follows:

1. Relating product cost to revenues to determine gross profit.
2. Relating other expenses of the period to gross profit to determine net income.

Revenue is ordinarily recognized as being realized when a sale occurs although exceptions exist in installment sales, long-term contracts, and other transactions. In addition, the practical aspects of measurement may modify the ideal matching of revenues with costs. The depreciation of production equipment is difficult to determine and even more difficult to relate to the actual goods produced. A survey of accounting literature of the past 40 years shows general agreement on the proposition that revenues and costs should be matched by accounting period. There are, however, some points of divergence in theory and some difference in practice regarding when, and how precisely, income should be measured and how, and with what precision, and whether all costs can be matched to the applicable revenue.

Two basic factors seem to have contributed to the problems of applying the matching theory: business continuity and the accounting period. It is important to realize that any business, from a long-term viewpoint, is a single venture and that no completely accurate determination of profits can be made until all assets have been realized and all liabilities have been liquidated. Despite a need for reasonably precise periodic reporting of income in a continuing business, the inability to determine economic values, and changes in such values, gives rise to the estimates required by matching theory.

The matching of costs and revenues requires precise application in the deferring of all the expenditures of one period that might be fairly applicable to the revenue of a subsequent accounting period. Revenues represent what the business has accomplished; costs represent the sacrifice made to acquire this revenue; and profits are the excess of revenues over costs in each operating period.

Problems of Measurement

The primary measurement of income usually occurs when revenue is realized through services rendered or merchandise sold. This raises the question of whether there may be some right to return the merchandise, even after it has been paid for. Some form of probabilistic estimate can usually be made of the percentage of sales that will be returned.

There is also some justification for considering that a sale made on an installment plan does not produce revenue immediately but over the period of time during which the installment receivable is paid. This requires the deferral of income initially, followed by an estimate of the amount of income earned during each succeeding accounting period.

The depreciation of productive assets is another type of measurement problem. For example, depreciation may be taken on a straight-line basis, using an estimated useful life and an estimated salvage value. This would provide an equal annual charge that would be prorated to all the units produced, including those not sold but held in inventory at the end of the period. As volume fluctuates from year to year, the amount assessed against each product unit would change. In years of excessive production but limited sales, a substantial part of this cost might be deferred until the following year.

It has often been contended that depreciation of productive equipment should be based on use rather than on time, although difficulties arise in estimating technical obsolescence. A further theory that has been advanced is to combine the original cost of the equipment with the estimated repairs and maintenance over the useful life, and to compute annual charges that would amortize these combined amounts on an actuarial basis.

Fortunately, theoretical measurement errors that presently exist in accounting practice would have no further effect on sample estimates made of income and expense transactions for accounting purposes. This type of measurement error would continue to occur, even with complete coverage, so that it is reasonable to say that sample estimates made from accounting data will not have measurement errors of great magnitude or of the type usually comprehended by statisticians as a part of the nonsampling error. To this extent they are more efficient estimates.

REVENUE

The principal uses of estimation sampling in connection with revenues would be in the areas of revenue recognition, revenue allocation, and revenue analysis.

Revenue Recognition

In companies where the operating cycle is short, the determination of revenue is easy, as is that of sales cutoffs. In some lines of business, though, the operating cycle is long enough that prepayments or advanced billings are often made, and accounting principles permit a determination of income on a percentage of completion basis, provided that there is evidence of the ultimate proceeds and that a better measure of periodic income results. In other instances, the sale is made but the payments are to be made in installments or otherwise deferred over long periods of time. With a long period intervening between the sale and the receipt of all the proceeds, a question arises as to when it may be concluded that the income will be fully realized. Here again, accounting principles specify the basis on which this may be done.

Percentage of Completion.   When revenue is recognized based on the percentage of completion, some type of measurement of the amount of work performed under the contract must be made. The measurement may be in terms of the proportion of estimated total dollars or labor hours already expended, or possibly may be based on some informed person's judgment as to the percentage of work physically completed compared to that remaining to be done.

Consider, for instance, a manufacturing company that manufactures, under long-term contracts, certain types of equipment made to the customer's specification. The equipment may be delivered over a period of years. At any point in time, therefore, some pieces of equipment under the contract may be completed and delivered, others may be partially completed, and the work on still others may not have even started. In such a situation, advance payments are often made to cover both the cost of the materials to be used in the manufacture and some part of the direct labor costs and overhead cost already incurred. The problem is to determine, for each such long-term contract, the percentage of the contract that is completed. By multiplying the expected revenue from the full contract by this percentage, the amount of the revenue earned to date can be matched with the cost incurred on each contract to date to arrive at the anticipated gross profit from all such long-term contracts.

Where there may be thousands of such contracts open at one time, it may be easier to select a sample from these contracts to determine, for each contract in the sample, the percentage and amount of revenue that has been earned. From these sample contracts, the entire amount of revenue earned under all the contracts can be estimated.

A similar situation could exist in a professional organization where retainers or progress payments have been billed to clients, with some portion of these revenues unearned at the end of the fiscal period. A sample could be taken from these billings to determine whether the work for that client has been completed or whether some part still remains undone. In this way an estimate could be obtained, from the sample, of the amount of revenue that is unearned and which should be deferred until the following period.

Installment Sales. Another problem area encountered in revenue recognition is the installment sale. Many installment sales are made on the assumption that a significant portion of the installment payments will never be made and thus the merchandise will be subject to repossession or will not be deeded to the purchaser. In some such cases, as in connection with land sales, the profit on the sale is recorded at the time the contract is signed, but only if certain conditions are met. In other cases, and in other transactions treated as installment sales, part of the revenue is considered to be earned when each payment is made.

A somewhat different type of revenue recognition problem occurs when a commodity or service is paid for in advance and the revenue cannot be recognized until the commodity is delivered or service is performed. We have discussed previously the problem that arises when airline transportation is prepaid and the revenue is not earned until the flight coupons are lifted. The sheer volume of such transactions makes this type of revenue recognition problem suitable for estimation sampling. An estimate can be made of the entire amount of earned revenue based on a fairly small sample.

A similar problem occurs also in connection with the interest earned on installment loans. In banks or finance companies where interest must be accrued on large volumes of loans, a sample can be used effectively to determine the applicable revenue earned on a very large number of individual loans.

Revenue Allocation

The problem of revenue allocation has been described previously in connection with interline billing among airlines. In this situation a travel agent, or an airline, may sell transportation over one or more airlines and the revenue must be apportioned to the airlines that provide the actual transportation. In some cases, because of delays or overbookings, travel scheduled on one airline may actually take place on another airline. In light of the vast number of flight coupons that would have to be exchanged on a cash basis, the major trunk airlines, as discussed before, agreed to a sampling procedure to determine the amount of money due to or from each of them to the others. The possible inaccuracy caused by the sampling procedure is so slight in comparison with the clerical cost that would be incurred to gain a more precise figure that each airline saves money by using an estimation sampling procedure.

Truckers have found that they can settle interline freight bills on a sampling basis and some of the railroads have settled less-than-carload freight bills in this way. While the opportunities for sampling in revenue allocation are more apparent in the transportation industry, they exist in other industries as well.

Revenue Analysis

From time to time the need will arise for a certain type of information about sales made by a company that cannot be obtained directly from the company records. Although most companies provide for types of sales analysis such as sales by customer, salesmen, and districts or territories, the particular information that is now required may not be available. Often the information is needed on a one-time basis and it may not be economically feasible to program the computer for such a limited purpose. Furthermore, the information may be required promptly, without the normal delays inherent in computer programming. Estimation sampling is particularly useful for obtaining this type of information quickly and easily.

An example is reporting by industry segments. In many companies the sales may have been recorded by divisions or product groups, which is not necessarily consistent with the reporting requirements by industry segments. While reporting procedures can be altered to obtain this type of information more readily in the future, there exists a need to determine sales by industry segments for the past periods for comparative purposes.

There is also a need from time to time for geographic analysis of sales that might be different from the available analysis. For instance, data might be required on sales by standard metropolitan statistical area, whereas the basic records are broken down by states, or on sales by certain groups of adjacent counties to assist in the formation of new sales territories. Once obtained for a given purpose, this information might not be required again and estimation sampling would be useful to achieve this single aim.

When prices are changed it may be useful to monitor the effects of price changes through the use of estimation sampling. One becomes aware of the total effect of the price change because it is reflected in the gross profit percentage, but it may also be useful to know the way in which price changes have affected sales volume in certain components of sales. This type of analysis could be done quickly enough to be useful in adjusting price changes where necessary.

COSTS AND EXPENSES

The analysis of costs and expenses is an ongoing problem for financial management. It seems that, no matter what breakdowns of costs may be available, there is always a need for further information. Many of these analyses are time consuming and are rarely obtained as quickly as may be desired.

Cost of Sales

It is customary in many companies that have large volumes of transactions to use a standard gross profit percentage against sales each month to determine both monthly net income and a cumulative standard cost of sales for use until the actual cost of sales is determined at the end of the fiscal year when a complete inventory will have been taken. If interim financial statements are to be relied upon by informed investors, it may be necessary to obtain a more precise measure of gross profit that will take into consideration any changes in volume or product mix.

An example of this type occurred in connection with the sale of a company in the middle of a fiscal year. The problem was solved by taking a statistical sample of all sales in the covered period and costing out the sales for the sample items to obtain an estimate of the cost of sales and, consequently, of the gross profit percentage. Because of seasonal factors involved, the gross profit percentage for the interim period was significantly different from the standard gross profit percentage derived from the data for the previous year.

Failure to Observe Inventory.   When a company goes public for the first time, it is required to file a registration statement with full financial statements for a period of three years. Occasionally it occurs that the accountant of record was not the accountant for the full 3-year period and thus was not in a position to have observed the annual inventories at the four times necessary to be satisfied with the income data as presented. In such cases the accountant must seek to confirm these data by alternate means.

One alternate method would be to estimate the cost of sales for the three annual periods and, by application of these estimates, make sure that the inventory values as shown are realistic under the circumstances. This would require that individual samples be taken from the sales invoices for each of the three annual periods and each sales invoice costed at the costs then current. This can prove to be a very satisfactory alternate method of substantiating the value of a physical inventory when the necessary observation was not made.

Replacement Basis of Cost of Sales.   The Securities and Exchange Commission has, for some time past, required companies to disclose data relating to inventory profits which the Commission defined as the difference between the cost of sales on an historical basis and on a current cost basis. This type of information is useful in the interpretation and use of financial statements and the Commission recognized that this requirement would necessitate the use of estimation sampling techniques in many cases.

The cost of sales on a replacement cost basis is now required to be disclosed by SFAS 33 and can be obtained by taking a sample from the sales invoices and costing the sample items on a current replacement cost basis.

Payroll

The payroll records are a source for numerous analyses that are requested from time to time. Most of them can be accomplished while preparing the payroll, but others must be made on a one-time basis.

Vacation, Illness, and Holiday Pay.   An accrual is required by SFAS 43 for the amount of pay for compensated absences that is due workers for vacations, illness, or holidays that have not been taken. To the extent that this information is not readily available, a sample could be taken to determine the amount of vacation or the amount of sick leave that should be accrued at that time. The sample could be taken from the annual payroll in terms of dollars paid to each worker and the amount of vacation, sick leave, and holidays due, also in dollars, would be determined for each individual in the sample. This would result in a direct estimate of the annual pay for compensated absences that should be accrued.

Payroll Budgets.   Information might also be required about payroll costs by product or by process. This type of information is often needed in the development of standard costs or in the budgetary process. Data regarding the amount of labor used directly for the product, if not otherwise available, could be obtained by taking a sample from the cost records to arrive at an estimate of the labor costs for each product. Since many products are not produced uniformly throughout the production period, the sample must be taken randomly over the entire period to obtain satisfactory results.

Category Analysis.   Often some type of knowledge is required about the payroll by category. Many of these requests may be for nonmonetary information by age, ethnic surname, or marital status, for example.

To determine the amount of money paid to workers between the ages of 30 and 50 or the percentage of the payroll paid to unmarried individuals, it would be appropriate to take a sample from the entire payroll and determine for each of the sample items whether such amount was paid to workers between the ages of 30 to 50 or to an unmarried individual.

In payroll situations, the amounts paid are likely to be quite similar or to fluctuate within a fairly narrow range. Consequently, there will not be too much advantage to monetary stratification. In some of these situations an unstratified regression estimate will give satisfactory results.

When numerical values are required in the sample, such as the number of people on the payroll age 50 and over, an unstratified mean estimate can be used without any particular loss of precision. A sample would be taken and a value of one set in the sample card for each person who fell in the category of age 50 and over. All others would be set at zero. The evaluation would provide an estimate of the number of people on the payroll aged 50 and over.

Depreciation

The cost of any asset that provides benefits for only one fiscal year is recognized as an expense of that year. Assets such as property and equipment usually provide benefits over a number of years so that the cost of these assets must be allocated to each of these years in a systematic and rational manner unless there should be a more appropriate basis for associating cause and effect.

Most property records provide a systematic way to obtain the annual depreciation of property and equipment to be included as depreciation expense in the financial statements. This amount will be applied either individually or in total as an offset against the original cost of the property and equipment. Because the useful life of many types of property and equipment may outrun by far the estimated life used for the systematic allocation, or the property records may be lost or submerged through mergers and acquisitions, the need will arise occasionally for an up-to-date study and analysis of the remaining useful life of partially or fully depreciated property and equipment. Such studies have been required at times for public utilities by the applicable regulatory commission to determine a fair rate structure.

In most cases it would be appropriate to start with the property records although some preliminary effort would be required to be sure that they were up-to-date and contained a complete record of all the property and equipment. If doubt existed as to whether all the property was recorded, it might be necessary to take the sample from the actual property and equipment. In those cases where the property records could be relied upon, a sample could be taken from this record and a determination made for each of the sample items as to its remaining useful life. Using this information in relation to the original purchase date, the recorded depreciation expense and the current depreciated value of the property and equipment could be calculated.

The depreciation over the remaining useful life of the property and equipment would be equal to the net value of the property and equipment or the original cost less the depreciation that should have been taken to date. Consequently, an estimate could be obtained directly of the estimated net value of the property and equipment based on the original cost.

Depreciation on Replacement Costs. When the property and equipment have been revalued at current replacement cost, either in full or by the use of estimation sampling, it becomes necessary to determine depreciation on replacement cost for the current year and the prior year so that comparative statements can reflect the service potential used up in those two periods. Similar calculations would be required for depletion on current replacement cost and for amortization on current replacement cost.

A sample could be taken from the property and equipment records in the same way as would be done to estimate current replacement cost. In fact, the sample used to estimate the current replacement cost could be used to estimate the depreciation, thus avoiding the necessity of taking two samples. In this case, the selected values would be the equipment cost and the estimated values would be the depreciation on a current replacement cost basis. In those property and equipment records that contain the annual depreciation charge, the monetary precision surrounding the estimate could be improved by selecting from the depreciation charges rather than the property and equipment values. This improvement would come about because both the amounts going into the evaluation would be annual expense amounts and the difference would be only that one amount is calculated on a current replacement cost basis. The correlation between these two amounts should be somewhat higher and thus would produce a better regression estimate.

Expense Analysis

There always seems to be a need for expense analysis that is not readily available from the accounting records in the form required. Management may need to have certain types of information to make informed decisions. It is usually difficult to obtain such information quickly from a highly structured accounting system and thus many managers are forced to make quick decisions on the basis of less than full pertinent data. Many of these needs could be satisfied readily by estimation sampling from the existing records.

Similar needs arise within the accounting department for such special purposes as the preparation of budgets for varying levels of volume or the development of a standard cost system. Estimation sampling can be used to advantage in gaining the necessary information at a reasonably low cost. The need to set volume price differentials may require an analysis of distribution and selling costs by quantity sold, territory, or class of merchandise. Studies of this type usually require an inordinate amount of time, as such information is not readily available in the accounting records; however, it could be obtained rather easily by estimation sampling. Samples could be taken from all types of expenses and broken down by quantity, territory, and class of merchandise to provide the necessary estimates.

Repairs and Maintenance

In public utilities, and other large companies that have a considerable volume of work orders for repairs and maintenance, it may be necessary to compile information from time to time for specialized purposes. The volume of work orders may be staggering, indicating estimation sampling as the way to obtain the required information. These work orders may contain expense items that more properly should be capitalized for tax purposes and it is necessary to estimate the amount of capital expenditure that has been improperly classified. This amount may be estimated by taking a sample from the work orders and determining, for each item in the sample, the amount of expense that should properly be capitalized. Once these amounts for all work orders in the sample are on hand, an estimate can be made of the amount that should be capitalized but has been included in the repairs and maintenance work orders.

Sales Tax

Sales taxes have been adopted by many states and cities to meet their current expenditures. As these expenditures have climbed, the various taxing authorities have applied the sales tax law more rigorously, and at times perhaps a little aggressively.

There have been cases where companies have been challenged by taxing authorities on the amount of taxes paid on sales. These assessments are rarely made on the basis of a valid sales analysis but more often than not are based on arbitrary judgment. The obvious defense in such a situation would be to refute the arguments of the taxing authorities by developing a valid statistical sample that would provide the required sales analysis.

Often the tax law does not clearly state which items are taxable. A favorite ploy of the taxing authorities is to take a small sample, usually improperly and incorrectly, and make a claim for additional tax based on the results of this sample. As the tax is often collected on a cash basis, the taxpayer is in a poor position to refute such a claim.

Even though the claim is unfairly assessed, the cost of disproving it may outweigh the settlement costs. Several such claims have been successfully resisted by the use of estimation sampling. Companies that have suffered such claims, or expect to experience such claims, should consider the use of estimation sampling to bolster their position.

Selections can be made from the sales journal or cash register tapes, and the applicable sales tax can be computed on each of the sales items sampled. Based on this sample information, a satisfactory regression estimate could be made of the total amount of sales tax that should have been collected. In cases like this that might eventually reach a litigation stage, the taking of the sample and the evaluation of the sample should be carefully documented and perhaps supervised by a statistical consultant or observed by an external auditor.

CHAPTER 10

ESTIMATION FOR BUSINESS AND REGULATORY PURPOSES

In most businesses of even moderate complexity there are a number of reports that are, or need to be, prepared to keep management abreast of everchanging conditions. In addition, the many regulatory agencies, both state and federal, require numerous detailed and time-consuming reports. The purpose of this chapter is to show how a number of such reports could be prepared quickly and efficiently by the use of estimation sampling. The list is by no means complete but should serve to stimulate the reader's imagination as to ways in which estimation sampling might be useful.

COMPARISONS BY OFFICE OR DIVISION

Companies that have many offices or divisions may find it useful to make comparisons between such offices or divisions through the use of estimation sampling.

Accounts Receivable. For example, a company with accounts receivable at 50 locations might like to compare certain characteristics, such as collectibility or credit worthiness. Often the accounts receivable records will be on a computer at a central location which helps to simplify the sampling procedure. In any case, if a sample is taken from each location, using the same upper cutoffs and the same sampling intervals for each stratum, the results obtained for the evaluated samples will be comparable from division to division.

After the sample is taken it may be necessary to send the data to the various offices for further information. When the results have been evaluated, it should be possible to rank the offices on the basis of these evaluations. A similar procedure could be used in the case of banks or small loan companies for evaluating the loans at each location and forming an opinion about the relative efficiency of the various locations.

Inventories.   The opportunity to make this type of comparison for various warehouse locations was alluded to in the coverage of inventories in prior chapters but the point was not fully developed at that time.

When there are inventories of similar types of materials or supplies at different warehouse locations, it is possible to determine the relative efficiency of these warehouses, provided that the samples are taken with the same upper cutoffs and the same sampling intervals. If the monetary precision as a percentage of the total inventory is lower in one location than in another, there can be a reasonable presumption that the warehouse with the lower percentage is being run more effectively. The monetary precision is a direct reflection of the correlation between book and physical inventory, weighted by the dollar values. The differences between book and physical reality reflect errors, losses, and possible pilferage. A statistical inference can be made that the degree to which these differences occur is a reflection of the control exercised over the warehouse operations.

CONTRACT CANCELLATION

A large number of companies have had the experience, at one time or another, of having a substantial contract terminated or canceled unexpectedly. This situation has occurred more frequently when a company does business with the government or is a subcontractor for another company with a defense contract. Contract cancellation can come about for many reasons and often produces unhappy consequences for the parties involved, including possible lawsuits.

The company that is on the receiving end of the canceled order may have made substantial commitments based on the contract being completed and may have incurred considerable expense in the manufacture of assemblies and subassemblies. In such cases, the company will look to the government or other contractor to reimburse it for the out-of-pocket expenses involved in the cancellation.

Unfortunately, these costs are not always easy to determine and may require a great amount of clerical effort which will merely add to the cost. In such situations it would be well to make an arrangement between the parties that would permit estimation of the amounts involved, particularly in those situations where the development of complete cost data would be time-consuming and expensive.

Where the parties cannot agree on such a procedure, and it appears that the determination may eventually rest with the courts, the approach to the problem should, of course, be reviewed with legal counsel. It would be wise, in these situations, for the sample to be taken carefully, under the direction of the outside auditors or a consulting statistician who would be in a position to testify about the adequacy of the methods used.

CONTRACT PERFORMANCE

There are a growing number of instances where a unit of the government, or a third party, has an interest in contract performance. Among these types of contracts would be student loans, employee training programs, and various health and welfare activities such as Blue Cross and Medicare programs. As a result, program audits may be performed by independent public accountants, government auditors, or a special purpose inspection team.

The institution or company performing under the contract may not realize that it is violating certain provisions of the contract and consequently may have to make a refund or fail to receive payment for certain expenses incurred. The best defense against the development of this type of situation would be for the institution or company to take a sample of the transactions to evaluate whether the transactions fall within the boundaries of the contract.

In the case of student loans, the sample items selected could be reviewed as to whether the loans were properly made to parties eligible for these loans and whether the terms of repayment are being met at the time such payments are supposed to be made. In the case of Medicare payments, a representative sampling of such payments could be investigated to determine whether the work was properly done and the value of the work done. An estimate could then be made to determine whether the charges for all such services were reasonable under the circumstances. In the case of a hospital, a representative number of the patient billings could be sampled to determine whether the transactions appearing on the register are validly incurred and are appropriate costs for reimbursement in full or in part. An estimate of the total costs appropriate for reimbursement could be based on the sample items.

Giveaway Programs.   Companies that offer prizes as a means of stimulating sales usually subcontract the actual administration of the sales contest. To protect their own goodwill, they may require sufficient indication of the subcontractor's conformance with the terms of the sales contest and of the awarding of prizes. Such assurance could be gained by estimation sampling. Samples could be taken to evaluate whether specified postmark dates are observed by the subcontractor and other terms of the contest are satisfied by those eligible for prizes. Samples taken from the list of prizewinners could be followed up to verify their existence and their receipt of the prize.

Lotteries.   As more and more states initiate lotteries of various types, some assurance is required that those responsible for printing the tickets and administering the lottery are conforming with the applicable regulations. For example, if the lottery promises that 1 out of 100 tickets will win a $10 prize, there should be that ratio of winning tickets among the tickets sold. The purchaser of a lottery ticket has absolutely no way of determining whether this is so and is relying solely on faith in the state lottery division. The lottery division, in turn, may be relying upon the integrity of the printer that the specific number of winning tickets are printed and are turned over to the lottery administration.

There are several points in such a process where estimation sampling can be used to test the overall integrity and effectiveness of the lottery system.

Parimutuel Betting.   The same need to check contract performance exists in legalized betting on horse races, dog races, jai alai games, and other sporting events. In all cases it is a matter of public interest that winners be paid the right amounts. In most cases a percentage of the amount handled is due to a city or state as a tax upon the operations. Random samples could be taken on a continuous basis to police these matters of public interest.

DISTRIBUTION COSTS

Companies that manufacture products whose cost includes packaging, distribution, and sale of the product may offer quantity discounts to large customers who can buy and use these products in substantial volume. Under the Robinson–Patman Act the company offering quantity discounts must be able to show that these discounts are related to costs avoided through these larger sales. Whenever companies have been prosecuted for violation of the law, the burden of proof has been difficult because of the complexity of the distribution operation. In many cases the necessary information, such as the time spent by each salesman with each customer, has not been maintained or if it has been maintained, requires a great deal of processing and interpretation.

These cases usually arise from a specific complaint made by a competitor, and the company is faced with the need to support its position. It would be best if such an analysis were made on a continuing basis not only to support the company's position in the case of a lawsuit but to comply with the spirit of the law and to price products realistically with respect to order sizes. The considerable work required to make a complete analysis could be avoided by the use of estimation sampling.

EXPENSE REDUCTION

Cost reduction techniques become more important to a company at the onset of a business recession, but progressive companies utilize such techniques at all times as a means of maintaining or enhancing their position in a highly competitive society. Estimation sampling can be very helpful in supporting a continuing cost reduction program.

Flexible Budgeting. A good way to control expenditures at various levels of production is by way of a flexible budgeting procedure under which expense budgets are prepared for various levels of production. Although in use for many years, this type of budgeting has not gained wide acceptance because of the difficulty in constructing such a budget. Vast amounts of production data need to be analyzed to determine the necessary allowances at the various levels of production.

This work could be reduced considerably by the use of estimation sampling in the buildup of the flexible rates. With statistical assurance that the allowances are reasonable for the given level of production, the budgets arrived at in this manner can serve to control production costs at varying levels of production, whereas otherwise, costs tend to stay fixed even though the level of production drops substantially.

Invoice Checking. Estimation sampling could be used to reduce the cost of checking and approving invoices before vouchers are paid. In most companies it is customary to check everything on the invoice, matching items billed with receiving reports and recomputing all extensions.

In many companies this is not too burdensome a job and is a useful control measure. In railroads, public utilities, and certain other large companies, however, the volume of payments may be tremendous and many of the amounts are small routine payments to reputable suppliers. The cost of achieving complete control so as to avoid erroneous or duplicate payments may be more costly than the potential losses. In such a situation it might be desirable to take a representative sample of the vouchers payable and process these sample items in the usual manner so that the potential loss could be kept within tight bounds and the work considerably reduced.

SEGMENT REPORTING

Over the years many companies have expanded their business by merging with or buying companies that were in a similar line of business. Some companies have developed international markets in this way or by establishing branch operations overseas. The latter group includes companies of foreign parentage that have acquired American companies as subsidiaries.

In addition to horizontal mergers of companies in related businesses, there has been a considerable movement toward vertical integration. Large highly integrated companies have been formed, from numerous small companies, that control the process from the raw material production stages through marketing of the finished product. Also, to avoid the vagaries of the business cycle, many companies have diversified into completely unrelated lines of business to form the so-called conglomerates.

Consequently, much of the financial and statistical information available from the government and trade associations has been obscured by a reduction in the number of companies reporting on a separate basis.

When there are 50 or more companies reporting financial data in a given line of business, the law of large numbers will tend to iron out individual aberrations and provide workable standards for the entire industry. In view of the structural changes that have taken place, economists and statisticians in and out of government contend that some of the data become questionable when the number of reporting companies falls below 20, and that it is doubtful whether the effectiveness of competition within the economy can be measured statistically when the number falls below 5.

So that it can report to Congress and the general public on the need for appropriate legislation, the Federal Trade Commission has advocated that a company engaged in several lines of business should report pertinent financial information not only on a consolidated basis but by the various lines of business in which it is engaged. This approach has received considerable support from antitrust advocates and from economists and statisticians interested in measuring the effectiveness of competition in the American economy. Financial analysts, investment bankers, and institutional investors also have been interested in obtaining this data so that they can more effectively measure potential market values of the stocks of different companies.

Financial managers and professional accountants have not been ardent supporters of publishing this type of financial data, primarily because they realize that much of the information is based on arbitrary assumptions. The result would be that many people could misinterpret such data without understanding the full ramifications implicit in the various assumptions. Thus once two companies are merged into one, the general administrative costs are virtually joint costs, and even when great care is taken there will still be a considerable degree of arbitrary allocation. Similarly, the sales and distribution functions are also merged and it becomes impossible to allocate such costs directly. Suitable bases may be developed for internal purposes, and for establishing quantity discounts, but any such allocations must of necessity be arbitrary. Furthermore, patterns of financing may change drastically when two companies are merged. It is quite possible that one company would have a sizable cash flow and the other company might be expanding and thus be constantly in need of borrowed funds. The difference between the cost that the first company might have received on idle funds and the cost to the second company of borrowed funds could be large, but would be difficult to measure or allocate. Horizontally or vertically integrated firms are likely to engage in many intercompany transactions that require arbitrary transfer prices in lieu of prices set in the marketplace. Market prices include the cost to finance and market the inventories, so that, even with the best intentions, it is difficult to set satisfactory transfer prices.

Statement of Financial Accounting Standards. The Financial Accounting Standards Board has required by SFAS 14 that the financial statements of a business enterprise include certain information about the industry segments of the enterprise, its foreign operations, and its major customers. Revenue and profitability information are to be presented for each identified segment, together with the assets identifiable to that reportable segment. The use of "segments" in place of "line of business" is significant. Companies that have integrated vertically by combining individual lines of business that perform distinct processing steps in the eventual production of a single product would constitute one segment.

Clearly, these disclosures may differ significantly from those now provided by a company's accounting system, so that estimation sampling techniques could be used. For instance, if revenues are not broken down by reportable segments, a sample could be taken from total revenue to estimate the total revenue for each reporting segment. A similar approach could be taken for payroll and other costs which are aggregated by division or by company and must now be broken down by reportable segments. Eventually the accounting system could be adjusted to provide such information directly but the sampling approach could be continued indefinitely if necessary. It would also ease the burden in providing the data for the interim period required to completely change the accounting system.

MERGER STUDIES

Among the many possible reasons for a merger, the obvious economic reason is that the profits of the joint enterprise would be greater than the sum of the profits of each individual company. In other words, there will either be an increase in the joint revenue or a decrease in the joint costs that will permit the combined enterprise to be more profitable than each of the separate parts. Quite often these conjectures are not borne out, once the merger is consummated, for reasons that might have been obvious at the time of the merger if sufficient information had been developed. It is sometimes difficult to determine this on a pro forma basis, however, because of the excessive amount of paperwork that would be required, particularly in a fast-moving merger situation. The following illustrations show how estimation sampling could be useful in such situations.

Traffic Diversion. An example of possible revenue enhancement would be a proposed merger between two connecting railroads. At each junction point, the railroad carrying freight would give up the freight to any one of several railroads meeting at the junction point. A merger would enable the combined railroad to carry the freight, in many cases, over the combined railroad for a greater distance and thus increase the total revenues of the combined railroad over the revenues of the two separate railroads. The same principle would apply, of course, to two trucking companies or two airlines contemplating a merger.

To evaluate the effect on the joint revenues, the freight traffic could be analyzed for several years to measure the results satisfactorily. Such a detailed study would be a tremendous task, but estimation sampling could reduce the workload sufficiently to make this study eminently feasible. A sample could be taken from the freight bills for several years and each item in the sample studied for the net effect of a merger. The evaluated sample would provide an estimate of the additional revenue that would be produced by the merger.

A proposed merger of this type could well bring opposition either from the government or from competing railroads, truckers or airlines that might fear injury by this diversion of traffic. Consequently, they, too, might wish to make such a study to determine how much traffic they would lose and to have data available for any complaint that they might make. Samples have been used on many occasions in hearings before regulatory commissions, and specific rules of procedure have been set up for such samples. If there is a likelihood that such sample results may be introduced as testimony, the advice of counsel should be sought beforehand and care taken that the results are valid and well documented.

Overlapping Sales Areas. In a horizontal merger of companies in the same line of business, and to some extent when diversifying into other similar product lines, one of the primary advantages is that sales areas overlap and can be handled jointly by the salesman serving a particular area. This should lead to a reduction of selling costs, since a number of salesmen would be removed from the payroll, together with their associated selling expenses. The potential saving depends on the degree of overlap, which may not be readily apparent but may require a detailed study of the sales by various territories.

It is unlikely that a detailed study could be made quickly enough to provide information during the merger talks. It could be desirable, though, to take a sample from the sales records of each company, determine the amount of overlap within the sample items, and thus estimate the amount of overlap in the combined sales territories. With this information at hand, it might be easier to predict the potential savings from the combined selling operation.

METER TESTING

Public utilities have a large number of meters installed in private residences, apartment buildings, and commercial or industrial enterprises. Most of the regulatory commissions have some sort of arbitrary testing requirement to ensure that the installed meters are performing with reasonable accuracy and that customers are not being overcharged. A typical example would be a requirement that one tenth of the meters installed are to be removed and tested every year. Thus all meters would be tested within a 10-year period. As a practical matter, most of the meters that are pulled and tested may be operating well within the prescribed tolerances, and thus a great amount of effort would have been expended unnecessarily. In most companies the controls over possible overcharges are good enough so that it is unlikely for any overcharge to exceed the cost of inspecting and testing the meter. It would seem more logical to test where the possibility of overcharge was the greatest, and only to an extent that would provide sufficient assurance that the general public was not being intentionally or deliberately overcharged. Estimation sampling would provide a more precise answer to this problem and at the same time substantially reduce the inspection and testing costs.

Most public utilities have computerized meter and billing records, which would allow for the selection and testing of meters based on the total amount billed during a given period. If a meter was reading too high a consumption, the overcharge would likely be greater for meters registering the greatest consumption, as reflected by the amount billed. Meters might also be selected by type, since certain types of meters might have manufacturing defects leading to possible overbilling. Once selected, the meters could be sorted by route or street to facilitate testing. After all meters have been tested, the results could be evaluated and a measurement obtained of the potential overcharge in all installed meters. Samples could be drawn and evaluated periodically, such as by month or quarter, to provide the regulatory commission with sufficient assurance that customers were not being overcharged.

In those cases where the meter records are computerized but not integrated sufficiently with the billing records, the sampling could be done on a numerical or usage basis, with somewhat larger samples.

OPERATIONAL CONTROL

Often a company needs to measure and control operating performance. Statistical sampling has been used extensively to control production operations, and those operations that are under statistical control perform effectively. In the clerical and administrative areas, operations do not always seem to be going right and yet it is difficult to put a finger on just what is wrong. Estimation sampling may be able to provide an answer on this point.

For example, it is generally agreed that inventories should be maintained at such a level that the cost of lost sales does not exceed the cost of maintaining the inventory. This is undoubtedly a sound theoretical formulation but determining the cost of lost sales is a practical problem. This would require subsequent tracing of every order request that cannot be filled immediately to determine whether the sale was made subsequently or the customer obtained the merchandise elsewhere. Such a study would involve, in most cases, a great deal of time, so that it is unusual to make such a determination. A study could, however, be made by using estimation sampling. A sample of all unfilled order requests could be taken and each sample item investigated to determine whether there was a lost sale. Based on the sample items, an estimate could be made of the cost of all sales lost during a given period, together with the additional costs that would have been incurred by maintaining inventory at a sufficient level to fill all sales orders as received.

Back Orders.   Most companies maintain control over the total number of back orders, but it is unusual to further analyze how soon the back orders were filled. It would seem desirable to maintain a continuous review over the back order file and to compile statistics that would alert management to the need for improved performance. This could be done by sampling from the back order file at regular intervals, such as each week, to estimate the age and dollar value of back orders. A comparison of these estimates would provide operational control of the sales-order operation over a period of time.

PRICE CONTROL

Companies that distribute and sell a large number of different products may have difficulty in gauging the effect of price changes on earnings. Prices are changed on the individual commodities and need to be weighted by the sales of each product to arrive at the total increase in revenue. Some lessons learned during the era of price control could be used effectively to obtain a degree of control over prices and measure the effect of price changes.

A sample can be taken from all the products sold during a given prior period. Each sample item would be extended at the new price level and a regression estimate made of the likely overall effect of the price changes. During the years that price control was in effect, this procedure was used both by companies in establishing that their prices conformed to the regulations, and by government auditors in determining whether companies were violating the provisions of the law.

REPORTING REQUIREMENTS

Most companies are required to report to some government agency, or agree to report to trade associations, on certain important aspects of their business. Some doubt may exist at the agency or among the general public as to whether these reports are sufficiently accurate for some of the more important decisions that are based upon them. For instance, questions have been raised about the oil and gas reserves that are reported by the individual petroleum companies or by owners of oil leases.

The accuracy of such reported data could be estimated by sampling from the data reported by field location and having qualified personnel develop estimates for each location in the sample. A regression estimate, based on an evaluation of these sample items, would confirm the degree of reliance that could be placed upon the total reserves.

STATISTICAL DISCLOSURE

The Securities and Exchange Commission has encouraged registrants to disclose fully those factors that materially affect historical earnings. In recent years the Commission has defined quite clearly the type of information that it expects to obtain from registrants, and some of these requirements call for a great deal of analysis. For example, one release required certain disclosures by bank holding companies. Similar disclosure requirements may be required in the future from other companies in other lines of business.

If companies are required to file such information, it would obviously be to their advantage to use estimation sampling techniques in preparation of this data. Otherwise they would have to maintain a large clerical force to be able to supply this information regularly. While the need for such information may be justified, and it is undoubtedly within the province of the Commission to require the development of such information, the cost of compliance could clearly constitute a substantial burden unless estimation sampling techniques are used.

USEFUL LIFE

Determining the useful life of a class of property and equipment has always been difficult. In recent years tax regulations have prescribed guideline depreciation lives.

A company may, however, use a different useful life if it can prove its reasonableness. This could be established by sampling from the property and equipment records for a number of prior years and determining the actual life and salvage value for each item in the sample. This would provide the basis for an estimate of the useful depreciable lives that should be acceptable to the taxing authorities.

CHAPTER 11

COMPUTER PROGRAMS

One of the more compelling reasons for consideration of statistical sampling in the estimation of accounting data is the advent of electronic data processing into the accounting environment. For many years, most large companies have maintained accounting records in some form which may be readily updated and referred to for operational or control purposes. This has been particularly true in the case of inventory, accounts receivable, accounts payable, and property records where numerous detailed records are combined into one general ledger control total.

COMPUTER RECORDS

In the past, these accounting records were on loose-leaf sheets or cards and were one of the principal applications of tabulating equipment. Now that many companies maintain such records on computers, the ease with which such data may be assembled, and reassembled, simplifies the accounting and control procedures.

When unit records were introduced, it became possible to subdivide the general ledger controls into more convenient accounting groups so that these individual groups could be reconciled or proved separately as well as in total. The filing of accounts within these groups might be alphabetic, alphanumeric, or more closely allied to the particular type of account such as by due date, geographic area, class of property, or type of part. Dividing the accounting records into smaller control groups hastened the separation of operational control from accounting control. Rather than waiting for an annual inventory, certain counting procedures known as *cyclical counting* could be instituted, so that most parts would be counted more often during the year and on a rotating basis. This not only spread the counting more evenly throughout the year, when it often could be done as a fill-in job, but also provided greater assurance that the necessary parts would be on hand to meet the day-to-day operating requirements.

At that point, it should have been recognized that a statistical estimate of inventories would be acceptable for the determination of financial income and that the complete annual inventory could have been abandoned. This did not happen, probably because accountants, at that time, were not familiar with statistical techniques and statisticians were unaware of the problems of financial accounting. What in fact happened was somewhat the reverse. An effort was made, in many situations, to have the cyclical counts taken throughout the year serve as an annual physical inventory. This has never really been a satisfactory substitute, despite all the effort expended to ensure proper cutoffs and correct pricing. It also wasted considerable time, as the cyclical counts for operational control would not normally require pricing and extending. A statistical estimate could be made near to or at the end of the year and only a small sample would have to be priced and extended.

Flexibility

The general trend toward maintaining inventories of parts and supplies on an electronic computer makes the application of statistical procedures much more feasible than heretofore. The computerized perpetual inventory file not only provides considerable information as to the nature and distribution of the inventory data but serves as an effective frame for design and selection of a random sample.

When the perpetual inventory records are contained in a computer file, there is available, to a degree not always the case in statistical estimation, satisfactory knowledge of the frame from which the sample is to be taken. It should be pointed out that the physical counts often will not agree with the counts obtained from the book inventory. The perpetual inventory record is, nevertheless, a reasonable proxy for the physical inventory. The true feature of sampling interest is the degree to which the book inventory is representative of the physical inventory.

Computation

Having prepared, in the file preparation stage, a computer file that provides part number and extended inventory cost for each different item in the inventory, it becomes relatively easy to process this file and obtain the necessary data to design a sample, making due allowance for the expected relationship between the book and physical inventory. The advance information from the book inventory enables the statistician to design the sample more carefully than would otherwise be the case. As the nature and characteristics of an inventory tend to remain fairly stable from year to year, there should be continued improvement in the design process over time.

The type of analysis that can be made from the computer file is more comprehensive than anything that could be done manually. The information contained in the file may be classified, sorted, multiplied, or summarized, as the case may be, to provide the necessary input to the sampling program.

Prior to the development of the Deloitte Haskins & Sells computer programs for estimation sampling, a certain amount of statistical estimation of accounting populations had been done on a manual basis. Most of these statistical estimates were mean estimates, some were stratified estimates, and a few were stratified ratio estimates of large inventories where the calculations were quite complex. The first computer program, part of a series of programs that culminated in the present statistical estimation programs included in the Auditape system, was one that duplicated the manual evaluation process for ratio estimation. Control totals were supplied from client computer runs, giving the necessary sums of squares and sums of cross-products that were required for a ratio estimate and for the related precision.

Program Development

The use of generalized computer programs enables the accountant who has a limited knowledge of statistical principles and computer processing to design and select a stratified random sample with optimum stratification and with optimum allocation of the sample among the various strata. When the sample items have been physically counted and correctly collated with the appropriate book values, all of which one knows how to do, the accountant can proceed to make a satisfactory stratified regression estimate within the desired range of precision. The savings in time, money, and physical effort will be worthwhile.

The success of the first evaluation program led to the development of a more sophisticated program to process the sample data directly in order to obtain the necessary control totals from the sample data and to calculate estimates in any one of several ways—as a regression, ratio or mean estimate. Additional refinements that were added later include the calculation of combined and separate regression estimates, and combined and separate ratio estimates in addition to mean estimates selected on a monetary basis with probability proportional to size. The final product has been included in the Auditape System as the Estimation Sample Evaluation Routine.

Since the manual selection procedure was inefficient as well as arbitrary in selecting strata limits, effort was put into developing a sampling program that would design and select a sample while saving the necessary data for subsequent evaluation of the sample results. This second program was still arbitrary in regard to the number of strata and the upper limits of each stratum. Allocation of the sample size to the strata was proportional to size. Optimum allocation[1] and optimum stratification[2] were subsequently added as were other options. The final product has been included in the Auditape System as the Estimation Sample Design and Selection Routine.

GENERAL PURPOSE PROGRAM

The statistical estimation of a computer-based inventory, as stated previously, is a problem that requires accounting, statistical, and computer knowledge. It is only one of many situations in recent years in which accountants have found themselves to be insufficiently knowledgeable about either computers or statistics. Accounting has traditionally been peripheral to other professions such as law, engineering, and marketing, but now statistics and computer science must also be included. It was this need for computer knowledge that led Deloitte Haskins & Sells to develop the Auditape general-purpose computer program for auditing purposes.

Auditape System

Formerly, an auditor was able to get directly all the information required from the general ledger, the subsidiary ledger, and the journals. As companies grew larger, the bound books were replaced by loose-leaf ledgers or punched cards until today the auditor is faced with the fact that not only are many of the necessary client records large but they are only available in the form of computer records.

For many years, auditors were auditing around rather than through the computer and were relying solely on reports prepared by the computer. This, of course, was far from satisfactory. If the computer does not give the auditors the information they want, in the way they want it, they really have no alternative but to get this information themselves, preferably without assistance from the client's programming staff. The problem for auditors is how to get this information and use it to make a better audit.

Audit Solution. The Auditape System was developed as an answer to this problem, and the procedure is so simple that people can decide what information they wish to obtain and then proceed to obtain it. The programmer is

---

[1] See any book in statistical theory; for example, W. Edwards Deming, *Sample Design in Business Research*, Wiley, New York, 1960, pp. 291–301.
[2] *Ibid.*, pp. 487–496.

eliminated, and the auditor controls the entire information-gathering process as would be the case with a manual accounting system.

The Auditape System is a collection of general-purpose programs that can be used in various combinations to do specific things. For example, a person might need to obtain certain specific information on invoices from a voluminous computerized invoice file. A specification sheet is filled in, giving the format of the data in the client file and the specific data fields required. As soon as these specifications are keypunched, the problem is ready for the computer. In its simpler form, the Auditape is mounted, the cards are inserted in the reader, and the rest is just button pushing. The data will be translated from the original computerized file to an Auditape work file. The totals, and subtotals if any are specified, will be printed. A Print/Punch Routine may then be employed to print out a detailed listing, and cards may be punched if they are required.

Once the data are in the Auditape format, any other Auditape routine, or a variety of general routines that operate on this format, may be used to process the data further. Also, since the data have been transcribed to a work file, they are portable and can be processed elsewhere at a later date.

Using the Include Routine, specific data on the file may be included on or excluded from a new file and control totals may be developed during the run.

Using the Mathematical Routine, fields may be added to or subtracted from each other and fields may be multiplied or divided by each other, or by a user-specified constant value. Tests as to whether one field is greater than, equal to, not equal to, or less than another field or a constant factor may also be made.

The Summarize Routine provides a summary record on another file for a group of records having some specified common characteristic. Any fields in the Auditape record such as account number, customer number, or product code may be specified as the field for controlling summarization.

The Match-Merge Routine compares two separate files of Auditape records on as many as five control fields and writes an output file consisting of records from either input file or from both input files as specified.

The Insert Routine inserts data selected from fields in one file of Auditape records into corresponding fields of another file of Auditape records. The selected data are inserted whenever both input records match as to the control field specified.

The Print/Punch Routine provides the capability of printing any selected fields of the Auditape record, with column headings as an option. This routine also punches information in specified Auditape fields into an 80-column card.

The Audit Sample Routine embodies the Deloitte Haskins & Sells audit sampling plan that takes a highly sophisticated stratified sample from detailed items of audit interest, giving proportional weight to monetary values. The Audit Evaluation Routine computes the results after the selected items have been investigated.

Auditape License.   The Auditape System has proved that persons having no specialized knowledge of computers or programming languages can use the computer to obtain computerized information in usable form. At the request of clients and other accountants, Deloitte Haskins & Sells has made the Auditape System available to any interested party under a simple licensing agreement that provides for a modest annual license fee which is based on actual usage. As stated earlier, the fee is waived for colleges, universities, or other not-for-profit research institutions.

An Auditape System Manual which is available on request[3] provides a general description of the System. Instruction in the use of Auditape is provided at training seminars conducted at various times and locations. The seminars do not require any prior data processing experience and deal with Auditape Systems designed for use on computers and operating systems of various manufacturers.

Statistical Routines.   It is to this basic Auditape System that the previously discussed statistical routines such as Estimation Sample Design and Selection, and Estimation Sample Evaluation have been added.

High Speed Input/Output

The original versions of the statistical routines were written entirely in FORTRAN, a programming language designed particularly for mathematical and statistical purposes. Although the most complicated formulas can be quickly translated into computer codes using the FORTRAN language and compiler, this advantage was offset somewhat by the low input and output speeds compared with those of programs written in a computer assembly-language.

Generality.   A comparison of the input/output characteristics of the FORTRAN system against similar characteristics of an assembly-language system shows that much of the time lost can be attributed to the generality of the FORTRAN system. Since it is required to handle input data in any conceivable form, and to write output data in a similarly unpredictable number of ways, a substantial part of the FORTRAN compiler is devoted to situations that never would arise in handling accounting records prepared on tape or disk in a prescribed manner. The input to these statistical programs is

---

[3] Deloitte Haskins & Sells, Computer Services Department, One World Trade Center, New York, NY 10048.

specifically oriented to the Auditape System and does not require the generality of the FORTRAN system.

Blocking Factor. Another reason for the slower input/output in a FORTRAN system was that the system was not designed to handle blocked records. Blocking is a computer process whereby file handling is reduced by grouping a number of individual records for input and output operations. This blocking procedure increases file handling speed considerably, permits the computer to work faster, and also reduces the amount of tape or file space required. If an inventory record can be maintained on one tape instead of two, thus avoiding tape changes, the handling time is further reduced.

A further decrease in running time can be achieved if the conversion can be limited to the numerical fields required by the computer program and if all other data could be passed directly from the input file to the output file without conversion and reconversion by the FORTRAN system.

Input/Output Routine. Proceeding on this basis, a set of programs was developed in assembly-language which provide high speed input and output from an Auditape file to a FORTRAN program. These subprograms handle a number of unit records blocked into a single computer record. The two or three numerical input fields required by the program are transferred to the FORTRAN memory, and the remaining numerical fields are transferred, without conversion, to the output file.

The increased operating speed due to these subprograms is roughly a factor of ten to one. This is an enormous gain in operating performance over a standard FORTRAN program and means that inventories of over 100,000 items can be handled in the same time that would otherwise be required for inventories of 10,000 items. The size of the inventory will not be a deterrent to the use of the program.

In recent years, the improvement in operating speeds and efficiency of FORTRAN compilers is such that input/output time would only be a problem in processing very large files. For those who may want to develop their own estimation sampling procedures following the principles outlined in this book, consideration should be given to using assembly-language macros for input and output and FORTRAN for the statistical routines.

STATISTICAL SAMPLING ROUTINES

The statistical principles that have been discussed here have been known for years. They may be found in the standard statistical textbooks or authoritative literature. The procedural problems of achieving optimum stratification, stratifying large populations, and making stratified regression estimates are sufficiently complicated that they were unlikely to be used on a large scale until high-speed data processing became available.

The unique characteristic of the statistical sampling programs in the Auditape System is the way in which known statistical concepts have been put together in an accounting-oriented approach to obtain sufficiently precise estimates of assets or liability values for financial statement purposes. The statistical principles and formulas required have also been discussed previously. The following discussion is primarily for the benefit of those who wish to have a better understanding of how these statistical sampling routines are accomplished by the computer programs. The reader will find in Appendix 5 a number of subroutines or pertinent parts of programs that will supply a more detailed comprehension of the statistical aspects of the programs.

Specification Sheets

The statistical sampling routines start, as do all other Auditape routines, with the user filling in the necessary specification sheets for the particular routine. Copies of the specification sheets for the Estimation Sample Design and Selection routine and for the Estimation Sample Evaluation routine are given in Appendix 2. These forms can be filled out quite readily with the information gained from previous chapters.

When the Estimation Sample Design and Selection routine is used for design purposes only, the necessary selection specification cards for the subsequent use of the routine for selection purposes are punched out automatically or the specific information may be retained on a computer disk for later use as a designated selection specification file. This avoids the necessity of filling out specification sheets and punching cards for the selection stage unless changes are required.

When the Estimation Sample Design and Selection routine is used for both design and selection or for selection only, the necessary specification cards for the Estimation Sample Evaluation routine are also punched out automatically or the specific information may be retained on a computer disk for subsequent use as an evaluation specification file. Filling out specification sheets and punching specification cards have been kept to a bare minimum for the use of these statistical sampling procedures.

Design Stage

Several specific operations are accomplished in the design stage of the design and selection program. First, all counters and control totals are cleared and certain data that have been specified and punched into specification cards, as shown in Appendix 1 (Exhibit 1), must be read into the computer. These data are subjected to a series of tests to be sure that the specifications are valid and reasonable. If all these tests are passed satisfactorily, the specifications are printed out, as shown in Exhibit 2.

Upper Cutoff. The first statistical step (Appendix 5) is to compute the upper cutoffs for each stratum as illustrated in Exhibit 3. The average or mean value is computed by dividing the dollar total of the population by the number of items. As shown in Exhibits 1 and 2, the number of items specified is 2500 and the book population is $10,000,000. The mean value, therefore, is $4000. This value is doubled to achieve optimum stratification, as discussed in Chapter 4, so that it now becomes $8000.

In the given example of a 21-stratum design, only 19 cutoffs have to be determined. The lowest upper cutoff will be zero so as to contain all the zero and most of the minus values. The upper cutoff for the top stratum will be infinity. To find these intervening 19 values, a formula that can be used is

$$[\text{Ln } 20 - \text{Ln}(n)] \cdot 2 \, \mu(X) \tag{11.1}$$

where Ln is the natural logarithm and where the variable n decreases from 19 down to one for each successive stratum. The calculation of the upper cutoff for the twentieth stratum would be

$$\text{Ln } 20 = 2.99573$$
$$\underline{\text{Ln } \quad 1 = 0.00000}$$
$$(\text{Ln } 20 - \text{Ln } 1) = 2.99573 \ (\$8000) = \$23,965$$

In the situation where an upper cutoff is specified, the calculation is reversed to get a substitute mean or, in effect, a new value to substitute for the $8000. If $24,000 had been specified as the upper cutoff, the remaining upper cutoffs would be approximately the same as those shown in Appendix 1 (Exhibit 3). Each factor would be multiplied by $8011.40 obtained by dividing $24,000 by 2.99573 above.

In an exponential distribution the mean and variance are the same. If we divide all values by the mean, then the mean, variance and standard deviation will all be equal to one. Therefore, in the case where an exponential distribution is assumed, so as to avoid the design stage completely, the standard deviation is taken to be the same as the mean, and all cutoffs and other calculations are made on that basis. If an estimated standard deviation is also specified with the exponential assumption, this value will be used as the substitute mean for determining the upper cutoffs.

If stratification is to be made completely on all units of the population, the program would move immediately to that point. If, however, stratification is to be based on a sample from the population, some preliminary steps are necessary.

Pilot Sampling Rate. The pilot sampling rate is set by specification at whatever rate appears to be useful. This rate could be any number, such as 5, 10, 25, up to 99, but it is helpful to use squares of numbers, such as 4, 9, 16, or 25, to preserve the multiple relationship of standard deviations.

The interval chosen is divided into the random number specified, and the remainder is used as the random start. If we were sampling at a rate of one in 25, with a random number given as 585789, the remainder would be 14. The fourteenth item in the file would be selected, and stratified, followed by the thirty-ninth, sixty-fourth, eighty-ninth, and so on.

Input File. If both book values and physical values are contained in the input file, these two values would be transferred to the program memory for statistical calculations, but only one would be stratified. This would normally be the book value, although it could be the physical value if so specified.

Unusual Differences. In basing the sample design on a previous physical inventory, where both book values and physical values would be available for design purposes, any unusual differences could distort the variance and upset the logical allocation of the sample. Similar tests are made as are used in the evaluation procedure to isolate these unusual differences (Appendix 5). Any item having a physical value that is greater than the upper cutoff and four times greater than its comparable book value is included in the upper stratum and treated as an unusual difference.

Stratification. The book value assigned to a particular part number, or such other value as may have been specified as the X variable for stratification, is compared to each of the upper cutoffs in succession from 1 to 20. If it is less than or equal to zero, it is included in the lowest stratum, unless it should also exceed the cutoff for minus values. In the latter case, the excessive minus value would be included in the upper stratum.

If the item does not fall in the first stratum, it would be compared with the upper cutoff of the second stratum, and if it is less than or equal to that cutoff, it would be included in the second stratum (Appendix 5). Items falling in the upper stratum will have been tested 20 times to see whether they fall in any one of the lower strata. The stratum number assigned is carried into the next stage of the program.

Squares and Cross-Products.   Six preliminary calculations by stratum are now performed (Appendix 5) that will ultimately provide 126 control totals for statistical purposes: six totals for each of 21 strata. The first step is to add one to the item count for the particular stratum. The second step is to add the book value or independent variable to the sum of the X variables by stratum. The third step is a similar step to obtain the sum of the Y variables by stratum. The next step is to square the X variable and add it to the sum of squares of X variables by stratum. A similar step is performed for the Y variable to obtain the sum of squares of Y variables by stratum. Finally, the X and Y variables are multiplied together to obtain a sum of cross-products of X and Y variables by stratum. These mathematical calculations are made for each variable in turn as each record is read in and is stratified. The program continues until all variables have been stratified and all calculations have been made.

At this stage, most of the data shown in the first five columns in Exhibit 3 (Appendix 1) have been calculated. A summarization step is required to obtain the three totals shown for the number of items, the total book value, and the total physical value. All the necessary data are now available to proceed with the sample design.

Sample Design.   In most accounting situations where we would use statistical estimates, we have an accounting record of an item and an unknown value to be ascertained that is the supposed equivalent of the accounting record. In the case of inventory, the accounting record would be the book value, or perpetual record, and the supposed equivalent would be the physical count and value that are to be determined. In statistical terms these are the X, or independent, value and the Y, or dependent, value. The design should be based, wherever possible, on both of these values as they may be available from past history or from a preliminary sample. The design will be so much the better for using all available information. There are some situations, however, when only the X value, or book value, will be available for design purposes, and yet it is the Y value, or physical value, that must be determined.

The sample design will be based on both values if they are present in the computer file and specified as input. In this situation all calculations will be based on a regression relationship, and the evaluated sample results are likely to be quite close to those desired.

In the situation where only book value is available or specified for entry into the program, the design will be based upon deviations from book mean values. As the physical values are likely to vary considerably from the book mean values, the evaluated sample results may be less than satisfactory. When only the book values are used for design, a considerable amount of conservatism should be built into the monetary precision desired. Specifying the monetary precision at 25 percent or less of the desired precision may not be excessive.

Standard Normal Deviate.   A number of separate calculations have to be made before the actual calculation of sample size. One of these is the determination of the standard deviate corresponding to the reliability specified. If 95 percent reliability is specified on the usual two-tailed test, the standard normal deviate required is approximately 1.96. This is obtained by a special subroutine (Appendix 5) that calculates the standard deviate for any given percentage. Most computer manufacturers have statistical subroutines that will give the normal probability for a given standard deviate. It is not as easy to find one that will do the reverse and give the standard deviate for a normal probability as is required in this situation.

Some mathematical functions are available that may be programmed on the computer to provide a rational approximation of the value desired. Such an approximation will usually be sufficiently accurate for this purpose.

Correction to the Mean.   The next step deals with the statistical procedure of correcting the sums of squares and the sum of the cross-products to the mean. This step (Appendix 5) is performed for each of the 21 strata in turn. The means of the X and Y values are determined from the sums previously compiled. With these mean values, and other totals previously compiled, the corrected sums of squares and cross-products may be obtained. These, in turn, provide the values necessary to determine the regression coefficient, and to develop the variance of the population within each stratum.

Standard Deviation.   The square root of the variance within each stratum provides the standard deviation within each stratum. If both book values and physical values are available, this standard deviation will be the standard deviation of regression as shown in Exhibit 3. In the event that only one value is available, this column will be headed Standard Deviation of Mean, and the values shown would be determined from the mean.

In the special situation where a pilot sample has been used for stratification purposes, the standard deviation from the sample is itself a random variable and will have a standard error of its own. It is necessary (to make sure that the sample size is not too small) to increase the standard deviation determined at this point by two standard errors.[4] When this option is specified (Appendix 5), each standard deviation will be increased at this point by two standard errors before proceeding further. The population standard deviation is also determined during this process.

---

[4] Deming, *Sample Design*, p. 439.

Weighted Average Deviation.   In the next step (Appendix 5), the standard deviation of each stratum from 2 to 20 is multiplied by the number of items in that stratum to produce an allocation factor for the sample size. These allocation factors are summed to provide the denominator for the allocation of the total sample to each stratum. In addition, the division of this amount by the total number of items in those strata provides a weighted average standard deviation for use in determining the overall sample size. This standard deviation will be different from the population standard deviation in that two strata have been omitted. Stratum 1 is not used because in most situations there will be only zero values and therefore no standard deviation in this stratum, and Stratum 21 is omitted because that stratum will be sampled in its entirety and will therefore contribute nothing to the variance or the determination of sample size.

In the event that an option has been used to substitute an estimated standard deviation in the determination of sample size, the adjustment will be made at this point. The estimated standard deviation to be substituted will be divided by the actual standard deviation determined for the population, and this factor relationship will be used to multiply and adjust all the stratum standard deviations.

Determination of Sample Size.   Having determined the weighted average standard deviation, and the number of standard normal deviates for the prescribed percentage of reliability, the first approximation to the sample size is obtained (Appendix 5) by multiplying the number of items in the population by the number of standard deviates and by the weighted average deviation. This amount is divided by the monetary precision required, and the result is squared. The formula, as given previously, is

$$n_0 = \left(\frac{NtS}{P} \right)^2 \qquad (4.1)$$

The desired sample size is then found by dividing this first approximation by an adjustment[5] for the finite population correction as follows:

$$n = \frac{n_0}{1 + [(n_0 - 1)/N]} \qquad (4.2)$$

While this adjustment for sampling without replacement is not really necessary when the sample[6] is less than 20 percent of the frame, it does no harm and is included for those situations where a larger sample is required.

[5] William G. Cochran, *Sampling Techniques*, 2nd ed., Wiley, New York, 1963, p. 75.
[6] Deming, *Sample Design*, pp. 387–388.

Optimum Allocation.   When the sample size has been determined, it is then necessary to allocate the sample size to each of the strata. The principle of optimum,[7] or Neyman, allocation is that the total sample size as determined will be allocated to each stratum in accordance with the weighted standard deviation within each stratum. These factors were calculated at an earlier stage and were used in arriving at overall sample size. A simple computation (Appendix 5) is now required to allocate the total sample size in order to find the sample size required in each stratum. So that the sample required in each stratum will not exceed the number in that stratum, nor 1000 items in any case, certain adjustments are made to the indicated sample size in each stratum, as the allocation factor may produce a fractional number. After intervals have been determined, the sample size is rounded off to the nearest whole number.

The sampling interval is then determined for each stratum by dividing the total number of items classified in each stratum by the number of sample items required in that stratum. This interval is computed and rounded off to two decimal places. For example, if the population in Stratum 9 was 152 and the sample required was 13, the sampling interval would be 11.69. Actual program calculations may differ slightly as sample size is rounded later. As an arbitrary rule, limits between one and 1000 are placed on the sampling interval.

Highest Stratum.   The sampling interval for the top stratum is set at one, which means that each item above the upper cutoff will be selected in the sample. This procedure tends to reduce the variance considerably and thus tighten the precision surrounding the estimate.

Lowest Stratum.   The principle of optimum allocation depends on the weighted standard deviation, as discussed earlier, and does not work satisfactorily in the lowest stratum where most of the items are zero values and the rest are small minus values. To overcome this deficiency, the interval for the lowest stratum is set arbitrarily at the same interval as the second stratum.

Interval Specified for Lowest Stratum.   There will be times when it may be desirable to select a larger sample in Stratum 1 by specifying a lower sampling interval if it is likely that a large proportion of the zero values may, in fact, have physical values. The user may specify a particular sampling rate for the first stratum alone.

At this point, all the information contained in Exhibit 3, except for the footnote, is available to be printed.

[7] *Ibid.*, pp. 289–294.

Stratum Sample Size.   The formula[8] for the variance of a regression estimate contains an $(n - 2)$ term that would vanish or become negative with
less than three items in a sample. As a consequence, there is a requirement of
at least three items in each stratum for a valid stratified regression estimate.
One method of accomplishing this is to set the monetary precision sufficiently tightly so that samples larger than three will be required in every stratum.
Another way of overcoming this requirement is to reduce the number of
strata, which will have the effect of increasing the sample size in each stratum. The situation could also be corrected in the selection stage by changing
the sample selection interval. Obviously, a combination of these methods
could also be used to increase stratum sample sizes to three or more in every
stratum.

Collapsing Strata.   As an alternative to increasing stratum sample sizes by
specification, and to prevent unintentional oversight of a size deficiency that
would prevent the Estimation Sample Evaluation Program from functioning
properly at a later point, a special collapsing feature (Appendix 5) is incorporated into the design stage. This feature combines any stratum having less
than three sample items with the next higher stratum and, if necessary, with
the next succeeding stratum so that the combined stratum will contain a
large enough sample. This overcomes any resulting deficiency from using too
many strata or from specifying monetary precision at too wide a range. As
discussed elsewhere, this collapsing procedure, as shown in Appendix 1 (Exhibit 3), would normally only affect one or two strata at most. The top and
bottom strata are not considered in the collapsing procedure so that the full
21-stratum design could never be reduced to fewer than three strata.

Sample Selection Cards.   At this point in the program, the design stage is
completed. The program may continue into the selection stage, if so specified, or it may terminate at this point. If design only has been specified, the
necessary selection data will be punched out into cards, as shown in Exhibit
4, so that the selection procedure may be continued at another time and
perhaps with an inventory record of a later date or another location. It may
be desirable, when the inventories are large, to design the sample at a period
before the actual selection date. This will minimize the amount of computer
time that will be needed at the selection date, when time may be at more of a
premium. The differences in sample design that would occur from using a
prior week's or a prior month's file are likely to be minimal.

---

[8] Cochran, *Sampling Techniques*, p. 195.

Selection Phase

If the design and selection procedure has been specified, the program will continue into the selection phase without punching out the sample selection cards shown in Appendix 1 (Exhibit 4). If selection only is specified, these cards or similar cards would be required to initiate the program. The essence of the design, as contained in these sample selection cards, may be modified in any way that is considered necessary or desirable. A sample design determined for one location might well be used at other similar locations with or without modification.

Random Start. The random number included in the specifications is used as an entry point to a random number program (Appendix 5) that develops new random numbers for each stratum. The random number developed for a particular stratum is divided by the sampling interval for that stratum, and whatever amount remains, to two decimal places, is used as the random start within that stratum.

As the calculations of the intervals made in the design stage are carried to two decimal places and the random numbers are computed in the selection stage, no conceivable pattern of selection could develop that would not be random selection. If the same random number is used with the same inventory file, the items selected should be identical, assuming the same type computer is used. There are differences in accuracy between computer systems such that the computer of one manufacturer may select a sample different from that selected by another manufacturer's machine. In either case, however, the selection would have to be considered as random.

Monetary Amount Selection. The program deals sequentially with each item as it appears in the file. The sequence is dependent, of course, on the manner in which the company maintains its records, or the way in which the file has been sorted. The selection will be random regardless of the method of sequencing used for the file. Whether the first item on the file is selected will depend on the stratum in which it is classified and what the random number is for that stratum. The same holds for the second, third, fourth, and all subsequent items in the input file.

The particular value to be considered for selection is read from the input file to the FORTRAN program memory. As this is done, the item is stratified (Appendix 5), and population and stratum counters are advanced for both items and dollars. Similar counters are maintained, by number and dollars, for the sample items selected in each stratum.

An additional item count is maintained within each stratum for selection purposes. This item count is advanced by 100 for each item read in. As stated before, the sampling intervals are carried to two decimal places. These values are multiplied by 100 so that they may be handled as integers. For example, a sampling interval of 20.19 would be converted to 2019.

When the item count equals or exceeds the random number, that item is selected for the sample. If the random number is 593, the sixth item on the file that fell in Stratum 6 would be selected. At this point, the selection counter would stand at 600, the counter would be reset by subtracting the interval, 2019, and the counter would then stand at −1419. This counter would be incremented each time an item appeared and was classified in that stratum. Eventually the counter would again equal or exceed 593, the random number, with that item being selected and the whole process repeated.

The use of two decimal places in the interval injects a further note of randomness into the systematic selection procedure. If the random number is 593 and the sampling interval is 20.19, the sixth item will be selected, followed by the twenty-seventh rather than the twenty-sixth. The selection counter will stand at 581 and will not exceed the random number when 20 additional items have been processed in that stratum. The two decimal places in the interval have their own effect on the periodicity of the systematic selection of items.

The items that fall in the top stratum are selected automatically without reference to counters or random numbers, but otherwise the program continues sequentially through the file, keeping track of 20 separate intervals, counters, and random starts so that the final sample is selected in a completely random manner.

Sample Output File.   A separate assembly-language subroutine is used to create an output file from those items that are selected. When each item is selected, the item record is transferred from the input file to the output file, along with the stratum number and sequence number from the computer memory. If the fields assigned to the stratum and sequence numbers already contain data, the stratum and sequence numbers will replace the data stored in those fields when they are carried to the output file.

Sample Summary.   When the sample has been selected, the actual sampling intervals are obtained by dividing the number of items in the population by the number of items in the sample. A summary of the population and of the sample selected is printed out as shown in Appendix 1 (Exhibit 5). This summary establishes control over each stratum and shows the population data, sample data, stratum cutoffs and selection intervals. The sample file would also normally be printed out as a record of the sample to be taken, and as a safeguard against unintentional destruction or erasure of the sample file before the evaluation can be completed. An example of part of such a printout is shown in Appendix 1 (Exhibit 6).

Evaluation Specifications.   The final step in the sample selection process is to punch out the specification cards or create a second output file that will be required in the sample evaluation procedure. These card images are shown in Exhibit 7, and most of the data contained therein can be traced to the original specification cards (Exhibit 1) or to the summary information as shown in Exhibit 5. These cards may be modified as circumstances require but normally are usable exactly as they are determined by the selection procedure.

Punched cards may also be produced from the sample output file to serve several purposes in connection with taking and evaluating the sample. One set may be used for control purposes, and this set would contain all the information available in the input file, or as much as could be contained in a single card. Another set might be used as a master set for preparing the evaluation cards at a later date. A third set could be used to provide a basis for the actual count in the stockroom or warehouse. This count set would not normally contain book quantities or unit prices to ensure specific counting but should contain the part number, part description, and location of the item within the warehouse.

Sample Simulation.   When a tape or disk file is available containing both book values and physical values, either from a previous complete inventory or by reconstruction, it is possible to simulate samples from this file for instructional or empirical purposes. The physical values contained in the input file will be carried over to the output file, provided that the particular field is not used for either the stratum or sequence number and thus will not be overridden by one of these numbers. By punching cards from the output file, both the book values and physical values will be carried into the sampling item cards as if the sample items had been counted, priced, and extended. The sample cards would thus be ready immediately for the evaluation procedure.

A number of samples taken in this way from an existing file will convince many otherwise skeptical people of the effectiveness of statistical sampling. It is also helpful to go through such a procedure on a dry run basis so that all those concerned with taking and evaluating the sample will understand the way in which the final data will be processed.

Evaluation Procedures

The Estimation Sample Evaluation Program that is contained in the Auditape System will evaluate sample data in any one of six different statistically permissible ways, providing, as output, a specified estimate with the associated monetary precision at the specified reliability. The program was designed as a companion to the Estimation Sampling Design and Selection

Program to provide a means of evaluating the samples selected by the sampling program. It is not necessary, however, for the sample to have been selected by the sampling program for the sample data to be evaluated by the evaluation program. Samples may be drawn manually, or by some other selection procedure, and still be evaluated by this program. This takes care of the burdensome calculations that are a part of any sample evaluation.

Specification Cards.   Two distinct files are required to operate the sample evaluation program, and these files may be on card, tape, or disk as the occasion demands. One of these files contains the specification cards, and the other contains the sample item cards. The sample evaluation specification cards are, in most cases, the same cards that are the output of the estimation sampling program, as shown in Appendix 1 (Exhibit 7). In those cases where the sample has not been selected by the estimation sampling program, similar cards must be punched up containing all the necessary data for evaluation purposes.

The specification cards are read into the computer, and various codes are translated to their literal definitions at which time the specifications are printed, as shown in Exhibit 8. If any options have been specified, these will also be printed out, as also shown in Exhibit 8, where the number of strata has been specified at 20. This specification was an amendment to the original specifications used in the sampling procedure brought about by use of the collapsing feature, as shown in Exhibit 3, to join the original Strata 2 and 3 together.

Specification Review.   Since failure to specify certain parameters would be fatal to the evaluation process, an editing routine is used to check all the specifications for reasonableness. When errors are encountered, printed messages describe the nature of the error and the action to be taken. In some cases it will be possible for the Program to supply automatically what is missing, but most errors are of the type that necessitate correcting the specification cards and starting again. If no errors are detected in the specification cards, the process will continue.

Sample Data Cards.   The evaluation specification cards contain information as to the number of sample items in each stratum. The sample items may be read into the computer directly from cards or may be set up on tape or a disk file and read from the tape or disk as required.

The sample data cards must contain, at a minimum, the physical value, even where selection has been made manually. In most cases, the cards will also contain the book value and the stratum number into which the sample item was originally classified. Both values would be required for a regression estimate, but only the physical value would be required for a mean estimate. If selection has been made proportional to size, based on the book values, both the book and the physical values would be required for evaluation purposes.

As the sample data cards are read in, the necessary squares and cross-products are calculated, and the sums accumulated by stratum. A test, similar to that already described, is made for unusual differences to avoid major errors in the evaluation process. If the number of items in a particular stratum does not agree with the number indicated in the specification card, this fact will be printed out and the program will continue. This provides a warning to the user that sample cards may be missing and therefore the evaluation may not be valid.

Statistical Calculations. When all the sample data cards have been entered and checked against the predetermined totals, the statistical calculations (Appendix 5) are made to correct the sums of squares and cross-products to the mean. Coefficients, estimates, variances and precision are calculated for each stratum and printed, as shown in Exhibit 9. This is the end result of the sampling process and provides the best estimate that can be made, from that particular sample, by the estimating procedure that has been specified.

The exhibit shows a combined regression estimate of $10,035,509.96 and a precision range of plus or minus $132,832 at 95 percent reliability. We may infer from this, with 1 chance in 20 of being wrong, that the unknown physical inventory population lies between the two limits shown on the exhibit. These precision limits are the estimate plus or minus the precision.

A larger sample would most likely produce tighter precision but not necessarily a better estimate. We know, because this is a simulation, that the estimate is very close to the actual population value as shown in Appendix 1 (Exhibit 3). Another sample might not give as good an estimate even if the sample were larger. The precision band narrows as the sample increases until it ultimately disappears with a full complete count. The extent of sampling in this situation gets down to how precise one wants or needs to be. The example given here should be sufficient for estimating physical inventories and for most other accounting purposes.

The basic regression formula for estimating the unknown mean of the physical population values, as given previously, is

$$\mu(\hat{Y}) = \bar{y} + b[\mu(X) - \bar{x}] \tag{6.1}$$

where X represents the book value and Y the physical value. Lowercase letters indicate the sample statistics and capital letters indicate the population statistics. The value of the regression coefficient, b, changes according to the type of estimate that is being made.

Tentative Design.   As a supplementary follow-up procedure, the computer has been programmed to continue, after printing out the results of the evaluation, and to compute the sample that would have been required, based on the sample results, in order to achieve the design precision. The results of such a tentative design are shown in Appendix 1 (Exhibit 10). The purpose of this procedure (Appendix 5) is to show what the sample design should have been if the knowledge gained from the present sample had been available when the sample was designed. Such information is helpful in designing the next sample or, as in the case of a pilot sample, can be used to replace the design stage.

Where a pilot sample has been taken and is to be evaluated to form a basis for the sample design, the pilot sample will be evaluated with the normal evaluation procedure. The tentative design becomes more important now as it, in effect, takes the place of the design procedure in the estimation sampling program. If specification cards have been requested, they will be printed and punched out, as shown in Exhibit 11. These cards are now ready to enter the selection procedure and obtain a new and larger sample, based on the design as determined from the smaller pilot sample. The program terminates at this point.

These descriptions of the various steps taken in the program will serve to acquaint the user with the manner in which the various statistical procedures are undertaken and to indicate that all the necessary statistical procedures have been followed. It will also help those who would prefer to design such programs from the beginning and help them avoid some of the pitfalls they might otherwise encounter.

EMPIRICAL OBSERVATIONS

Some distillation of experience may be useful to the individual taking a sample and deciding on various specifications and options. The following observations are based on samples taken from a constructed exponential file of 2500 items and a population total of $10,000,000. Monetary precision was set in all cases at $200,000 at 95 percent reliability. These observations are based on the evaluation of specific samples, and they provide relative indications of some of the problems that may be encountered in the use of various options.

Two-Variable Design

With both the book and physical values available from a previous inventory for design purposes, some of the results were as follows:

Sample size	347
Strata	21
Precision	$149,134

One-Variable Design

With all other factors the same, but with only book values available, the results change dramatically:

Sample size	109
Strata	11
Precision	$731,091

This points out quite clearly that a design based solely on book values can be unsatisfactory without some knowledge of the variability of the unknown physical population.

Lower Precision

This can be corrected fairly well by reducing the design precision from $200,000 to $40,000 with the following results:

Sample size	491
Strata	21
Precision	$144,374

These results approximate the precision achieved with the two-variable design, although the sample size is larger. Conceivably, a reduction to $50,000 design precision could reduce the sample size and still achieve the desired precision. A four- or fivefold reduction is conservative and works out well in practice when only book values are available.

The remaining observations are based on samples from a typical live data file of about 2500 items and somewhat less than $5,000,000 in the population. Monetary precision was set at $150,000 for design purposes.

Pilot Sample

For a population of 100,000 items or more, and with some conservatism in the design precision, good results may be achieved through the use of a pilot sample approach to the design of a sample. If this approach is used on a small population at an extreme sampling rate, however, the results may not be too satisfactory. Using a sample rate of one in 25, which means that the sample size is determined through analysis of 100 items out of 2500, the results achieved were:

Sample size	112
Strata	8
Precision	$380,509

Using the entire population for design purposes, without any other changes, the results were:

Sample size	186
Strata	18
Precision	$143,554

One would not normally use a pilot sample approach with such a small population, and certainly not at such a high sampling rate, so the results are not as inconsonant as they may appear. The indicated sample size of 112 is too small primarily because the pilot sample of 100 items was too small for this purpose. If the population had been larger or the sampling rate had been one in four or five, the results undoubtedly would have been much better. Some protection would also be available through a more conservative use of monetary precision which, by itself, would enlarge the sample size.

Unstratified Sample

The question is often raised as to the effect of stratification and whether stratification is worthwhile, particularly if manual methods must be employed in selection. The effect of stratification can be clearly shown by comparing the sample taken above with another sample taken on an unstratified basis, as shown below:

	Unstratified	Stratified
Sample size	559	186
Strata	1	18
Precision	$219,539	$143,554

Thus, without stratification, the sample size increased threefold from 186 to 559 and the monetary precision achieved increased approximately 50 percent, and considerably over the design precision of $150,000.

Fewer Strata Specified

It is evident that stratification is highly desirable, but it is often contended that no more than 10 strata are really useful in sample design. By specifying 10 strata without any other changes in design, the comparative results were as follows:

	10 Strata	20 Strata
Sample size	305	186
Strata	8	18
Precision	$227,371	$143,554

The sample size on a 10-stratum basis is considerably less than on an unstratified basis but not nearly as small as with the 20-stratum design. The precision achieved was in the same range as for the unstratified sample and not nearly as good as for the full 20-stratum design. Although 10-stratum designs may be sufficient for statistical samples in other areas, the 20-stratum design seems much more suitable for accounting purposes. This number has been arrived at empirically, as stated earlier in the book, and the results speak for themselves.

Upper Cutoff

The upper cutoff as determined by the program, and based on the exponential distribution, will be approximately six times the population mean. There may be reasons why a different upper cutoff should be selected. For example, when a number of similar inventories are being taken at one time, the use of a standard cutoff will make comparisons between the inventories more useful than if each one has a different upper cutoff.

Some inventories will have a distribution that is somewhat skewed to the right, with a large number of fairly expensive parts or supplies. In this case, it will be desirable to increase the upper cutoff and thus minimize the variance and sample size. The effect of changing the upper cutoff can be best indicated by the several examples shown below:

Upper Cutoff	Sample Size	Precision
$ 8,000	198	$156,381
10,000	186	143,554
12,000	184	135,561
14,000	181	108,100

If the design data show an unusual concentration of high value items in the upper strata or, conversely, a low number of items in the upper strata, it is worth considering an increase or decrease in the upper cutoff. Where the data are distributed reasonably on an exponential basis, it is unlikely that there will be important gains in efficiency from moving the upper cutoff.

Estimated Standard Deviation

In most accounting situations where estimation sampling will be used, the need is to estimate a relationship between two different records such as between the physical inventory and the perpetual record. This relationship is evidenced by the standard deviation of regression as shown in Exhibit 3. In those situations where this relationship is not known and cannot be determined because only book values are available, it may be possible to use an estimated standard deviation. The effect on sample size and precision, using estimated standard deviations, is shown below:

Estimated Standard Deviation	Sample Size	Precision
$ 800	199	$143,554
1800	513	98,721
7800	1587	17,273

It can be seen that by increasing the estimated standard deviation, the sample size will increase substantially and the precision will be reduced, although not as substantially on a relative basis. Using a higher standard deviation than expected will introduce conservatism into the sample, and this is particularly desirable the first time through it.

Exponential Assumption

The complete pass of the input file that is necessary for a normal design phase, or even for a pilot sample approach, may be avoided completely by use of the exponential assumption. The assumption is made that the population is distributed exponentially, and the design proceeds on that basis. The stratification and the allocation of the sample to strata are satisfactory with this approach. A comparison of a sample taken using the exponential assumption to the standard procedure follows:

	Exponential Assumption	Standard Procedure
Sample size	107	186
Strata	8	18
Precision	$237,524	$143,554

The weakness, as indicated by the data above, lies in the fact that the book value is being used as the basis for design and no recognition is being given to the relationship between the physical and book values. It is about as effective as a design based on book values and saves half the time. The exponential assumption will normally underestimate the sample size unless an estimated standard deviation is available and can be used to offset this underestimate. The same effect could be gained by using more conservative precision.

APPENDIX 1

CASE STUDIES

ESTIMATION SAMPLING SPECIFICATION CARD IMAGES

```
........10........20........30........40........50........60........70........8
ES 2    EXPONENT TESTDS      BOOK INVENT    2500       10000000 7PHYS INVENT   9
........10........20........30........40........50........60........70........8
ES 3    1500009500    687514NY    1012   0   0       0     0  0     0      000
```

Exhibit 1

SPECIFICATION CARD DATA

ROUTINE TO BE USED FOR   DESIGN AND SELECTION

INPUT FILE

    VARIABLE X
        DESCRIPTION   BOOK INVENT
        NUMBER OF ITEMS   2500
        ACTUAL OR APPROXIMATE TOTAL   10000000
        AUDITAPE FIELD ASSIGNMENT   7
    VARIABLE Y
        DESCRIPTION   PHYS INVENT
        AUDITAPE FIELD ASSIGNMENT   9
    SAMPLE DESIGN SPECIFICATIONS
        MONETARY PRECISION   150000
        RELIABILITY LEVEL (PERCENTAGE)   95.00
    RANDOM NUMBER   687514
    OUTPUT FILE

    AUDITAPE FIELD ASSIGNED TO STRATUM NUMBER   1C
    AUDITAPE FIELD ASSIGNED TO SEQUENCE NUMBER   1

NO ERRORS HAVE BEEN DETECTED IN SPECIFICATION CARDS. PROCESSING IS CONTINUING.

Exhibit 2

CALCULATED DESIGN AND SELECTION DATA

STRATUM NUMBER	UPPER CUT-OFF	POPULATION DATA			INDICATED SAMPLE		STANDARD DEVIATION OF REGRESSION
		ITEMS	BOOK INVENT	PHYS INVENT	INTERVAL	SIZE	
1	0	31	-28.62	.00	10.33	3	.00
2	410	233	46973.89	45975.71	152.74	2	34.28
3	842	223	138694.21	137972.52	61.71	4	84.83
4	1300	211	225059.37	224728.17	39.95	5	131.04
5	1785	200	307537.97	312499.91	24.76	8	211.47
6	2301	188	383237.56	378398.47	20.20	9	259.12
7	2853	176	452612.76	451596.29	14.23	12	367.96
8	3446	165	518668.93	530799.51	13.28	12	394.13
9	4086	152	571196.65	566820.34	11.73	13	446.20
10	4782	142	628281.58	628073.58	7.66	19	683.44
11	5545	129	664745.49	658291.12	8.52	15	614.67
12	6387	117	696154.02	701106.00	6.88	17	760.86
13	7330	106	724800.81	744887.74	5.36	20	975.90
14	8398	94	737005.51	745780.38	5.72	16	915.10
15	9631	82	736987.54	744189.64	5.14	16	1019.30
16	11090	69	711984.72	695869.94	5.06	14	1035.17
17	12875	58	691344.22	703728.13	3.30	18	1588.64
18	15176	45	626880.55	633308.62	3.53	13	1484.60
19	18420	33	548469.54	532863.54	2.29	14	2288.52
20	23965	21	433920.39	421385.01	2.16	10	2425.58
21		25	155472.91	161574.88	1.00	25	422.23
TOTAL		2500	10000000.00	10019849.50		265	685.51

THE NUMBER OF STRATA HAS BEEN REDUCED TO 20
BY COMBINING WITH THE NEXT STRATUM ANY STRATUM
WHERE SAMPLE SIZE WOULD BE TOO SMALL FOR A PROPER
EVALUATION.

Exhibit 3

SPECIFICATION CARD IMAGES FOR SAMPLE SELECTION

```
........10........20........30........40........50........60........70........80
```

```
........10........20........30........40........50........60........70........80
ES01
```

```
........10........20........30........40........50........60........70........80
ES02   EXPONENT TEST S     BOOK INVENT   2500       10      0 7PHYS INVENT  9
```

```
........10........20........30........40........50........60........70........80
ES03   1500009500    357894      1012                         20Y  0    000
```

```
........10........20........30........40........50........60........70........80
ES041      0    1033      842  11400    1300   3995    1785   2476    2301  2020
ES042   2853    1423     3446   1328    4086   1173    4782    766    5545   852
ES043   6387     688     7330    536    8398    572    9631    514   11090   500
ES044  12875     330    15176    353   18420    229   23965    216
```

Exhibit 4

SUMMARY OF POPULATION AND SAMPLE SELECTED

STRATUM NUMBER	UPPER CUT-OFF	POPULATION		SAMPLE		
		ITEMS	BOOK INVENT	INTERVAL	ITEMS	BOOK INVENT
1	0	31	-28.62	10.33	3	-28.62
2	842	456	185668.10	114.00	4	1739.40
3	1300	211	225059.37	35.17	6	6527.09
4	1785	200	307537.97	25.00	8	11488.39
5	2301	188	383237.56	18.80	10	19913.70
6	2853	176	452612.76	14.67	12	31064.18
7	3446	165	518668.93	12.69	13	40562.93
8	4086	152	571196.65	11.69	13	48550.28
9	4782	142	628281.58	7.89	18	80558.87
10	5545	129	664745.49	8.60	15	76727.06
11	6387	117	696154.02	6.88	17	100464.9
12	7330	106	724800.81	5.30	20	135066.3
13	8398	94	737005.51	5.53	17	131960.2
14	9631	82	736987.54	5.12	16	147099.9
15	11090	69	711984.72	5.31	13	134581.1
16	12875	58	691344.22	3.22	18	210236.1
17	15176	45	626880.55	3.75	12	170836.1
18	18420	33	548469.54	2.36	14	235543.9
19	23965	21	433920.39	2.10	10	202871.9
20		25	155472.91	1.00	25	155472.9
TOTAL		2500	10000000.00		264	1941237.0

Exhibit 5

AUDITAPE SYSTEM   RELEASE 2.0   (c)1979   PARTIAL OUTPUT OF SAMPLE

LINE NO.	BOOK INVENTORY	PHYSICAL INVENTORY	STRATUM NUMBER	SEQUENCE NUMBER
1	21099.65	19335.31	19	6
2	1899.48	1581.14	5	10
3	1099.27	1236.75	3	11
4	15899.22	15899.22	18	12
5	2898.96	2898.96	7	17
6	598.74	598.74	2	21
7	7497.06	7497.06	13	61
8	10997.01	10997.01	15	63
9	11096.66	11709.44	16	75
10	4896.41	4493.87	10	83
11	6996.20	8355.27	12	86
12	3595.93	3595.93	8	91
13	6095.70	6095.70	11	98
14	9195.52	9195.52	14	107
15	19694.69	19694.69	19	125
16	11493.60	12156.73	16	147
17	6293.17	6293.17	11	159
18	4592.86	4592.86	9	168
19	27392.82	27392.82	20	169
20	2492.67	2492.67	6	175
21	6492.49	6492.49	12	180
22	8092.13	8092.13	13	188
23	2991.54	2991.54	7	206
24	12791.11	15909.79	16	215
25	9490.97	9490.97	14	221

Exhibit 6

SAMPLE EVALUATION SPECIFICATION CARD IMAGES (FROM SELECTION FUNCTION)

```
........10........20........30........40........50........60........70........8C
```

```
........10........20........30........40........50........60........70........8C
EE01
```

```
........10........20........30........40........50........60........70........8(
EE02   EXPONENT TEST   BOOK INVENT 7PHYS INVENT  910      19500
```

```
........10........20........30........40........50........60........70........8(
EE03   1500009500     20    00
```

```
........10........20........30........40........50........60........70........8(
EE04  1       31    3        0       -29   456    4      842    18566:
EE04  2      211    6     1300    225059   200    8     1785    30753:
EE04  3      188   10     2301    383238   176   12     2853    45261
EE04  4      165   13     3446    518669   152   13     4086    57119
EE04  5      142   18     4782    628282   129   15     5545    66474
EE04  6      117   17     6387    696154   106   20     7330    72480
EE04  7       94   17     8398    737006    82   16     9631    73698
EE04  8       69   13    11090    711985    58   18    12875    69134
EE04  9       45   12    15176    626881    33   14    18420    54847
EE0410        21   10    23965    433920    25   25        0    15547
```

Exhibit 7

SPECIFICATION CARD DATA

  INPUT SPECIFICATIONS

    VARIABLE X

      DESCRIPTION   BOOK INVENT

      AUDITAPE FIELD   7

    VARIABLE Y

      DESCRIPTION   PHYS INVENT

      AUDITAPE FIELD   9

      STRATUM NUMBER - AUDITAPE FIELD   10

  TYPE OF ESTIMATE TO BE MADE   COMBINED REGRESSION

  RELIABILITY LEVEL (PERCENTAGE)   95.00

  TEST FOR UNUSUAL DIFFERENCES   YES

  TENTATIVE DESIGN DATA FOR NEXT SAMPLE

    MONETARY PRECISION   150000

    RELIABILITY LEVEL (PERCENTAGE)   95.0

  STRATIFICATION SPECIFICATIONS

    NUMBER OF STRATA   2

NO ERRORS HAVE BEEN DETECTED IN SPECIFICATION CARDS. PROCESSING IS CONTINUING.

Exhibit 8

SAMPLE EVALUATED AS A COMBINED REGRESSION ESTIMATE

STRATUM NUMBER	UPPER CUT-OFF	POPULATION		INTERVAL	SAMPLE			ESTIMATED PHYS INVENT
		ITEMS	BOOK INVENT		ITEMS	BOOK INVENT	PHYS INVENT	
1	0	31	-29	10.33	3	-28.62	.00	255.57
2	842	456	185668	114.00	4	1739.40	1738.31	186072.14
3	1300	211	225059	35.16	6	6527.09	6762.18	233513.73
4	1785	200	307538	25.00	8	11488.39	11429.05	305203.60
5	2301	188	383238	18.80	10	19913.70	19489.14	374885.39
6	2853	176	452613	14.66	12	31064.18	31524.04	459482.98
7	3446	165	518669	12.69	13	40562.93	41584.04	531468.85
8	4086	152	571197	11.69	13	48550.28	47291.05	556325.85
9	4782	142	628282	7.88	18	80558.87	84085.20	656403.79
10	5545	129	664745	8.60	15	76727.06	77330.05	669725.93
11	6387	117	696154	6.88	17	100464.97	98361.71	681481.11
12	7330	106	724801	5.30	20	135066.36	138428.83	742247.49
13	8398	94	737006	5.52	17	131960.29	140782.56	785480.59
14	9631	82	736988	5.12	16	147099.92	142704.23	715167.45
15	11090	69	711985	5.30	13	134581.12	132062.19	698712.83
16	12875	58	691344	3.22	18	210236.16	218665.69	717923.31
17	15176	45	626881	3.75	12	170836.11	174437.79	640963.03
18	18420	33	548470	2.35	14	235543.98	217968.58	507324.43
19	23965	21	433920	2.10	10	202871.96	192256.75	411297.01
20		25	155473	1.00	25	155472.91	161574.88	161574.88
TOTAL		2500	10000002		264	1941237.06	1938475.87	10035509.96

PRECISION AT 95.00 PERCENT RELIABILITY LEVEL

PRECISION RANGE – PLUS OR MINUS   132832.16

UPPER PRECISION LIMIT   10168342.12

LOWER PRECISION LIMIT   9902677.80

Exhibit 9

191

TENTATIVE DESIGN DATA FOR NEXT SAMPLE AS COMBINED REGRESSION ESTIMATE

STRATUM NUMBER	UPPER CUT-OFF	INDICATED SAMPLE	
		INTERVAL	ITEMS
1	0	10.33	3
2	842	181.46	2
3	1300	26.72	7
4	1785	22.47	8
5	2301	18.24	10
6	2853	14.91	11
7	3446	13.15	12
8	4086	12.16	12
9	4782	8.74	16
10	5545	9.29	13
11	6387	7.67	15
12	7330	6.18	17
13	8398	6.31	14
14	9631	5.88	13
15	11090	5.90	11
16	12875	4.16	13
17	15176	4.39	10
18	18420	3.50	9
19	23965	3.25	6
20		1.00	25
TOTAL			227

EXPECTED MONETARY PRECISION

AT RELIABILITY OF 95.00 PERCENT

WOULD BE $ 150000.

Exhibit 10

CARD IMAGES OF PUNCHED TENTATIVE DESIGN DATA FOR NEXT SAMPLE SELECTION

```
........10........20.........30........40.........50........60........70........

........10........20.........30........40.........50........60........70........
ES01

........10........20.........30........40.........50........60........70........
ES02   EXPONENT TEST S       BOOK INVENT   2500      10     2 7PHYS INVENT  9

........10........20.........30........40.........50........60........70........
ES03   1500009500                    10                        20Y

........10........20.........30........40.........50........60........70........
ES041      0   1033      842  18146     1300   2672    1785   2247    2301   18
ES042   2853   1491     3446   1315     4086   1216    4782    874    5545    9
ES043   6387    767     7330    618     8398    631    9631    588   11090    5
ES044  12875    416    15176    439    18420    350   23965    325
```

Exhibit 11

192

SAMPLE EVALUATED AS A SEPARATE REGRESSION ESTIMATE

STRATUM NUMBER	UPPER CUT-OFF	POPULATION		INTERVAL	SAMPLE			ESTIMATED PHYS INVENT
		ITEMS	BOOK INVENT		ITEMS	BOOK INVENT	PHYS INVENT	
1	0	31	-29	10.33	3	-28.62	.00	.00
2	842	456	185668	114.00	4	1739.40	1738.31	185511.23
3	1300	211	225059	35.16	6	6527.09	6762.18	233343.19
4	1785	200	307538	25.00	8	11488.39	11429.05	302248.88
5	2301	188	383238	18.80	10	19913.70	19489.14	379674.52
6	2853	176	452613	14.66	12	31064.18	31524.04	458650.15
7	3446	165	518669	12.69	13	40562.93	41584.04	530148.17
8	4086	152	571197	11.69	13	48550.28	47291.05	557021.81
9	4782	142	628282	7.88	18	80558.87	84085.20	656821.86
10	5545	129	664745	8.60	15	76727.06	77330.05	669245.98
11	6387	117	696154	6.88	17	100464.97	98361.71	681961.78
12	7330	106	724801	5.30	20	135066.36	138428.83	745159.92
13	8398	94	737006	5.52	17	131960.29	140782.56	788361.62
14	9631	82	736988	5.12	16	147099.92	142704.23	696479.12
15	11090	69	711985	5.30	13	134581.12	132062.19	697304.94
16	12875	58	691344	3.22	18	210236.16	218665.69	736328.91
17	15176	45	626881	3.75	12	170836.11	174437.79	651334.62
18	18420	33	548470	2.35	14	235543.98	217968.58	505030.72
19	23965	21	433920	2.10	10	202871.96	192256.35	403382.24
20		25	155473	1.00	25	155472.91	161574.88	161574.88
TOTAL		2500	10000002		264	1941237.06	1938475.87	10039584.53

PRECISION AT 95.00 PERCENT RELIABILITY LEVEL

PRECISION RANGE - PLUS OR MINUS   126551.04

UPPER PRECISION LIMIT   10166135.58

LOWER PRECISION LIMIT   9913033.49

Exhibit 12

SAMPLE EVALUATED AS A COMBINED RATIO ESTIMATE

| STRATUM NUMBER | UPPER CUT-OFF | POPULATION | | INTERVAL | SAMPLE | | | ESTIMATED |
		ITEMS	BOOK INVENT		ITEMS	BOOK INVENT	PHYS INVENT	PHYS INVENT
1	0	31	-29	10.33	3	-28.62	.00	266.36
2	842	456	185668	114.00	4	1739.40	1738.31	185561.70
3	1300	211	225059	35.16	6	6527.09	6762.18	233332.70
4	1785	200	307538	25.00	8	11488.39	11429.05	306025.59
5	2301	188	383238	18.80	10	19913.70	19489.14	375243.67
6	2853	176	452613	14.66	12	31064.18	31524.04	459361.87
7	3446	165	518669	12.69	13	40562.93	41584.04	531623.79
8	4086	152	571197	11.69	13	48550.28	47291.05	556468.67
9	4782	142	628282	7.88	18	80558.87	84085.20	656111.12
10	5545	129	664745	8.60	15	76727.06	77330.05	669923.76
11	6387	117	696154	6.88	17	100464.97	98361.71	681671.91
12	7330	106	724801	5.30	20	135066.36	138428.83	742609.36
13	8398	94	737006	5.52	17	131960.29	140782.56	785777.52
14	9631	82	736988	5.12	16	147099.92	142704.23	714484.13
15	11090	69	711985	5.30	13	134581.12	132062.19	698618.61
16	12875	58	691344	3.22	18	210236.16	218665.69	718486.02
17	15176	45	626881	3.75	12	170836.11	174437.79	640406.86
18	18420	33	548470	2.35	14	235543.98	217968.58	507051.86
19	23965	21	433920	2.10	10	202871.96	192256.35	411616.00
20		25	155473	1.00	25	155472.91	161574.88	161574.88
TOTAL		2500	10000002		264	1941237.06	1938475.87	10036216.37

PRECISION AT 95.00 PERCENT RELIABILITY LEVEL

PRECISION RANGE - PLUS OR MINUS   146372.44

UPPER PRECISION LIMIT   10182588.81

LOWER PRECISION LIMIT   9889843.94

Exhibit 13

SAMPLE EVALUATED AS A SEPARATE RATIO ESTIMATE

STRATUM NUMBER	UPPER CUT-OFF	POPULATION		SAMPLE				ESTIMATED
		ITEMS	BOOK INVENT	INTERVAL	ITEMS	BOOK INVENT	PHYS INVENT	PHYS INVENT
1	0	31	-29	10.33	3	-28.62	.00	.00
2	842	456	185668	114.00	4	1739.40	1738.31	185551.65
3	1300	211	225059	35.16	6	6527.09	6762.18	233165.08
4	1785	200	307538	25.00	8	11488.39	11429.05	305949.50
5	2301	188	383238	18.80	10	19913.70	19489.14	375067.37
6	2853	176	452613	14.66	12	31064.18	31524.04	459313.28
7	3446	165	518669	12.69	13	40562.93	41584.04	531725.70
8	4086	152	571197	11.69	13	48850.28	47291.05	556382.08
9	4782	142	628282	7.88	18	80558.87	84085.20	655784.00
10	5545	129	664745	8.60	15	76727.06	77330.05	669969.16
11	6387	117	696154	6.88	17	100464.97	98361.71	681579.84
12	7330	106	724801	5.30	20	135066.36	138428.83	742844.88
13	8398	94	737006	5.52	17	131960.29	140782.56	786278.90
14	9631	82	736988	5.12	16	147099.92	142704.23	714965.07
15	11090	69	711985	5.30	13	134581.12	132062.19	698656.91
16	12875	58	691344	3.22	18	210236.16	218665.69	719063.80
17	15176	45	626881	3.75	12	170836.11	174437.79	640097.32
18	18420	33	548470	2.35	14	235543.98	217968.58	507545.25
19	23965	21	433920	2.10	10	202871.96	192256.35	41121.442
20		25	155473	1.00	25	155472.91	161574.88	161574.88
TOTAL		2500	10000002		264	1941237.06	1938475.87	10036731.09

PRECISION AT 95.00 PERCENT RELIABILITY LEVEL

PRECISION RANGE - PLUS OR MINUS   146402.35

UPPER PRECISION LIMIT   10183133.44

LOWER PRECISION LIMIT   9890328.73

Exhibit 14

195

SAMPLE EVALUATED AS A MEAN ESTIMATE

STRATUM NUMBER	UPPER CUT-OFF	POPULATION		SAMPLE				
		ITEMS	BOOK INVENT	INTERVAL	ITEMS	BOOK INVENT	PHYS INVENT	ESTIMATED PHYS INVENT
1	0	31		10.33	3		.00	.00
2	842	456		114.00	4		1738.31	198167.34
3	1300	211		35.16	6		6762.18	237803.33
4	1785	200		25.00	8		11429.05	285726.25
5	2301	188		18.80	10		19489.14	366395.83
6	2853	176		14.66	12		31524.04	462352.59
7	3446	165		12.69	13		41584.04	527797.43
8	4086	152		11.69	13		47291.05	552941.51
9	4782	142		7.88	18		84085.20	663338.80
10	5545	129		8.60	15		77330.05	665038.43
11	6387	117		6.88	17		98361.71	676960.00
12	7330	106		5.30	20		138428.83	733672.80
13	8398	94		5.52	17		140782.56	778444.74
14	9631	82		5.12	16		142704.23	731359.18
15	11090	69		5.30	13		132062.19	700945.47
16	12875	58		3.22	18		218665.69	704589.45
17	15176	45		3.75	12		174437.79	654141.71
18	18420	33		2.35	14		217968.58	513783.08
19	23965	21		2.10	10		192256.35	403738.33
20		25		1.00	25		161574.88	161574.88
TOTAL		2500			264		1938475.87	10018771.16

PRECISION AT 95.00 PERCENT RELIABILITY LEVEL

PRECISION RANGE - PLUS OR MINUS   156124.00

UPPER PRECISION LIMIT   10174895.16

LOWER PRECISION LIMIT   9862647.16

Exhibit 15

SPECIFICATION SHEETS

ESTIMATION SAMPLE DESIGN AND SELECTION ROUTINE

Note – The following rules apply to the completion of these specification sheets:

- Right justify all quantitative entries.
- Leading zeros are not required for quantitative data.
- Leave blocks blank unless otherwise instructed.

AUDITAPE ROUTINE SPECIFICATIONS

Constants

E	S	0	1
01	02	03	04

Constants

E	S	0	2
01	02	03	04

Application Identification

Enter the name of the company, division, etc.

05	06	07	08	09	10	11	12	13	14	15	16	17	18	19	20

Routine Identification

This routine may be used to design a sample, to select a sample using a previous design, or to design and select a sample concurrently.

If the routine is to be used to *design* a sample, or to *design* and *select* a sample concurrently, enter a D . Otherwise, leave this block blank.

21

If the routine is to be used to *select* a sample, or to *design* and *select* a sample concurrently, enter an ⬜ S . Otherwise, leave this block blank.

⬜ 22

Blocks to be left blank

▨ 23   ... to ...   ▨ 29

Input File Specifications (Population)

Variable X:

Enter a description of the values upon which stratification is to be based (variable X).

30	31	32	33	34	35	36	37	38	39	40	41

Enter the input file record count or a reasonable approximation.

42	43	44	45	46	47

Enter the input file total for variable X (monetary amounts should be entered in whole dollars and may be estimated if necessary).

48	49	50	51	52	53	54	55	56	57	58	59	60	61

Enter the number of the Auditape field that contains variable X (0 7 to 1 2).

62	63

Variable Y:

It is often desirable, for design purposes, to use some prior values of the variable to be estimated so that sample size may be determined on the basis of standard deviations measured from a regression line. When such values are not available (leave blocks 64 to 77 blank), the calculations will be based on standard deviations from the mean.

Enter a description of the values to be estimated (variable Y).

64	65	66	67	68	69	70	71	72	73	74	75

Enter the number of the Auditape field that contains variable Y (0 7 to 1 2).

76	77

Constants

E	S	0	3		
01	02	03	04	05	06

Sample Design Specifications

This section is required if DESIGN has been specified (entry of [D] in block 21 of the ES02 card). If DESIGN has not been specified leave blocks 07 thru 18 blank.

07 08 09 10 11 12 13 14

Enter the precision limit to be used (monetary precision should be entered in whole dollars).

15 16 17 18

Enter the reliability level to be used (enter as a percentage with two integers and two decimals—e.g., enter 95 percent as [9][5][0][0]).

19 20 21 22

Blocks to be left blank

Random Number

Enter a six-digit random number.

23 24 25 26 27 28

Output File Specifications (Sample)

Blocks to be left blank

29 ... to ... 35

Enter the number of the Auditape field ([0][7] to [1][2]) in the output record into which the stratum number associated with each sample item is to be placed. If the stratum number is not desired, leave these blocks blank.

36 37

200

The sequence number, denoting the relative position of each sample item on the input file, may be obtained in the output record by entering the number of the Auditape field into which it is to be placed ([0][7] to [1][2]). If the sequence number is not desired, leave these blocks blank.

38 39

Blocks to be left blank

40 41 42

Optional Design Specifications

This section is optional and may be used only if DESIGN has been specified (entry of [D] in block 21 of the ES02 card). If these options are not desired, leave blocks 43 thru 62 blank.

Pilot Sample—Sample design is normally based upon stratification and analysis of the entire input file. For very large files, an alternative is to draw a numerical sample as a basis for design.

43 44

If a pilot sample is to be used, enter the sampling interval ([0][2] to [9][9]), and enter the reliability level (enter as a percentage with two integers and two decimals—e.g., enter 95 percent as [9][5][0][0]).

45 46 47 48

Assumed Exponential Distribution—The stratification phase may be bypassed completely if an exponential distribution of the input data (variable X) is assumed.

49

If an assumed exponential distribution of variable X is to be used, enter a [Y].

Estimated Standard Deviation—Where prior values of variable Y are not available for design purposes or an exponential distribution is assumed, the design may be improved by using an approximation to the standard deviation.

50 51 52 53 54 55 56

If the approximate standard deviation is known, enter the approximate standard deviation in whole dollars.

Optional Design Specifications (cont.)

Upper Cutoff—The internally computed upper cutoff will approximate six times the mean value of variable X. The design may be improved for highly skewed distributions, by specifying a higher value for the upper cutoff. For more compact distributions, the value may be lowered. This option *will not be available* if the "Assumed Exponential Distribution" option has been specified (entry of Y in block 49 on the previous page).

If the upper cutoff is to be changed, enter the desired cutoff in whole dollars.

57 58 59 60 61 62

Optional Stratification Specifications

The ES program will determine optimum cutoffs automatically for 21 strata or for a lesser number if so specified. Selection intervals will be determined by optimum allocation. Cutoffs or selection intervals different from those calculated may be specified on ES04 cards. Negative values up to $100 (lower cutoff) will be grouped together with zero values in stratum one and the selection interval for this stratum will be set at the same interval as for stratum two.

If a lesser number (0 3 to 2 0) of strata is desired for a stratified design or if an unstratified (0 1) sample is required, enter the number of strata. Otherwise leave blank.

63 64

202

If cutoff or interval determinations are to be changed by specification on the ES04 cards, enter a $\boxed{Y}$ and complete ES04 cards
as indicated on the following page.

If a different selection interval is desired for stratum one, enter
that interval in whole numbers.

If a different lower cutoff for the negative values is to be used
for stratum one, enter that amount (in whole dollars without
a minus sign).

AUDITAPE ROUTINE SPECIFICATIONS

The following ES04 cards must be used under the following conditions:

a) When *both* the DESIGN and SELECTION routines are specified
   (entry of $\boxed{D}$ in block 21 and $\boxed{S}$ in block 22 of the ES02 card)
   and upper cutoffs and/or selection intervals are to be specified.

b) When *only* the SELECTION routine is specified ($\boxed{}$ in block
   21 and $\boxed{S}$ in block 22 of the ES02 card). Normally these cards
   are punched by a previous DESIGN routine, but they may be
   specified.

From one to four cards are required, depending on the number of
strata required.

203

Auditape Routine Specifications (cont.)

E	S	0	4	1
01	02	03	04	05

E	S	0	4	2
01	02	03	04	05

STRATUM

UPPER CUTOFF
(in whole dollars)

SELECTION INTERVAL
(includes 2 decimals
with implied decimal point)

STRATUM	UPPER CUTOFF (in whole dollars)				SELECTION INTERVAL (includes 2 decimals with implied decimal point)				
1	06 07	08 09	10 11	12 13	14 15	16 17	18	19	20
2	21 22	23 24	25 26	27 28	29 30	31 32	33	34	35
3	36 37	38 39	40 41	42 43	44 45	46 47	48	49	50
4	51 52	53 54	55 56	57 58	59 60	61 62	63	64	65
5	66 67	68 69	70 71	72 73	74 75	76 77	78	79	80
6	06 07	08 09	10 11	12 13	14 15	16 17	18	19	20
7	21 22	23 24	25 26	27 28	29 30	31 32	33	34	35
8	36 37	38 39	40 41	42 43	44 45	46 47	48	49	50
9	51 52	53 54	55 56	57 58	59 60	61 62	63	64	65
10	66 67	68 69	70 71	72 73	74 75	76 77	78	79	80

204

E S 0 4 3
01 02 03 04 05

E S 0 4 4
01 02 03 04 05

11

12

13

14

15

16

17

18

19

20

06 07 08 09 10 11 12 13
21 22 23 24 25 26 27 28
36 37 38 39 40 41 42 43
51 52 53 54 55 56 57 58
66 67 68 69 70 71 72 73

14 15 16 17 18 19 20
29 30 31 32 33 34 35
44 45 46 47 48 49 50
59 60 61 62 63 64 65
74 75 76 77 78 79 80

END OF APPLICATION (ROUTINE) INDICATOR

If this is the last routine or program in this application, enter in blocks 01 and 02
a / / . Otherwise, enter a / * |

01 02

205

ESTIMATION SAMPLE EVALUATION ROUTINE

NOTE – The format for the Estimation Evaluation cards is shown below for reference only, in case changes are to be made. Ordinarily these cards are punched as output from the Estimation Sample Selection routine.

The following rules apply to the completion of these specification sheets:

- Right justify all quantitative entries.
- Leading zeros are not required for quantitative data.
- Leave blocks blank unless otherwise instructed.

AUDITAPE ROUTINE SPECIFICATIONS

Constants

E	E	0	1
01	02	03	04

Constants

E	E	0	2
01	02	03	04

Application Identification

Enter the name of the company, division, etc.

```
05 06 07 08 09 10 11 12 13 14 15 16 17 18 19 20
```

Blocks to be left blank

```
21 22 23 24
```

Input Specifications

Variable X:

Enter a description of the values upon which stratification was based when the sample was selected (variable X).

```
25 26 27 28 29 30 31 32 33 34 35 36
```

Enter the number of the Auditape field that contains variable X (0 7 to 1 2).

```
37 38
```

Variable Y:

Enter a description of the values to be estimated (variable Y).

```
39 40 41 42 43 44 45 46 47 48 49 50
```

Enter the number of the Auditape field that contains

variable Y ($\boxed{0}\boxed{7}$ to $\boxed{1}\boxed{2}$).

51 52

Stratum number:

If an Auditape field was used to contain the stratum number when the sample was selected, enter the number of that field ($\boxed{0}\boxed{7}$ to $\boxed{1}\boxed{2}$). Otherwise, leave these blocks blank.

53 54

Blocks to be left blank

55

60

Type of Estimate to be Made

Indicate the type of estimate to be made by entering one of the following codes:

Combined regression 1
Separate regression 2
Combined ratio 3
Separate ratio 4
Mean 5
Probability proportional to size 6

61

Reliability Level

Enter the reliability level to be used (enter as a percentage with two integers and two decimals—e.g., enter 95 percent as $\boxed{9}\boxed{5}\boxed{0}\boxed{0}$).

62 63 64 65

Blocks to be left blank

66 67

Unusual Differences

Enter $\boxed{N}$ if test for unusual differences is not desired, otherwise leave blank.

68

Constants

```
┌─┬─┬─┬─┐
│E│E│0│3│
└─┴─┴─┴─┘
 01 02 03 04
```

Tentative Design for Next Sample (optional)

Given the sample data and the inherent variability, this procedure determines the sample size necessary to obtain the indicated precision and reliability.

A small sample may be taken as a basis for design in which case interval and cutoff specification cards for use with the selection routine will be punched based upon the tentative design.

This information may also be useful for design purposes when other samples are taken at later dates.

Enter the monetary precision limit in whole dollars.

```
┌─┬─┬─┬─┬─┬─┬─┬─┬─┬─┐
│ │ │ │ │ │ │ │ │ │ │
└─┴─┴─┴─┴─┴─┴─┴─┴─┴─┘
 05 06 07 08 09 10 11 12 13 14
```

Enter the reliability level to be used (enter as a percentage with two integers and two decimals—e.g., enter 95 percent as $\boxed{9}\boxed{5}\boxed{0}\boxed{0}$).

```
┌─┬─┬─┬─┐
│ │ │ │ │
└─┴─┴─┴─┘
 15 16 17 18
```

Interval and cutoff specification cards (ES04) for possible future use with the Estimation Sample Design and Selection Routine will be punched based upon the tentative design. If punched output is not desired, enter an $\boxed{N}$. Otherwise, leave this block blank.

```
┌─┐
│ │
└─┘
 19
```

Blocks to be left blank

□□□□ 20 21 22 23

Stratification Specifications

Enter the number of strata to be evaluated.

□□ 24 25

If a different lower cutoff for the negative values is to be used for stratum one, enter that amount (in whole dollars without a minus sign).

□□□□□□ 26 27 28 29 30 31

Enter □1□ to print standard deviation.

□ 32

Block to be left blank

□ 33

Enter total negative values in dollars and cents (without minus sign and with implied decimal) in bottom stratum of population (required *only* for PPS—Code 6 on EE02 card, block 61) —e.g., enter −$350.75 as □□□□□□□□□ 3 5 0 7 5 .

34 35 36 37 38 39 40 41 42 43 44 45

Stratification Specification Cards

(From 1 to 11 cards may be required, with two strata per card.)

Constants   `E E 0 4`   01 02 03 04

Card number (`0 1` to `1 1`)   0506

Blocks to be left blank   07 08

First Stratum On Card

Number of Population items in stratum.   09 10 11 12 13 14 15 16

Number of Sample items in stratum.   17 18 19 20 21

Upper cutoff of stratum (in whole dollars).   22 23 24 25 26 27 28 29 30 31

Variable X Population amount in stratum (in whole dollars).   32 33 34 35 36 37 38 39 40 41 42 43 44

Second Stratum On Card

Number of Population items in stratum.   45 46 47 48 49 50 51 52

Number of Sample items in stratum.   53 54 55 56 57

Upper cutoff of stratum (in whole dollars).

Variable X Population amount in stratum (in whole dollars).

Punched Card Input File

If the input file is on tape or disk, cross out the three following lines of blocks.

Otherwise:

Use the following three lines of blocks.

Constants

Insert the data cards at this point. Make certain that an Auditape Record Specification Sheet is completed to define this field usage and the corresponding card included with the Auditape Routine Specification cards as indicated on page 1 of this routine.

Constant, following last data card.

END OF APPLICATION OR ROUTINE INDICATOR

If this is the last routine in this application, enter $///$. Otherwise, enter $/\cdot$.

58 59 60 61 62 63 64 65 66 67

68 69 70 71 72 73 74 75 76 77 78 79 80

/	·
01	02

/	/	S	T	E	P	A	U	D	·	C	A	R	D			D	D	·	
01	02	03	04	05	06	07	08	09	10	11	12	13	14	15	16	17	18	19	20

L	A	S	T		C	A	R	D
01	02	03	04	05	06	07	08	09

01	02

211

DEFINITIONS

ACCOUNTING TERMINOLOGY

Application Control   An accounting control relating to a specific data processing routine. The control may be over input, processing, or output and is designed to ensure that recording, calculating, summarizing, and reporting are performed properly.

Book Record   The accounting books of record such as cash books, sales journals, and the general ledger are rarely found these days but have been replaced by loose-leaf ledgers, punched card files, magnetic tape, and computer printouts. The name still persists in referring to any quantity or value to be found in the company records as a unit or aggregate. Associated terms are "book quantity" and "book value," which often are used to distinguish them from actual quantity or actual value.

Breakage   Items may be purchased and placed in inventory at a price per dozen and priced out of inventory in twos or threes at a price not exactly divisible into the price per dozen. The amount over or short is known as "breakage." As an example, if a part costs $7.60 per dozen and is priced out at 64¢ a unit, there would be a negative balance of 8¢ for each dozen parts sold.

Conservatism   Managers, investors, and accountants prefer any errors in measurement to be such as to understate rather than overstate net income and net assets. This has led to the modifying convention of conservatism, which is expressed in rules adopted by the accounting profession such as the rule for pricing inventory at the lower of cost or market, that may result in stating net income and net assets at lower amounts than would otherwise be the case.[1]

---

[1] Basic Concepts and Accounting Principles Underlying Financial Statements of Business Enterprises, Statement of the Accounting Principles Board No. 4, American Institute of Certified Public Accountants, October 1970, Paragraph 171.

Count Date   A count date is established as a basis for reconciling the physical counts and values to the books of record. If an inventory count date is November 30, the accounting records will be cut off at the close of business on November 30 although the actual recording of these closing transactions may not be completed until December 5. The actual counting might take place before any movement of goods in or out of the warehouse on the first business day following November 30, which could be December 3.

Cutoff   Accounting transactions do not always enter the accounting records in chronological sequence because of delays in transit and remote locations. When a reconciliation is required, or at the end of an accounting period, an effort will be made to cut off the transactions properly so that all existing transactions are included and all transactions subsequent to the cutoff date are excluded.

Cyclical Count   The problem of counting and reconciling hundreds of thousands of different parts can take more time than can be made available without disrupting production too much. This has led to counting smaller quantities more often on a regular cyclical basis, such as once a week, and reconciling each count as it is made. The more valuable or more critical parts may be counted more times a year than the less sensitive items.

Estimates   Financial statements are prepared at the end of periods of continuous enterprise activities but most commonly at the end of a yearly period. The accounting measurements that involve allocations among relatively short periods of time and among complex and joint activities often preclude definitive measurement; therefore, estimates which involve a substantial area of informed judgment are necessary.[2] In past and present practice, these estimates are unlikely to be statistical estimates.

Hash Total   A summarization of one or more fields of a file, that would not usually be added, to provide a check on processing of input documents.

Internal Control   Comprises the plan of organization and all the coordinate methods and measures adopted within a business to safeguard its assets, and check the accuracy and reliability of the data produced by the financial accounting system.

Locator Record   A stock room, warehouse, or any other place where inventoriable items are stored requires some kind of locator record to which the generic name bin record is often applied. This record may contain quantities and/or locations together with an identification number and

[2] Ibid., Paragraph 123–124.

description. It may be a loose-leaf file, a bound book, a computer record, or a card attached to each bin or storage location.

Master File   A file of customers, vendors, or other more or less permanent list that provides authoritative information when required. Entry into such files is usually controlled.

Obsolescence   Parts and supplies may be stocked, in anticipation of future demand, at a higher level than actually necessary so that the parts are no longer usable and thus become obsolete. This obsolescence may occur because the part is replaced by a more efficient or less costly part or because the machinery and equipment of which it is a part is retired from use. These costs, which may have been recorded as assets in a prior period, are now associated with the current accounting period as expenses because they have no discernible future benefit.[3]

Perpetual Record   An accounting record that maintains, in detail by part or other identification, an ongoing record of quantities received and shipped is called a perpetual inventory record. Perpetual records may be maintained for other assets such as tools and dies, or property and equipment. These records may also be maintained at purchase cost or standard cost so that the entire record may be reconciled to the general ledger control total.

Physical Inventory   In the process of taking an annual physical count and pricing and extending the actual value of the physical inventory, a record is prepared that is often referred to as the physical inventory. This record is usually on accounting worksheets but, in recent years, often appears on computer tape. A perpetual record would most probably also be priced and extended and incorporated in the same tape so that detailed comparisons by part number of differences between actual and book would be available.

Posting   In manual records, transactions are recorded in journals or daybooks and transferred or posted to the subsidiary ledgers or the general ledger. These postings are usually in summary form by day, week, or month. The term continues in use with computer records and mostly in connection with summary transactions, although the ledgers may not exist except as computer printouts.

Principle   Generally accepted accounting principles is a technical term that encompasses the conventions, rules, and procedures necessary to define accepted accounting practice at a particular time. It includes not only broad guidelines of general application, but also detailed practices and procedures.[4] These accounting principles are "generally accepted" to

[3] Ibid., Paragraph 160.
[4] Ibid., Paragraph 138.

the extent that they have substantial authoritative support or are promulgated by authoritative bodies.

Purchase Investigation   A company, when considering the acquisition of another company, would usually conduct a purchase investigation. This may be carried out by a team of lawyers, marketing specialists, engineers and accountants or it may be limited to a review of financial statements and other important matters which is often called a businessman's review.

Selection Date   Since several days or weeks may be needed to arrive at an accounting cutoff, it may well be necessary to use an earlier accounting record for selecting a sample in order to be ready for the actual count. If this earlier record was at the close of business on November 15, this would be the selection date. The record might not be available and the selection might not be made until a later date such as November 25.

COMPUTER TERMINOLOGY

Block   A block of records is more or less the analogical equivalent of a box of cards. It is a grouping of records that is read in or out of the electronic computer memory at one time. The computer separates the block into records, so that it operates on one record at a time, and then groups the records back into a block at output time. The purpose of blocking is to more nearly match the slower speeds of the peripheral units such as tape or disk drives with the lightning fast speeds of the computer.

Buffer   While the computer is working on one block of data, another block is moved from a peripheral unit into an input storage area, or buffer, to be held until required by the central processing unit. Similarly, the computer moves data that have been processed to an output buffer for subsequent transmission to the slower speed units such as tape drives, printers, and card-punches. It functions as a variable-speed connection between the computer and the peripheral units.

Central Processing Unit   The principal part, or mainframe, of the computer that contains the counters, storage areas, and main memory required to execute the programmed instructions and process the data in millionths of seconds. The peripheral units such as tape drives, disk drives, additional memory units, and printers operate at relatively much slower speeds under command of the central processing unit.

Character   Letters of the alphabet, numerals, and other common symbols such as $, %, &, etc. are called characters. These characters may be represented in a number of different ways; as a punch or double-punch in a card column, as a magnetic representation on a magnetic tape or disk, and in numerous binary-based codes within the computer. Groups of characters within a numeric field may comprise whole numbers or decimal numbers and may be represented by various notations.

Code As characters move from original documents to the computer and back to the printed report, they are represented at different stages in the process by various codes. Most of these coded character representations are invisible except by means of computer memory dumps which may be read only with considerable difficulty.

Conversion The process of changing from one form of representation to another, such as from decimal to binary.

Counter In much the same way as an adding machine accumulates numbers, a section of computer memory may be used as a counter, or register, to summarize specified values. The addition is performed in a register by transferring the previous balance from memory, adding the specific value, and returning the new balance to memory. The number of different counters that may be used at one time is, for all practical purposes, unlimited.

Data In computer processing, the term data is usually used to differentiate transaction input from program instructions, program specifications or control lists. Many general-purpose programs may require specifications to be introduced as input data ahead of, or interspersed with, the transaction data.

Disk Random-access disks have supplanted tape files in many operations, such as large inventories, where it is easier to process transactions out of sequence. Programs and data may be stored on the same disk so that the time required to mount tapes on tape drives may also be eliminated.

Edit A programmed routine that checks input data for errors or omissions prior to further processing.

Floating-Point Computer calculations are usually made using exponential notation or floating-point arithmetic. In the computer, a floating-point number is represented in two parts by the significant digits and by a separate signed integer value representing the number of places to the right or left of the decimal. This form of representation increases the precision of the arithmetic. Such a value is usually printed by converting the exponential notation to decimal format and rounding the number to the positions specified after the decimal, such as dollars and cents.

General Purpose System This is a collection of computer programs organized into a system so that they may be adapted to provide a solution to specific problems. Such a system avoids the time and effort necessary to develop programs specifically for occasional usage, but at some loss of computer efficiency. The principal advantage of a general purpose system is that results are obtained quickly and do not require a specialized knowledge of computer programming. It serves somewhat the same purpose as does a programming language.

Hardware Physical data processing equipment.

Input At some point in time, the necessary programs, control statements, and transaction data must be coded and converted to a medium that will provide input to the computer. Punched cards are commonly used for the initial recording of transactions and programs. Time-sharing terminals provide a method of manual input for subsequent input to the computer. Programs and data may be stored on magnetic tape sequentially and on magnetic disks randomly for reentry as input to the computer at a later time or date. Manual input directly to the computer is feasible but not usually practicable.

Integer In computer programming, the term integer implies more than a whole number. It also describes format, storage, and mathematical method. Integers are usually stored in some form of binary notation and binary mathematics is used for calculations involving integers. Integers can be converted to floating-point numbers to use exponential notation and mathematics. Literal constants made up of alphanumeric characters are also stored as integers in most computers and thus can be manipulated through mathematical operations.

Language The earliest computer programs were written in a machine language that could be used directly by the computer. This placed a barrier between those who knew what they wanted done and those who could get the computer to do it. This barrier has been removed partially through the development of various higher level languages. An assembly-language is a shorthand substitute for a machine language code into which it will be translated directly by compiler. The assembly-language may include macro instructions which translate into groups of instructions for a specific purpose such as reading an input tape. The FORTRAN language permits a complicated mathematical formula to be converted into sets of macro instructions and compiled into machine code which provides a close link between the user and the machine. The COBOL language is a business-oriented language that permits business types of instructions to be set up in macro terms, such as read and write, and compiled into machine language.

Macro A symbolic instruction equivalent to a number of machine language instructions that can be called upon by the programmer.

Memory   One of the characteristics of an electronic computer that sets it apart from all other types of machine processing is its ability to retain instructions and data in readily accessible memory. This permits the executive of programmed instructions at rates measured in millionth parts of seconds. High-speed memories are usually of the magnetic core type, and larger computers have considerable amounts of core storage that increase their processing capability. Memory can become virtually unlimited by use of peripheral units such as tapes, disks, drums and auxiliary core storage to feed instructions and data to the computer as required.

Output   The information that is developed within the computer as a result of processing with a specified program is generically described as output. This output may be in printed form, such as reports, in which case the data are not available for further processing. The output may be transferred to magnetic tapes or disk files so that it can be recaptured or reprocessed later as in the case of master files or inventory records. The output may be punched into cards for visual reference or other handling and may be transferred to a terminal such as those at airport ticket counters for ready reference or answering customers' questions.

Peripheral Unit   Units such as tape drives, disk drives, magnetic drums, printers, and auxiliary magnetic core storage that are accessed and controlled by the central processing unit. They are subsidiary to and act on the periphery of the mainframe of the computer at considerably slower relative speeds.

Program   A series of machine language instructions that will accomplish a specific procedure is called a computer program. The program may be written in a high-level language such as FORTRAN or COBOL but it must be translated into a machine language program that will be understood by the computer. Most programs accomplish several specific procedures, and some are sufficiently general to accomplish numerous procedures.

Record   In accounting usage, a record is usually a master file, a balance, or a transaction affecting either of these. It is the smallest unit on which a computer operates and there must be a defined record format for program usage. A record is somewhat akin to an 80-column punched card and most programs use a record length of 80 for that reason. Records may be fixed in length or variable up to the specified capacity of the computer. The record format is vital to an understanding of the computer process.

Software   The programs, compilers, library and supervisory routines, and associated documentation prepared by the manufacturer, user, or third parties.

Subroutine Particular procedures that are required over and over again may be programmed as subroutines. This requires only one program that may be entered with specific arguments and that returns specific results to the main program. Subroutines are used to obtain mathematical functions such as natural logarithms, sines, cosines, tangents, and square roots. Subroutines may also be used in place of tables of probability distributions and to determine random numbers, as well as for commonly used procedures such as reading from or writing to a tape or disk file.

Tape Computers became effective in business with the advent of magnetic tape for input/output purposes, including both programs and data. The high speeds at which tapes could be read or written upon, relative to the speeds at which cards could be read or punched, more closely matched the computer processing speeds. Tape files were readily adaptable to many accounting records, such as payroll or accounts receivable, in which the input and updating can be done sequentially.

STATISTICAL TERMINOLOGY

Allocation When a population that is to be sampled is stratified, by dollar value or otherwise, a decision has to be made as to how to allocate the total sample to the various strata. This allocation of the sample size may be proportional to the number in each stratum, it may be arbitrary, or it may be based on the weighted standard deviation in each stratum. The last method, known as the optimum or Neyman method of allocation, is designed to minimize the variance for a given sample size.

Coefficient of Variation This is the standard deviation of a distribution divided by the mean of the distribution. It provides a useful manner of comparing the variability of two or more distributions.

Distribution Any given finite population may be analyzed by number and specified class into a frequency distribution. This may be expressed graphically or mathematically in the form of a frequency function. If the total frequency is taken as unity, the frequency function represents the proportion of the total population falling into a given class of x. If we equate probability with frequency, the frequency function is referred to as a probability distribution. In an infinite or continuous population, the function is referred to as a probability density function, and if the probabilities are cumulative, as a cumulative probability distribution.

Efficiency One estimator would be considered more efficient than another possible estimator if it would produce a smaller variance. Thus efficiency is a way of measuring the relative merits of several possible estimators.

Estimators   If we know or may safely assume the shape of the distribution of a given population, we may describe it adequately by certain parameters such as the mean and standard deviation. These values may be derived from the population or developed as a statistic from a sample. If we estimate these statistics from a sample, the statistics become the estimators from which we may estimate the parameters of the population.

Evaluation   After a sample has been taken, the process of evaluation begins. The actual values for the sample items are processed to obtain estimators such as the mean and standard deviation. Other useful estimators would be the mean of the sample book values and the mean of the book population. Some or all of these would be used in the estimating equation to obtain the population estimate.

Exponential Distribution   Most accounting populations, such as a parts inventory, tend to have a large number of small value items with the numbers decreasing as the value increases. A frequency distribution of such a population would approximate an exponential distribution whose properties are well known and extensively tabulated. The mean and standard deviation of the standard exponential distribution are equal so that any exponential population may be described adequately if the average value is known.

Feature of Interest   When sampling, it is important to keep in mind what the sample is expected to produce. In the sciences and social sciences, the sampling feature of interest is often a specific value. In most accounting applications, however, the feature of interest is a relationship between the actual value and the book value. Sampling for a relationship improves the efficiency of the estimating procedure considerably.

Mean   The arithmetic mean, or average value, is primarily used in estimation sampling as a measure of location or location parameter. As this statistic is readily estimated from a sample, or a series of samples, it provides the basis for developing a distribution of sample means. The expected mean value of this distribution of sample means would be the true population mean, and from this distribution we may infer, at a given level of probability, that the population estimate is within a determined range of precision.

Moment   Using the term in the same way that it is used in physics, the various moments provide a mathematical description of the distribution. The first moment, measured from zero origin, is the mean. The second moment about, or measured from, the mean is the variance. The third moment about the mean which measures the degree of skew in the distribution is sometimes helpful to an understanding of the shape of a distribution.

Normal Distribution A continuous frequency distribution that is well tabulated and more popularly known as a bell curve because of its shape. This distribution is important in estimation sampling because it may be shown that a distribution of sample means from any population, regardless of the shape of its own distribution, will tend to a normal distribution. This allows statistical inference as to the range of the population mean to be based on normal distribution theory.

Parameter A type of distribution, such as the normal distribution, has certain values that define the distribution. These values, called parameters, are usually unknown and may vary over a wide scale. They are constants, however, for a specific population and, in the case of the normal distribution, the mean and the standard deviation are the essential parameters. The mean value is a location parameter and the standard deviation is a scale parameter. Greek letters are commonly used as symbols for population parameters.

Population In statistical usage, the terms universe and population are synonymous, with the latter being the more current usage. The population could consist of people, farms, customers, parts, or anything else that we wish to study. In an accounting context, it is usually the collection of units from which we want to sample and estimate the value of the population or other characteristics.

Precision In making statistical estimates of accounting data, the user will want to be assured that he can rely on the answers with a reasonable margin of error. The measure of this range of error is the precision surrounding the estimate, at a given level of reliability. Precision and reliability are statistically inseparable in that neither should be quoted without the other. All else being equal, the precision of a particular estimator will normally vary inversely with the square root of sample size. For this reason, larger samples do not produce proportionately better precision.

Probability The cornerstone of statistical sampling is the theory of probability. The sample must be drawn in such a way that the probability of selecting any sample unit is either equal to that of selecting any other sample unit or is otherwise determinable. A probability sample, often termed a random sample, is drawn at random so that it will conform to the laws of probability. Probability theory enables us to obtain a measure of the precision of an estimate at a specified reliability level.

Regression One of the earlier social scientists, Sir Francis Galton, made an historic analysis of the heights of fathers and sons. He determined that, to the extent that the father deviated from the average height of fathers, the son would deviate from the average height of sons to a lesser degree and thus tend to return or regress to the average. Thus the term regression has come to be associated with the statistical method used to investigate relationships. A regression line is obtained by the least squares method and is the mathematical equivalent of a graph containing numerous paired (x, y) points through which a line is fitted.

Reliability   When we take a probability sample and arrive at an estimate of a population parameter, the theory of probability enables us to express the degree of confidence that the estimate is within a certain range of the result that would be obtained from equal complete coverage, or full coverage using methods equal to those used for the sample. This degree of confidence is expressed as a reliability level or percentage so that a 95 percent reliability level indicates that the unknown population total should fall within the evaluated range of precision, of say, plus or minus $10,000, in 19 out of 20 samples. If we increase the reliability to 99.7 percent—this is known as statistical certainty—we widen the range by one-half to plus or minus $15,000 for the same sample size. Reliability and precision are related so that a change in one will change the other and neither should be quoted separately.

Risk   As the term is used generally in statistical sampling, statistical risk is the chance that the user takes of being wrong in the inference made from a sample. The risk is the complement of the reliability level, so that a reliability level of 95 percent implies a five percent risk.

Sampling Interval   A term used in systematic selection to describe the interval between sample items in the population sequence. It is approximately equal to the expansion factor which is the number of items in the population divided by the number of items in the sample.

Selection   The procedure for the selection of a sample requires certain rules such as assigning numbers to the sampling units, and the actual process of selection generally using random numbers. The nature of accounting data lends itself readily to systematic selection with one or more random starts. One process begins with selection based on a random start in the first interval of each stratum and, if the sampling interval is 24, would select every twenty-fourth item thereafter.

Standard Deviation   The principal unit in use to measure dispersion in a frequency distribution is the standard deviation. If we added the deviations of all values from the mean, the sum would be zero, providing no significant statistical information. It has thus become customary to square the deviations of all values from the mean, add them, and obtain the average. This summation is known as the variance and the square root of this value is the standard deviation. The standard deviation is sometimes divided, for comparative purposes, by the mean, and the resulting value is referred to as the coefficient of variation.

Standard Error   The standard deviation of a sampling distribution that is used to measure the precision of an estimate. It is based on the divergences between the observed values and the expected value which we tend to regard as the true value.

Statistic   In a specialized sense, any quantity that can be determined from the sample values is called a statistic. These statistics, such as the mean and standard deviation of the sample, are used as estimators of the corresponding population parameters.

Stratification   Any given set of data is likely to have certain characteristics by which the data may be classified. Data might be classified geographically, by states, or by urban/rural location. Similarly, data might be classified by age group or income level. Likewise, parts might be classified as purchased parts, manufactured parts, engine parts, or small parts. The process of classifying the data into such separate groups, or strata, is called stratification. The primary purpose of stratification is to make use of existing information to improve the estimating procedure and reduce the variance. Each stratum is sampled separately and combined to form an overall estimate. A useful characteristic for stratification of accounting populations is the monetary value.

Sufficient   In a statistical sense, an estimator is classed as sufficient when it makes use of all the information that can be obtained from the sample. As applied to accounting estimates, we usually have information about book values that may be used to improve estimates of actual or physical values. In this context, mean estimates of actual values would not make use of book value in the estimating process and therefore would not be considered as sufficient estimates.

Unbiased   For any given estimator that may be obtained from a sample, there is the possibility of mathematical bias. If we were to sample over and over again, for the same estimator, such as the sample mean—and these sample means, on the average, equal the population mean—the sampling procedure would be unbiased.

Variance   The second moment about the mean is of considerable importance in statistics and is called the variance. Moments about the mean portray mathematically the shape of a frequency distribution. The variance is the principal indicator of the variability of the underlying data.

FORMULAS, CONSTANTS, AND RELATIONSHIPS

Formulas

2.1 Regression equation

$$\bar{y} = a + b\bar{x}$$

2.2 Mean estimate

$$\hat{Y} = \frac{N}{n}\, y \qquad \text{or} \qquad \hat{Y} = N\bar{y}$$

2.3 Mean estimate of differences

$$\hat{Y} = X + \frac{N}{n}\,(y - x)$$

2.4 Mean estimate with probabilities proportional to size

$$\hat{Y} = \frac{N}{n}\sum_{i=1}^{n}\left[\, y_i \cdot \frac{\mu(X)}{x_i}\,\right]$$

2.5 Ratio estimate

$$\hat{Y} = \frac{\bar{y}}{\bar{x}}\, X$$

2.6 Regression estimate

$$\hat{Y} = \frac{N}{n}\, y + Nb\, [\mu(X) - \bar{x}]$$

2.7 Difference in means

$$\mu(Y) - \bar{y} = b[\mu(X) - \bar{x}]$$

2.8 Finite population correction

$$\frac{N - n}{N - 1}$$

3.1 Exponential function

$$e^{-x} \qquad \text{where } e = 2.71828$$

3.2 Determination of cutoff

$$X = -\mathrm{Ln}\,(\%) \cdot \bar{x} \cdot 2$$

4.1 Preliminary sample size

$$n_0 = \left(\frac{NtS}{P}\right)^2$$

4.2 Final sample size

$$n = \frac{n_0}{1 + [(n_0 - 1)/N]}$$

6.1 Rearrangement of (2.6) and (2.7) for ease of computation of estimate

$$\mu(\hat{Y}) = \bar{y} + b[\mu(X) - \bar{x}]$$

6.2 Determination of slope of regression line

$$b = \frac{\Sigma\, xy}{\Sigma\, x^2}$$

6.3 Finite population correction

$$\frac{N - n}{N - 1}$$

6.4 Variance of a mean estimate

$$V(\hat{Y}) = \sum_{i=1}^{n} (y_i - \bar{y})^2$$

6.5 Rearrangement of (6.4) for ease of computation

$$V(\hat{Y}) = \sum y^2 = \sum_{i=1}^{n} y_i^2 - n\bar{y}^2$$

6.6 Variance of ratio estimate

$$V(\hat{Y}_R) = \sum (y_i - Rx_i)^2$$

6.7 Rearrangement of (6.6) for ease of computation

$$V(\hat{Y}_R) = \sum_{i=1}^{n} y_i^2 - 2R\sum_{i=1}^{n} x_i y_i + R^2 \sum x_i^2$$

6.8 Formula 6.7 using corrected values

$$V(\hat{Y}_R) = \sum y^2 - 2R \sum xy + R^2 \sum x^2$$

6.9 Formula to correct variance of ratio estimate for understatement

$$1 + \frac{5}{n}$$

6.10 Variance of a regression estimate

$$V(\hat{Y}_{reg}) = \sum_{i=1}^{n} (y_i - \hat{y}_i)^2$$

6.11 Rearrangement of (6.10) and use of corrected values for ease of computation

$$V(\hat{Y}_{reg}) = \sum y^2 - b \sum xy$$

11.1   Cutoff determination

$$[Ln\ 20 - Ln(n)] \cdot 2\ \mu(X)$$

Constants

Calculation of value for exponential function

$$e = \lim_{n \to \infty} \left(1 + \frac{1}{n}\right)^n = 2.71828$$

$$e^1 = 1 + \frac{1}{1!} + \frac{1}{2!} + \frac{1}{3!} + \frac{1}{4!} + \frac{1}{5!} + \frac{1}{6!} + \frac{1}{7!} + \frac{1}{8!} + \frac{1}{9!} \ldots$$

$$= 1 + 1 + 0.5 + 0.16667 + 0.04167 + 0.00833$$
$$+ 0.00139 + 0.00020 + 0.00002 \ldots$$

$$= 2.71828$$

$$e^{-1} = 1 - 1 + 0.5 - 0.16667 + 0.04167 - 0.00833$$
$$+ 0.00139 + 0.00020 + 0.00002 \ldots$$

$$e^{-1} = \frac{1}{e} = \frac{1}{2.71828} = 0.36787$$

$$e^0 = 1$$

Relationships

A.   Regression estimate (2.6) to mean estimate (2.2)

$$\hat{Y} = \frac{N}{n}\ y + Nb\ [\mu(X) - \bar{x}] \tag{2.6}$$

If we disregard the difference in means (2.7) and set $b = 0$ then

$$\hat{Y} = \frac{N}{n}\ y \tag{2.2}$$

B.   Regression estimate (2.6) to ratio estimate (2.5)

$$\hat{Y} = \frac{N}{n}\ y + Nb\ [\mu(X) - \bar{x}] \tag{2.6}$$

If we disregard the constant in the regression equation (2.1), force the line through the origin by setting $b = \dfrac{\bar{y}}{\bar{x}}$, and simplify, then

$$\hat{Y} = \frac{N}{n} y + N \frac{\bar{y}}{\bar{x}} [\mu(X) - \bar{x}]$$

$$\hat{Y} = \frac{N}{n} y + \frac{\bar{y}}{\bar{x}} X - N\bar{y}$$

$$\hat{Y} = \frac{\bar{y}}{\bar{x}} X \qquad\qquad (2.5)$$

C. Regression estimate (2.6) to mean estimate of differences (2.3)

$$\hat{Y} = \frac{N}{n} y + Nb \, [\mu(X) - \bar{x}] \qquad\qquad (2.6)$$

If we disregard both constant and slope in the regression equation (2.1) and set $b = 1$ then

$$\hat{Y} = \frac{N}{n} y + X - x \frac{N}{n}$$

$$\hat{Y} = X + \frac{N}{n} (y - x) \qquad\qquad (2.3)$$

D. Ratio estimate (2.5) to mean estimate of differences (2.3)

$$\hat{Y} = \frac{\bar{y}}{\bar{x}} X \qquad\qquad (2.5)$$

A basic assumption of a mean estimate is that the sample and population means are the same. If we substitute Nx for X then

$$\hat{Y} = \frac{N}{n} y$$

$$\hat{Y} = \frac{N}{n} y + X - x \frac{N}{n}$$

$$\hat{Y} = X + \frac{N}{n} (y - x) \qquad\qquad (2.3)$$

E. Ratio estimate (2.5) to mean estimate with probabilities proportional to size (2.4)

$$\hat{Y} = \frac{N}{n} \sum_{i=1}^{n} \left[y_i \cdot \frac{\mu(X)}{x_i} \right] \qquad (2.4)$$

$$\hat{Y} = \frac{1}{n} \sum_{i=1}^{n} \left(\frac{y_i}{x_i} \right) \cdot X$$

If the ratio is computed after the individual items are summed rather than before, then

$$\hat{Y} = \frac{\sum y_i}{\sum x_i} \cdot X$$

$$\hat{Y} = \frac{\bar{y}}{\bar{x}} X \qquad (2.5)$$

PROGRAM SEGMENTS AND SUBROUTINES

```
C
C       DESIGNS STRATUM CUT-OFFS BASED ON STRATIFIED POPULATION
C
        CF = 0.
        DDF = 0.
        FNUM= NUM
        MST= NST - 1
        FST = MST
C          CF          (STRATUM NUMBER - 1) / (NUMBER OF STRATA - 1)
C          FNUM        NUMBER OF ITEMS IN POPULATION
C          MST         NUMBER OF STRATA MINUS ONE
C          FST         NUMBER OF STRATA - 1
        FM = XPOP / FNUM * 2.
C          FM          TWICE AN AVERAGE ITEM
C          XPOP        ACTUAL OR APPROXIMATE X POPULATION TOTAL
        IF (UCUT.GT.0.) FM = UCUT / DLOG(FST)
C          UCUT        SPECIFIED UPPER CUT-OFF
        ACF = 1./FST
        IF(NK.NE.2) GO TO 60
        PNS(NST) = 1.00
C          ACF         RECIPROCAL OF (NUMBER OF STRATA - 1)
C          NK          SELECTION BASIS  1=CONCURRENT, 2=PREVIOUS DESIGN
C          PNS         SAMPLE INTERVAL FOR EACH STRATUM
C          NST         NUMBER OF STRATA REQUIRED
        RETURN
     60 CONTINUE
        DO 40 I= 2,MST
        J = I-1
        CF = CF + ACF
        S(I) = ( DLOG(1.-CF))    * FM
        KSI = -S(I)
C          KSI         VARIABLE FOR TRUNCATING STRATUM CUT-OFF
        S(I) = KSI
     40 CONTINUE
```

Exhibit 1   Stratum Cutoffs.

```
C
C        FACTORS FOR ASSUMED EXPONENTIAL DISTRIBUTION
C
         IF(NB.NE.3) GO TO 40
         DO 40 I = 2,MST
         J = I - 1
         STDEV(I) = .2887 * (S(I)- S(J))
         SNS = SNS + (FX * STDEV(I))
         XA = (S(I) * 2.) / FM
C            SNS        SUM OF WEIGHTED FACTORS FOR ALLOCATION
C            FX         NUMBER OF ITEMS IN STRATUM (EXPONENTIAL POP. DIST.)
C            XA         STRATUM UPPER CUT-OFF / EST. STD. DEVIATION
C            S          UPPER CUT-OFF OF EACH STRATUM
C
         EX = .36787 ** XA
C
C            EX         FRACTION OF POPULATION IN THIS OR LOWER STRATA
C
         CX = (1.0 - EX) * FNUM
C
C            CX         EXPONENTIAL FREQUENCY DISTRIBUTION
C            FNUM       NUMBER OF ITEMS IN POPULATION
C
         FX = CX - TFX
C
C            TFX        EXPONENTIAL POPULATION SIZE, THROUGH PRIOR STRATUM
C
         NS(I) = FX
C
C            NS         NUMBER OF ITEMS IN EACH STRATUM OF POPULATION
C
         NNS = NNS + NS(I)
C
C            NNS        NUMBER OF ITEMS IN POPULATION - COUNTER
C
         TFX = TFX + FX
         FJ = 1.0 + XA
         CDF = (1.0 - (EX * FJ)) * XPOP
C
C            CDF        CUMULATIVE EXPONENTIAL DISTRIBUTION
C            XPOP       ACTUAL OR APPROXIMATE POPULATION TOTAL AMOUNT FOR X
C
         TX = CDF - DDF
C
C            TX         POPULATION AMOUNT IN CURRENT STRATUM
C            DDF        EXPON. POPULATION AMOUNT THROUGH PRIOR STRATUM
C
         SX(I) = TX
C
C            SX         SUM OF X VARIABLE BY STRATUM
C
         DDF = CDF
         TTX = TTX + TX
C
C            TTX        EXPONENTIAL POPULATION AMOUNT THROUGH PRIOR STRATUM
C
      40 CONTINUE
```

Exhibit 2   Assumed Exponential Distribution.

```
C
C       THE   FOLLOWING STATEMENTS ISOLATE ANY UNUSUAL DIFFERENCES
C               WHICH WOULD DISTORT THE VARIANCE IN DESIGN STAGE.
        NUD = 0
C
C           NUD         NUMBER OF UNUSUAL DIFFERENCES
C
        SMST = S(MST)
        X4 = 4. * X
        IF (Y.GT.SMST.AND.Y.GT.X4) GO TO 127
C
C           SMST        UPPER CUT-OFF OF STRATUM MST
C           X           INDEPENDENT DATA VARIABLE
C           Y           DEPENDENT VARIABLE BEING ESTIMATED
C           MST         NUMBER OF STRATA MINUS ONE
C
  127 CONTINUE
        NUD = NUD + 1
C           NUD         NUMBER OF UNUSUAL DIFFERENCES
C
  128 CONTINUE
        IX = NST
C
C           IX          STRATUM NUMBER DURING SAMPLE STRATIFICATION
C           NST         NUMBER OF STRATA REQUIRED


*   *   *   *   *   *   *   *   *   *   *   *   *   *   *   *   *   *   *   *   *   *   *   *   *   *   *   *   *   *


C
C       THE   FOLLOWING STATEMENTS ISOLATE ANY UNUSUAL DIFFERENCES
C               WHICH WOULD DISTORT THE VARIANCE IN EVALUATION.
C
        NERR = 0
  126 CONTINUE
        IF (NTUD.EQ.1) GO TO 125
C
C           NTUD        NO TEST FOR UNUSUAL DIFFERENCES IF SET TO ONE
C
C* * * THE FOLLOWING TEST FOR UNUSUAL DIFFERENCES IDENTIFIES THOSE ITEMS
C               IN STRATA 2 TO MST HAVING X AND Y VALUES WHICH DIFFER BY MORE
C               THAN 250 AND BY MORE THAN A 4-1 RATIO.
C
        DXY = DABS(X-Y)
        RXY = DXY / X
        IF (DXY.GT.250.AND.RXY.GT.3.) NERR = NERR + 1
C
C           NERR        NUMBER OF SUBSTANTIAL DIFFERENCES BETWEEN X AND Y
C
  125 CONTINUE
C
        IF (NERR.GT.0) WRITE (M3,53) NERR
   53 FORMAT (//29HOTEST FOR UNUSUAL DIFFERENCES /1H0,3X,25HTHE SAMPLE F
   1ILE CONTAINS ,I4,31H ITEMS WITH UNUSUAL DIFFERENCES /4X,31HTHAT MA
   2Y REQUIRE INVESTIGATION.  )
C
```

Exhibit 3   Unusual Differences.

```
C
C
C          STRATIFICATION OF POPULATION FOR DESIGN
C
  102 CONTINUE
      READ (7,28,END=150) NDES,FA
   28 FORMAT(11A4,6F12.1)
      X = FA(NV1)
C
C          X              INDEPENDENT DATA VARIABLE
C          NV1            AUDITAPE FIELD FOR INDEPENDENT (X) VARIABLE
C
      IF (NV2.NE.0) Y = FA(NV2)
C
C          Y              DEPENDENT VARIABLE BEING ESTIMATED
C          NV2            AUDITAPE FIELD FOR DEPENDENT (Y) VARIABLE
C
      IF(NMN.EQ.3) Y = X
C
C          NMN            ESTIMATE TYPE   1=REGRESSION, 2=RATIO, 3=MEAN
C
      IF(NST.EQ.1) GO TO 128
C
C          NST            NUMBER OF STRATA REQUIRED
      IF(X.LE.XLN) GO TO 128
C
C          XLN            LIMIT BELOW WHICH ALL MINUS VALUES WILL BE SELECTED
C
      IF(X.LE.0.)GO TO 115
      DO 120 K=2,MST
C
C          MST            NUMBER OF STRATA MINUS ONE
C
      IF(X.LE.S(K)) GO TO 122
C
C          S              UPPER CUT-OFF OF EACH STRATUM
C
  120 CONTINUE
      GO TO 128
  122 CONTINUE
      IX = K
C
C          IX             STRATUM NUMBER DURING SAMPLE STRATIFICATION
C
      GO TO 125
  115 CONTINUE
      IX=1
      GO TO 125
  128 CONTINUE
      IX = NST
  125 CONTINUE
      GO TO 102
  150 CONTINUE
```

Exhibit 4   Stratification.

```
C
C        DEVELOPMENT OF SUMS AND SUMS OF SQUARES AND CROSS-PRODUCTS
C
     NS(IX) = (NS(IX)+1)
C
C        NS          NUMBER OF ITEMS IN EACH STRATUM OF POPULATION
C
     SX(IX)= SX(IX) + X
C
C        SX          SUM OF X VARIABLE BY STRATUM
C        X           INDEPENDENT DATA VARIABLE
C
     SY(IX)= SY(IX) + Y
C
C        SY          SUM OF Y VARIABLE BY STRATUM
C        Y           DEPENDENT VARIABLE BEING ESTIMATED
C
     SXX(IX) = SXX(IX) +(X*X)
C
C        SXX         SUM OF SQUARES OF X VARIABLE BY STRATUM
C
     SXY(IX)=SXY(IX) +(X*Y)
C
C        SXY         SUM OF PRODUCTS OF X AND Y VARIABLES BY STRATUM
C
     SYY(IX) = SYY(IX) +(Y*Y)
C
C        SYY         SUM OF SQUARES OF Y VARIABLE BY STRATUM
C
 130 CONTINUE
```

Exhibit 5   Sums of Squares and Cross-Products.

```
C
C          DELIVERS NORMAL DEVIATE FOR ONE OR TWO TAILED RISK
C
           SUBROUTINE NDOUT
           IMPLICIT REAL*8 (A-H,O-Z),INTEGER*4 (I-N)
           COMMON/LBLND/QDIST,Z,NT
           DIMENSION C(6)
           DATA C/ 2.515517D0,.802853D0,.010328D0,1.432788D0,.189269D0,.00130
          18D0/
           NCZ = 0
           IF(NT.EQ.2) GO TO 40
           IF(QDIST - .5) 10,20,30
    10 CONTINUE
           NCZ = 1
           Q = QDIST
           GO TO 40
    20 CONTINUE
           Z = 0.
           GO TO 50
    30 CONTINUE
           Q = 1.0 - QDIST
    40 CONTINUE
           IF(NT.EQ.2) Q = QDIST /2.0
           RQ = 1.0 / Q
           RQ2 = RQ * RQ
           T =DSQRT(DLOG(RQ2))
           T2 = T * T
           T3 = T2 * T
           FNUM = C(1) + (C(2)*T) + (C(3)*T2)
           DENOM = 1.0 + (C(4)*T) + (C(5)*T2) + (C(6)*T3)
           Z = T - (FNUM / DENOM)

C          Z          STANDARD NORMAL DEVIATE FOR QDIST
C
    50 CONTINUE
           IF(NCZ .EQ.1) Z =  - Z
           RETURN
           END
```

Exhibit 6 Standard Normal Deviate.

```
C
C               CORRECTION OF SUMS,SQUARES,AND CROSS-PRODUCTS TO MEAN
C
      DO 140 I=1,NST
C          NST          NUMBER OF STRATA REQUIRED
      IF(NS(I).EQ.0) GO TO 140
      SN = NS(I)
C
C          SN           NUMBER OF ITEMS IN CURRENT STRATUM OF POPULATION
C
      XBAR(I) = SX(I) / SN
C
C          XBAR         MEAN OF X IN EACH STRATUM OF POPULATION
C          SX           SUM OF X VARIABLE BY STRATUM
C
      YBAR(I) = SY(I) / SN
C          YBAR         MEAN OF Y IN EACH STRATUM OF POPULATION
C          SY           SUM OF Y VARIABLE BY STRATUM
C
C
      CSSX = SXX(I) - (XBAR(I)* SX(I))
C
C          CSSX         CORRECTED SUM OF SQUARES OF X IN CURRENT STRATUM
C          SXX          SUM OF SQUARES OF X VARIABLE BY STRATUM
C
      CSSY = SYY(I) -(YBAR(I)* SY(I))
C
C          CSSY         CORRECTED SUM OF SQUARES OF Y IN CURRENT STRATUM
C          SYY          SUM OF SQUARES OF Y VARIABLE BY STRATUM
C
      CSXY = SXY(I) -(YBAR(I)* SX(I))
C
C          CSXY         CORRECTED SUM OF PRODUCTS OF X AND Y IN STRATUM
C          SXY          SUM OF PRODUCTS OF X AND Y VARIABLES BY STRATUM
  140 CONTINUE
```

Exhibit 7   Correction to the Mean.

```
C
C               ADJUSTMENT FOR STANDARD ERROR IN PILOT SAMPLE
C
      IF(NSAMP.GT.1) GO TO 135
C
C          NSAMP        SAMPLING RATE FOR PILOT SAMPLE
C
      GO TO 136
  135 CONTINUE
      STDEV(I) = STDEV(I) * ((SEC *(DSQRT(1./(2.*(SN-1.)))))+1.)
C
C          SEC          CONFIDENCE LEVEL FOR ESTIMATION
C
      VARY = STDEV(I) * STDEV(I)
C
C          VARY         VARIANCE IN CURRENT STRATUM
C
  136 CONTINUE
      SUMVAR = SUMVAR + VARY
C
C          SUMVAR       SUM OF VARIANCES FOR ALL STRATA
C
```

Exhibit 8   Standard Error in Pilot Sample.

```
C
C          DEVELOPMENT OF WEIGHTED AVERAGE DEVIATION
C
      IF(CSXY.EQ.0..OR.CSSX.EQ.0.) GO TO 122
      BETA = CSXY / CSSX
C
C          BETA          REGRESSION COEFFICIENT
C
  122 CONTINUE
      IF(NMN.EQ.3) BETA = 0.
C
C          NMN           ESTIMATE TYPE  1=REGRESSION, 2=RATIO, 3=MEAN
C
      IF(NMN.EQ.2) GO TO 125
      VARY = CSSY - (CSXY * BETA)
C
C          VARY          VARIANCE IN CURRENT STRATUM
C
      GO TO 130
  125 CONTINUE
      BETA = SY(I)/SX(I)
      BETA2 = BETA * BETA
      VARY = CSSY - (2.* CSXY * BETA) + (CSSX * BETA2)
  130 CONTINUE
      IF(VARY.LE.0.) GO TO 134
      STDEV(I) = (DSQRT(VARY / SN))
C
C          STDEV         STANDARD DEVIATION IN EACH STRATUM
C          SN            NUMBER OF ITEMS IN CURRENT STRATUM OF POPULATION
C
      GO TO 234
  134 CONTINUE
      STDEV(I) = 0.
  234 CONTINUE
      SN = NS(I)
      SUMVAR = SUMVAR + VARY
C
C          SUMVAR        SUM OF VARIANCES FOR ALL STRATA
C
      IF(I.EQ.1.OR.I.EQ.NST) GO TO 139
      PNS(I)= STDEV(I) * SN
C
C          PNS           SAMPLE INTERVAL FOR EACH STRATUM
C          STDEV         STANDARD DEVIATION IN EACH STRATUM
C          SN            NUMBER OF ITEMS IN CURRENT STRATUM OF POPULATION
C
      SNS = SNS + PNS(I)
C
C          SNS           SUM OF WEIGHTED FACTORS FOR ALLOCATION
C
  139 CONTINUE
  140 CONTINUE
```

Exhibit 9   Weighted Average Deviation.

```
C
C        DEVELOPMENT OF INDICATED SAMPLE SIZE
C
      NN=0
C
C        NN           TOTAL NUMBER OF ITEMS IN INDICATED SAMPLE
      DO 150 I=1,NST
C
C        I            STRATUM NUMBER
C        NST          NUMBER OF STRATA REQUIRED
C
      IF (NS(I).EQ.0) GO TO 50
      SN = NS(I)
      IF(NST.EQ.1) GO TO 128
      IF(I.EQ.1.OR.I.EQ.NST) GO TO 130
      FN = ALL * STDEV(I) * SN
C
C        NS           NUMBER OF ITEMS IN EACH STRATUM OF POPULATION
C        SN           NUMBER OF ITEMS IN CURRENT STRATUM OF POPULATION
C        FN           ALLOCATED SAMPLE SIZE
C        ALL          NEYMAN ALLOCATION FACTOR
C        STDEV        STANDARD DEVIATION IN EACH STRATUM
C
      N= FN + 0.5
      IF(N.LT.1) N = 1
      NSM = NS(I)
      IF(N.GT.NSM) N = NSM
      IF(N.EQ.1.OR.N.EQ.NSM) FN = N
      IF(FN.GT.SN) FN = SN
      IF(FN.GT.1000.) FN = 1000.
      PNS(I) = SN/FN
C
C        N            INDICATED SAMPLE SIZE FOR EACH STRATUM
C        NSM          NUMBER IN STRATUM FOR TESTING SAMPLE SIZE
C        PNS          SAMPLE INTERVAL FOR EACH STRATUM
C
      IF(PNS(I).GT.1000.) PNS(I)=1000.
      GO TO 126
  130 CONTINUE
      IF(I.EQ.1) N =(SN / PNS(1)) + 0.5
      IF(I.EQ.NST) N = NS(I)
      GO TO 126
  128 CONTINUE
      N = FNA + 0.5
C
C        FNA          SAMPLE SIZE
C
      PNS(1) = SN / FNA
  126 CONTINUE
      NT(I) =(PNS(I) * 100.)+0.5
C
C        NT           INTERVAL FOR SAMPLE STRATA
C
      NN=NN+N
C
  150 CONTINUE
```

Exhibit 10   Indicated Sample Size.

```
C
C
C           DEVELOPMENT OF OPTIMUM ALLOCATION FACTOR
C
      FNUM = NNS
C
C           FNUM        NUMBER OF ITEMS IN POPULATION
C           NNS         NUMBER OF ITEMS IN POPULATION - COUNTER
C
      XFN = NS(1) + NS(NST)
C
C           XFN         SUM OF ITEMS IN STRATA 1 AND 21
C           NS          NUMBER OF ITEMS IN EACH STRATUM OF POPULATION
C           NST         NUMBER OF STRATA REQUIRED
C
      FNM = FNUM - XFN
C
C           FNM         NUMBER OF ITEMS IN STRATA 2 TO 20
C
      IF(NST.EQ.1) FNM = FNUM
      WAD = SNS / FNM
C
C           WAD         WEIGHTED AVERAGE STANDARD DEVIATION
C           SNS         SUM OF WEIGHTED FACTORS FOR ALLOCATION
C
      FNO = (((FNM * ZORD * WAD) / PREC) **2)
C
C           ZORD        NORMAL STANDARD DEVIATE RETURNED BY NDOUT
C           FNO         PRELIMINARY SAMPLE SIZE
C           PREC        MONETARY PRECISION - INPUT PARAMETER
C
      FNA = FNO / (1. + ((FNO - 1.) / FNM))
      ALL = FNA / SNS
C           FNA         SAMPLE SIZE
C
C           ALL         NEYMAN ALLOCATION FACTOR
C
```

Exhibit 11   Optimum Allocation Factor.

```
C
C       FIRST STRATUM INTERVAL, IF NOT OTHERWISE SPECIFIED, IS SET TO SAME
C       INTERVAL AS NEXT FULL STRATUM.
C
        DO 115 I = 2,MST
C
C           MST         NUMBER OF STRATA MINUS ONE
C
C
        IF(NS(I).EQ.0) GO TO 115
C
C           NS          NUMBER OF ITEMS IN EACH STRATUM OF POPULATION
C
        SN = NS(I)
C
C           SN          NUMBER OF ITEMS IN CURRENT STRATUM OF POPULATION
C
        FN = ALL * STDEV (I) * SN
C
C           FN          ALLOCATED SAMPLE SIZE
C           STDEV       STANDARD DEVIATION IN EACH STRATUM
C
        N = FN + 0.5
C
C           N           INDICATED SAMPLE SIZE FOR EACH STRATUM
C
        IF(N.LT.3) N=3
        NSM = NS(I)
C
C           NSM         NUMBER IN STRATUM FOR TESTING SAMPLE SIZE
C
        IF(N.GT.NSM) N = NSM
        IF(N.EQ.3.OR.N.EQ.NSM) FN = N
        IF(FN.GT.SN) FN = SN
        IF(FN.GT.1000.) FN = 1000.
        PNS(1) = SN / FN
C
C           PNS         SAMPLE INTERVAL FOR EACH STRATUM
C
        IF (NB.EQ.3) GO TO 116
        SN = NS(1)
        TN = SN / PNS(1)
C
C           TN          TEST FOR ADEQUATE SAMPLE
C
        IF(TN.LT.3.0) PNS(1) =SN/3.0
        GO TO 116
 115 CONTINUE
 116 CONTINUE
```

Exhibit 12   First Stratum Interval.

```
C.      COMPLETES ALLOCATION OF SAMPLE

        IF(TN.LT.3.0) PNS(1) =SN/3.0
        DO 150 I=1,NST
C           I           STRATUM NUMBER
C           NST         NUMBER OF STRATA REQUIRED
        IF (NS(I).EQ.0) GO TO 150
C           NS          NUMBER OF ITEMS IN EACH STRATUM OF POPULATION
        SN = NS(I)
C           SN          NUMBER OF ITEMS IN CURRENT STRATUM OF POPULATION
        IF(NST.EQ.1) GO TO 128
        IF(I.EQ.1.OR.I.EQ.NST) GO TO 130
        FN = ALL * STDEV(I) * SN
C           FN          ALLOCATED SAMPLE SIZE
C           ALL         NEYMAN ALLOCATION FACTOR
C           STDEV       STANDARD DEVIATION IN EACH STRATUM
        N= FN + 0.5
C           N           INDICATED SAMPLE SIZE FOR EACH STRATUM
        IF(N.LT.1) N = 1
        NSM = NS(I)
C           NSM         NUMBER IN STRATUM FOR TESTING SAMPLE SIZE
        IF(N.GT.NSM) N = NSM
        IF(N.EQ.1.OR.N.EQ.NSM) FN = N
        IF(FN.GT.SN) FN = SN
        IF(FN.GT.1000.) FN = 1000.
        PNS(I) = SN/FN
C           PNS         SAMPLE INTERVAL FOR EACH STRATUM
        IF(PNS(I).GT.1000.) PNS(I)=1000.
        GO TO 140
    130 CONTINUE
        IF(I.EQ.1) N =(SN / PNS(1)) + 0.5
C           SN          NUMBER OF ITEMS IN CURRENT STRATUM OF POPULATION
        IF(I.EQ.NST) N = NS(I)
C           NST         NUMBER OF STRATA REQUIRED
C           NS          NUMBER OF ITEMS IN EACH STRATUM OF POPULATION
        GO TO 140
    128 CONTINUE
        N = FNA + 0.5
C           N           INDICATED SAMPLE SIZE FOR EACH STRATUM
C           FNA         SAMPLE SIZE
        PNS(1) = SN / FNA
    140 CONTINUE
        NT(I) =(PNS(I) * 100.)+0.5
C           NT          INTERVAL FOR SAMPLE STRATA
C           PNS         SAMPLE INTERVAL FOR EACH STRATUM
        NN=NN+N
    150 CONTINUE
```
Exhibit 13   Sample Allocation.

```
C
C               COLLAPSES SAMPLE DESIGN TO ELIMINATE STRATA WITH TOO FEW ITEMS
C
        NCS = 0
C           NCS         COLLAPSE STRATA IF SET TO 1
        I=2
     24 CONTINUE
        IP=I +1
        NSA=(NS(I)*100)/NT(I)
        IF(NSA.GE.3) GO TO 30
        IF(I.EQ.MST) GO TO 30
C           IP          COUNTER FOR NEXT STRATUM
C           NSA         SAMPLE SIZE IN STRATUM I
C           NS          NUMBER OF ITEMS IN EACH STRATUM OF POPULATION
C           MST         NUMBER OF STRATA MINUS ONE
C           NT          INTERVAL FOR SAMPLE STRATA
        GO TO 25
     16 CONTINUE
        IP = IP + 1
        IF (IP.GT.MST) GO TO 30
     25 CONTINUE
        IF (NS(IP).EQ.0) GO TO 10
        NS(I)=NS(I)+NS(IP)
        NSB=(NS(IP)*100)/NT(IP)
C           NSB         SAMPLE SIZE IN STRATUM IP
        NSC = NSA + NSB
C           NSC         SAMPLE SIZE IN COMBINED STRATUM I
        NT(I)=(NS(I)*100)/NSC
     10 CONTINUE
        DO 27 J = IP,MST
        JR = J+1
        JM = J-1
        S(JM)=S(J)
C           JM          COUNTER FOR PRIOR STRATUM
C           JR          COUNTER FOR NEXT STRATUM
C           S           UPPER CUT-OFF OF EACH STRATUM
        NS(J)=NS(JR)
        NT(J)=NT(JR)
     27 CONTINUE
        MST=MST-1
        NCS = 1
        IF (NS(IP).EQ.0) GO TO 16
        NSA = NSC
        NSE = (NS(IP) * 100) / NT(IP)
        IF(NSC.GE.3) GO TO 30
        IF (NSE.LT.3.AND.IP.EQ.MST) GO TO 25
C           NSE         TENTATIVE SAMPLE SIZE FOR STRATUM IP
        GO TO 25
     30 CONTINUE
        I=I+1
        IF(I.GE.MST) GO TO 32
        GO TO 24
     32 CONTINUE
        NST = MST + 1
C           NST         NUMBER OF STRATA REQUIRED
```
Exhibit 14   Collapsing Strata.

```
C
C      DETERMINE RANDOM START
C
       DO 300 I=1,NST
C
C          NST       NUMBER OF STRATA REQUIRED
C
       IF(NT(I).EQ.0) GO TO 280
C
C          NT        INTERVAL FOR SAMPLE STRATA
C
       CALL RANDOM (NRA,NAR)
C
C          NRA       RANDOM NUMBER
C          NAR       NEW RANDOM NUMBER
C
       NFR = NAR / NT(I)
C
C          NFR       INTERMEDIATE VARIABLE IN COMPUTING RANDOM START
C
       NR(I)= NAR - (NFR * NT(I))
C
C          NR        RANDOM START FOR EACH STRATUM FOR SAMPLE SELECTION
C
   280 CONTINUE
       IF(NT(I).EQ.0) NR(I)= 0
       NRA =NAR
   300 CONTINUE
    39 CONTINUE
       IF (NRA.LE.999999) GO TO 40
       NRA = NRA - 1000000
       GO TO 39
    40 CONTINUE



C
C
C          DEVELOPS RANDOM NUMBER FROM GIVEN NUMBER
C
       SUBROUTINE RANDOM (L,M)
       IMPLICIT REAL*8 (A-H,O-Z),INTEGER*4 (I-N)
       LD = L / 10000
C
C          LD        DIGITS TO RIGHT OF DECIMAL FOR INPUT DATA FIELDS
C
       LT = L - (LD * 10000)
       M = (LT *100) + L + 81569
     1 CONTINUE
       IF (M.LT.1000000) GO TO 2
       M = M - 1000000
       GO TO 1
     2 CONTINUE
       RETURN
C
       END
```

Exhibit 15   Random Start.

```
C
C           SELECTS AND WRITES SAMPLE TO BE EVALUATED.
C
      REWIND 7
      NSEQ = 0
  100 CONTINUE
      READ (7,101,END=200) NDES,FA
  101 FORMAT(11A4,6F12.2)
C           FA              DATA TO OR FROM  FIELDS 7 - 12
C           200             STATEMENT NUMBER TO GO TO AT END OF FILE
      X = FA(NV1)
      NSEQ = NSEQ + 1
C           X               INDEPENDENT DATA VARIABLE
C           NV1             AUDITAPE FIELD FOR INDEPENDENT (X) VARIABLE
  110 CONTINUE
      IF (NST.EQ.1) GO TO 128
      IF(X.LE.XLN) GO TO 128
C           XLN             LIMIT BELOW WHICH ALL MINUS VALUES WILL BE SELECTED
      IF(X.LE.0.) GO TO 115
      DO 120 K=2,MST
C           MST             NUMBER OF STRATA MINUS ONE
C           S               UPPER CUT-OFF OF EACH STRATUM
      IF(X.LE.S(K)) GO TO 122
  120 CONTINUE
      GO TO 128
  122 CONTINUE
      IX = K
C           IX              STRATUM NUMBER DURING SAMPLE STRATIFICATION
      GO TO 125
  115 CONTINUE
      IX = 1
      GO TO 125
  128 CONTINUE
      IX = NST
C           NST             NUMBER OF STRATA REQUIRED
  125 CONTINUE
C           ACCUMULATE POPULATION TOTALS
      J1= J1 + 1
      SJ1 = SJ1 + X
      NS(IX)= NS(IX)+ 1
      SX(IX)= SX(IX)+ X
C           J1              TOTAL NUMBER OF ITEMS IN POPULATION
C           SJ1             TOTAL AMOUNT IN POPULATION OF X VARIABLE
C           X               INDEPENDENT DATA VARIABLE
.C          NS              NUMBER OF ITEMS IN EACH STRATUM OF POPULATION
C           SX              SUM OF X VARIABLE BY STRATUM
      IF(NT(IX).EQ.100) GO TO 140
C           NT              INTERVAL FOR SAMPLE STRATA
C           IX              STRATUM NUMBER DURING SAMPLE STRATIFICATION
      IF(NST.EQ.1) GO TO 129
      IF(IX.EQ.NST) GO TO 140
      IF(NT(IX).EQ.0) GO TO 150
  129 CONTINUE
C     JP INCREMENTS BY 100 IN EACH STRATUM UP TO RANDOM NUMBER
C           JP              COUNTER FOR SELECTION OF SAMPLE ITEMS
C           NR              RANDOM START FOR EACH STRATUM FOR SAMPLE SELECTION
      JP(IX) = JP(IX) + 100
```

Exhibit 16   Sample Selection.

244

```
      IF(JP(IX).GE.NR(IX))GO TO 130
      GO TO 150
  130 CONTINUE
      JP(IX)=JP(IX)- NT(IX)
C           RESET STRATUM COUNTER BY ONE INTERVAL BASED ON RANDOM START
  140 CONTINUE
C           ACCUMULATE SAMPLE TOTALS
      J2 = J2 + 1
      SJ2 = SJ2 + X
      JQ(IX)= JQ(IX)+ 1
      SQ(IX)= SQ(IX)+ X
      FA(NV3) = IX
      FA(NV4) = NSEQ
C           J2          TOTAL NUMBER OF ITEMS IN SAMPLE SELECTED
C           SJ2         TOTAL AMOUNT IN SAMPLE OF X VARIABLE
C           X           INDEPENDENT DATA VARIABLE
C           JQ          NUMBER OF ITEMS SELECTED IN EACH STRATUM OF SAMPLE
C           IX          STRATUM NUMBER DURING SAMPLE STRATIFICATION
C           SQ          TOTAL AMOUNT OF SELECTED ITEMS IN EACH STRATUM
      WRITE (8,145) NDES,FA
  145 FORMAT(11A4,6F12.2)
  150 CONTINUE
      GO TO 100
  200 CONTINUE
      ENDFILE 8
C           THIS STATEMENT IS TO CLOSE FILE.
```

Exhibit 16   Continued.

```
C
C          COMPUTES STRATIFIED REGRESSION ESTIMATE OF Y POPULATION
C
       BETCR = WY(23)/WX(23)
C          BETCR       BETA FOR COMBINED RATIO
C          WY          SUM OF Y BY STRATUM AND IN TOTAL FOR SAMPLE
C          WX          SUM OF X BY STRATUM AND IN TOTAL FOR SAMPLE
       DO 950 I=1,22
       NH(I) = FN(I)
       IF(NS(I).EQ.0.AND.NH(I).EQ.0) GO TO 950
       IF(CSMXY(I).EQ.0..OR.CSSX(I).EQ.0.) GO TO 200
       BETA = CSMXY(I) / CSSX(I)
C          NH          TRUNCATED NUMBER OF ITEMS IN EACH STRATUM OF SAMPLE
C          FN          NUMBER OF ITEMS IN EACH STRATUM OF SAMPLE
C          NS          NUMBER OF ITEMS IN EACH STRATUM OF POPULATION
C          CSMXY       CORRECTED SUM OF PRODUCT OF X AND Y IN EACH STRATUM
C          CSSX        CORRECTED SUM OF SQUARES OF X IN EACH STRATUM
C          BETA        REGRESSION COEFFICIENT
       GO TO 210
  200 CONTINUE
       BETA = 0.
  210 CONTINUE
       IF(NS(I).EQ.0) GO TO 600
       IF(NH(I).EQ.0) GO TO 601
       PNS =(NS(I) * 100) / NH(I)
C          PNS         SAMPLE INTERVAL FOR CURRENT STRATUM
       PNS = PNS / 100.
       IF(EM(I).LT.1.0) GO TO 211
       XPBAR(I) = XPOP(I) / EM(I)
  211 CONTINUE
C          XPBAR       MEAN AMOUNT OF X POPULATION BY STRATUM AND IN TOTAL
C          XPOP        AMOUNT OF X POPULATION IN EACH STRATUM AND IN TOTAL
C          EM          NUMBER OF ITEMS IN EACH STRATUM OF POPULATION
       IF(CSMXY(I).EQ.0..OR.CSSX(I).EQ.0.) BETA = 0.
       IF(K3.EQ.1) BETA = 0.
       IF (K4.NE.1) GO TO 21
C          K3          MEAN ESTIMATE IF SET TO ONE
C          K4          RATIO ESTIMATE    1 = SEPARATE, 2 = COMBINED
       IF (WX(I).EQ.0.0.OR.WY(I).EQ.0.0) GO TO 20
       BETA = WY(I) / WX(I)
       GO TO 21
   20 CONTINUE
       BETA = 0.0
   21 CONTINUE
       IF(K4.EQ.2) BETA = BETCR
       IF(K5.EQ.2) BETA = BETCG
C          K5          REGRESSION ESTIMATE   1 = SEPARATE, 2 = COMBINED
C          BETCG       BETA FOR COMBINED REGRESSION
       REGES = EM(I)*(YBAR(I)+(BETA*(XPBAR(I)-XBAR(I))))
       IF (NS(I).EQ.NH(I)) REGES = WY(I)
       SUMEST = SUMEST + REGES
C          REGES       ESTIMATED SUM OF Y FOR STRATUM OF POPULATION
C          YBAR        MEAN OF Y BY STRATUM AND TOTAL FOR SAMPLE
C          BETA        REGRESSION COEFFICIENT
C          XBAR        MEAN OF X BY STRATUM AND TOTAL FOR SAMPLE
C          SUMEST      ESTIMATE OF Y POPULATION
```

Exhibit 17   Stratified Regression Estimate.

```
C
C          COMPUTATION OF PRECISION OF STRATIFIED REGRESSION ESTIMATE
C
       DO 40 I = 1,22
       IF(K4.GE.1) GO TO 75
       FR= CSSY(I) -(CSMXY(I)* BETA)
C          FR           INTERMEDIATE VARIABLE
C          CSSY         CORRECTED SUM OF SQUARES OF Y IN CURRENT STRATUM
C          CSMXY        CORRECTED SUM OF PRODUCT OF X AND Y IN EACH STRATUM
C          BETA         REGRESSION COEFFICIENT
       GO TO 80
   75 CONTINUE
       BETA2 = BETA * BETA
C          BETA2        BETA SQUARED
       FR = (CSSY(I) -(2.*(CSMXY(I)*BETA)) + (CSSX(I)*BETA2))
C          CSSX         CORRECTED SUM OF SQUARES OF X IN EACH STRATUM
       FR = FR + (FR *(5.0/FN(I)))
C          FN           NUMBER OF ITEMS IN EACH STRATUM OF SAMPLE
   80 CONTINUE
       FNDF = FN(I)-1.0
C          FNDF         DEGREES OF FREEDOM FOR STRATUM
       IF(K5.GE.1) FNDF = FN(I) - 2.0
       FL =((((EM(I)-FN(I))*(EM(I)**2))/((EM(I)-1.0)*FNDF*FN(I)))
C          FL           INTERMEDIATE VARIABLE
C          EM           NUMBER OF ITEMS IN EACH STRATUM OF POPULATION
C          VARY         VARIANCE FOR CURRENT STRATUM
       VARY = FL * FR
       IF(NS(I).EQ.1) VARY = 0.
C          NS           NUMBER OF ITEMS IN EACH STRATUM OF POPULATION
       SUMVAR = SUMVAR + VARY
C          SUMVAR       SUM OF STRATUM VARIANCES
C          VARY         VARIANCE FOR CURRENT STRATUM
       IF (VARY.LE.0.) GO TO 30
       SESD = CZ * DSQRT (VARY)
C          SESD         STRATUM STANDARD DEVIATION
       GO TO 31
   30 CONTINUE
       SESD = 0.
   31 CONTINUE
   40 CONTINUE
       IF (SUMVAR.LE.0.) GO TO 58
       STDEV = DSQRT(SUMVAR)
C          STDEV        STANDARD ERROR OF ESTIMATE
C          SUMVAR       SUM OF STRATUM VARIANCES
       FNUM=NS(23)
       XPBAR(23)=XPOP(23) / FNUM
C          XPBAR        MEAN AMOUNT OF X POPULATION BY STRATUM AND IN TOTAL
C          XPOP         AMOUNT OF X POPULATION IN EACH STRATUM AND IN TOTAL
C          FNUM         NUMBER OF ITEMS IN POPULATION
       PREC = STDEV * CZ
       SMINUS = SUMEST - PREC
       SPLUS = SUMEST + PREC
C          PREC         MONETARY PRECISION
C          CZ           NORMAL STANDARD DEVIATE
C          SMINUS       LOWER PRECISION LIMIT FOR ESTIMATE
C          SPLUS        UPPER PRECISION LIMIT FOR ESTIMATE
C          SUMEST       ESTIMATE OF Y POPULATION
```

Exhibit 18   Monetary Precision of Stratified Regression Estimate.

```
C
C        PREPARES TENTATIVE DESIGN DATA FOR NEXT SAMPLE
C

        IF (SUMVAR.LT.1.0) SUMVAR = 1.0
        ADJST =(((REQMP/CZ  )**2)/ SUMVAR)
C          ADJST      ADJUSTMENT FACTOR FOR NEXT SAMPLE
C          REQMP      MONETARY PRECISION REQUIRED IN NEXT SAMPLE
C          CZ         NORMAL STANDARD DEVIATE
C          SUMVAR     SUM OF STRATUM VARIANCES
        BETCG = (WXY(23)-(XBAR(23)*WY(23)))/(WXX(23)-(XBAR(23)*WX(23)))
  405 CONTINUE
C          BETCG      BETA FOR COMBINED REGRESSION
C          WY         SUM OF Y BY STRATUM AND IN TOTAL FOR SAMPLE
C          WX         SUM OF X BY STRATUM AND IN TOTAL FOR SAMPLE
C          WXY        SUM OF (X*Y) BY STRATUM AND TOTAL FOR SAMPLE
C          XBAR       MEAN OF X BY STRATUM AND TOTAL FOR SAMPLE
C          WXX        SUM OF SQUARES OF X BY STRATUM AND TOTAL FOR SAMPLE
        NNH = 0
C          NNH        TOTAL NUMBER OF ITEMS FOR NEXT SAMPLE
        SUMVAR = 0.
        DO 110 I=1,22
        NT(I) = 0
        IF(NS(I).EQ.0) GO TO 110
        IF (NST.LE.1) GO TO 50
C          NS         NUMBER OF ITEMS IN EACH STRATUM OF POPULATION
C          NST        NUMBER OF STRATA
        IF(I.EQ.1) GO TO 87
        IF(I.EQ.NST) GO TO 89
   50 CONTINUE
        BETA = CSMXY(I) / CSSX(I)
C          BETA       REGRESSION COEFFICIENT
C          CSMXY      CORRECTED SUM OF PRODUCT OF X AND Y IN EACH STRATUM
C          CSSX       CORRECTED SUM OF SQUARES OF X IN EACH STRATUM
        IF(K5.EQ.2) BETA = BETCG
C          K5         REGRESSION ESTIMATE  1 = SEPARATE, 2 = COMBINED
        FR= CSSY(I) -(CSMXY(I)* BETA)
C          FR         INTERMEDIATE VARIABLE
C          CSSY       CORRECTED SUM OF SQUARES OF Y IN EACH STRATUM
        FNDF = FN(I)-1.0
C          FNDF       DEGREES OF FREEDOM FOR STRATUM
        IF(K5.GE.1) FNDF = FN(I) - 2.0
        FL =(((EM(I)-FN(I))*(EM(I)**2))/((EM(I)-1.0)*FNDF*FN(I)))
        VARY = FL * FR * ADJST
C          FL         INTERMEDIATE VARIABLE
C          EM         NUMBER OF ITEMS IN EACH STRATUM OF POPULATION
C          VARY       VARIANCE FOR CURRENT STRATUM
C          ADJST      ADJUSTMENT FACTOR FOR NEXT SAMPLE
        FL = VARY / FR
        IF (FL.EQ.0.) GO TO 84
        FNO = EM(I) / (DSQRT(FL))
        IF(FNO.LT.3.0) GO TO 85
        FNT =(FL*(FNO-2.0))/(EM(I)-FNO)
C          FNO        PRELIMINARY ESTIMATE OF SAMPLE SIZE
C          FNT        SAMPLE INTERVAL IN NEXT SAMPLE
        GO TO 86
   84 CONTINUE
        FNO = FN(I)
```

Exhibit 19   Tentative Design for Next Sample.

```
    85 FNT =   EM(I) / FNO
    86 CONTINUE
       IF(FNT.LE.1.0) FNT = 1.0
       IF(FNT.GT.1000.) FNT = 1000.
       IF(FNT.GT.EM(I)) FNT = EM(I)
       SUMVAR = SUMVAR + VARY
C          SUMVAR     SUM OF STRATUM VARIANCES
       GO TO 90
    87 CONTINUE
       FN(1) = DSQRT(FN(1) * ADJST)
       IF (FN(1).LT.3.0)FN(1) = 3.0
       FNT = EM(1)/FN(1)
       GO TO 90
    89 CONTINUE
       FNT = 1.0
    90 CONTINUE
       NT(I) = (FNT * 100.) + 0.5
C          FNT          SAMPLE INTERVAL IN NEXT SAMPLE
       NH(I) = EM(I) / FNT
C          NH           NUMBER OF ITEMS IN EACH STRATUM OF SAMPLE
C          NNH          TOTAL NUMBER OF ITEMS FOR NEXT SAMPLE
       NNH = NH(I) + NNH
       IF (NST.EQ.1) GO TO 111
   110 CONTINUE
       IF (SUMVAR.LT.0.) SUMVAR = DABS(SUMVAR)
       STDEV = DSQRT(SUMVAR)
C          STDEV        STANDARD ERROR OF ESTIMATE
C          SUMVAR       SUM OF STRATUM VARIANCES
       FNUM=NS(23)
C          FNUM         NUMBER OF ITEMS IN POPULATION
       PREC = STDEV * CZ
C          PREC         MONETARY PRECISION
C          CZ           NORMAL STANDARD DEVIATE
   111 CONTINUE
       IF (NST.EQ.1) PREC = REQMP
C          REQMP        MONETARY PRECISION REQUIRED IN NEXT SAMPLE
```

Exhibit 19   Continued.

BIBLIOGRAPHY

BOOKS

Cochran, William G., *Sampling Techniques*, 2nd ed., New York, John Wiley & Sons, Inc., 1963.

Croxton, Frederick Emory, and Dudley J. Cowden, *Practical Business Statistics*, Englewood Cliffs, N.J., Prentice-Hall, Inc., 1960.

Deming, W. Edwards, *Some Theory of Sampling*, New York, John Wiley & Sons, Inc., 1950.

Deming, W. Edwards, *Sample Design in Business Research*, New York, John Wiley & Sons, Inc., 1960.

Draper, N. R., and H. Smith, *Applied Regression Analysis*, New York, John Wiley & Sons, Inc., 1966.

Ekeblad, Frederick A., *The Statistical Method in Business*, New York, John Wiley & Sons, Inc., 1962.

Ezekiel, Mordecai, and Karl A. Fox, *Methods of Correlation and Regression Analysis*, New York, John Wiley & Sons, Inc., 1965.

Freund, John E., *Mathematical Statistics*, Englewood Cliffs, N.J., Prentice-Hall, Inc., 1962.

Hansen, M. H., W. N. Hurwitz, and W. G. Madow, *Sample Survey Methods and Theory*, New York, John Wiley & Sons, Inc., 1953.

Kendall, Maurice G., and Alan Stuart, *The Advanced Theory of Statistics*, 3 volumes. New York, Hafner Publishing Co., 1966.

Kurnow, Ernest, Gerald J. Glasser, and Frederick A. Ottman, *Statistics for Business Decisions*, Homewood, Ill., R. D. Irwin, 1959.

Mood, Alexander M., and Franklin A. Graybill, *Introduction to the Theory of Statistics*, McGraw-Hill Book Co., New York, 1963.

Owen, D. B., *Handbook of Statistical Tables*, Reading, Mass., Addison-Wesley Publishing Co., Inc., 1962.

Raj, Des, *Sampling Theory*, New York, McGraw-Hill Book Co., 1968.

Ralston, Anthony, and Herbert S. Wilf, *Mathematical Methods for Digital Computers*, New York, John Wiley & Sons, Inc., 1966.

PERIODICALS

Armitage, P., "A Comparison of Stratified with Unrestricted Random Sampling from a Finite Population," *Biometrika*, **34** (1947).

INDEX

Ability to make estimates, credit and collection, 4
Abnormal data, sampling, 32
Acceptable alternative, sample estimate, 110
Acceptable codes, checking procedures, 95
Accessible memory, electronic computer, 16
Access to universe, statistical frame, 60
Accounting applications, regression estimates, 26
Accounting area, statistician, 16
Accounting control, inventory records, 61
Accounting data, change in variability, 50
Accounting entries, use of results, 108
Accounting knowledge, interdisciplinary scope, 15
Accounting period, revenue recognition, 136
Accounting populations: complete record, 47
    exponential distribution, 53
    internal control, 48
    statistical frame, 48
    statistical requirements, 47
    well defined, 47
Accounting practice, zero origin, 97
Accounting principles, APB statement No. 4, 212
Accounting procedures: adherence to proper cutoffs, 60
    check for missing records, 59
    choice of count date, 59
    choice of selection date, 59
    physical inventory, 58
    reduction of processing lag, 59
Accounting records: data processing, 16

frequency distribution, 50
Accounting terminology, definition, 212
Accounting viewpoint, McKesson & Robbins, Inc., 12
Account number, sampling unit, 49
Accounts payable: accrual, 128
    confirmation, 126
    estimation of, 126
    validation, 127
Accounts receivable: aging, 111
    appraisal, 4
    collectibility, 111
    comparison, 147
    computer selection, 113
    confirmation, 111, 112
    establish reserves, 4
    maturity spreads, 111
    monetary amount selection, 113
    numeric sample, 114
    sales characteristics, 111
Accrual, accounts payable, 128
Accrued illness pay, estimation of, 129
Accrued vacation pay: estimation of, 129
    sample selection, 129
Actual precision, evaluation of sample, 30
Adherence to proper cutoffs, accounting procedures, 60
Adjustment: sample size, 81
    strata limits, 57
Adjustment to selection date, physical quantity, 60
Advance information, sample design, 69
Aggregate data, normal distribution, 55

253